STYLIN'

Stylin'

African American
Expressive Culture from Its Beginnings
to the Zoot Suit

SHANE WHITE AND GRAHAM WHITE

CORNELL UNIVERSITY PRESS
Ithaca and London

First published 1998 by Cornell University Press
First printing, Cornell Paperbacks, 1999

Printed in the United States of America

Library of Congress Cataloging-in-Publication Data

White, Shane.
  Stylin' : African-American expressive culture from its beginnings
to the zoot suit / Shane White and Graham White.
      p. cm.
  Includes index.
  ISBN 0-8014-3179-4 (cloth : alk. paper)
  ISBN 0-8014-8283-6 (pbk. : alk. paper)
      1. Afro-Americans—social life and customs   2. Afro-Americans—
Clothing—History.   3. Hairstyles—United States—History.   4. Body
image—United States—History.   I. White, Graham J.   II. Title.
E185.86.W4388   1998
305.896'073—dc21   97-38507

Cornell University Press strives to use environmentally responsible suppliers and materials to the fullest extent possible in the publishing of its books. Such materials include vegetable-based, low-VOC inks and acid-free papers that are recycled, totally chlorine-free, or partly composed of nonwood fibers.

1 3 5 7 9   Cloth printing   10 8 6 4 2

1 3 5 7 9   Paperback printing   10 8 6 4 2

For Cornelia and Larry Levine,
Leon and Rhoda Litwack

CONTENTS

PREFACE

A few years ago, when one of the authors of this book (the younger one and, cruelly, the one with less hair) was flying from Australia to a conference somewhere on the east coast of America, he had his usual trouble getting past the ever-vigilant immigration officials guarding LAX at a ridiculously early hour of the morning. "What is it that you do for a living, Mr. White?" The reply—"I'm a historian"—elicited a raised eyebrow. "What sort of history ?" "I write about black Americans." The eyebrow got raised several notches higher and there was a long, ruminative pause. "Why are you coming to America ?" "To give a paper at a conference." By this time the official was getting a little bit agitated and fired back another question: "How long is this paper?" The answer—"Oh, about thirty minutes"—was just too much. A look of absolute incredulity passed across his face: "Why on *earth* didn't you just mail it ?" If you think about it for a moment, even at the best of times that is an almost unanswerable question, and all a jet-lagged Mr. White could manage was to stand there in stunned silence. Shaking his head sadly, the official stamped the passport and wearily waved the middle-aged Australian academic through.

Several things seemed to be troubling the immigration official, but looming largest among them was the self-evident preposterousness of the proposition that a foreigner could have anything to say to Americans about their history. It is not that difficult to find American historians with similar beliefs, usually, but not always, articulated in a more sophisticated fashion. For self-protection or at least to avoid being bored to death, foreign historians of America usually develop a series of one-liners such as "American history is too important a matter to be left to *Americans*," a glib retort to be sure, but one containing more than a kernel of truth. In fact, to turn on their heads many of the usual nostrums about who can or should write what, the idea that history ought ideally to be written from the "inside" (whether of a group or a country) is, for us, intellectually unappealing.

This, then, is a book about African American and American history. Each chapter is the work of both of us, although we have, of necessity, divided up some of the research tasks. It was conceived, mostly researched, and entirely written in Australia, and the first debts we wish to acknowledge are to Australian institutions and individuals. Writing American history from Australia has many pleasures, but conducting the necessary research in America is an expensive logistical nightmare. It is difficult to imagine how this book could have been completed in anything like its present form without the very generous financial support we have received in the form of a University of Sydney Institutional Grant for 1991 and an Australian Research Council Large Grant for 1992-94. For these, we are extremely grateful.

Both of us completed our graduate work in the History Department at the University of Sydney, were hired by the department before completing our respective doctorates, and have spent our entire university careers in the employ of this splendid institution. (In case this gives the wrong impression about the History Department, we should add that it has been known to hire graduates of other universities, and on occasion it has even employed people not named White). We are grateful to the department for its support (not the least example of which was the payment of a considerable sum of money for the rights to the illustrations used here) and, in particular, to Ros Pesman, Ian Jack, and Stephen Garton, heads of department over the last few years, who eased our path in the writing of this book in important ways. We would also like to single out a few people's contributions. Stephen Garton's attempt to teach Shane White something about humility by thrashing him on the golf course was a dismal failure (and not because he lost a single one of the weekly encounters), but he has offered much astute advice and help on all manner of other matters. Over the last five years, Glenda Sluga has heard rather more about fashion parades, the stroll, and the zoot suit than any normal person could desire (exacting her retaliatory pound of flesh in front of a large undergraduate audience by holding up one of the authors as an example of the possibilities of "outsider" history—after all, he wrote about beauty and beauty contests), but her smart questions and comments have been very helpful. Richard Waterhouse, supervisor of Shane White's dissertation, has continued to offer a mixture of criticism and encouragement that we have much appreciated. Christiana Campbell, who supervised Graham White's dissertation, has, as always, offered most thoughtful comments on chapter drafts. Ivan Coates, John Cook, Nick Gebhardt, Ian Gordon, Ian Hoskins, and Meg Miller were, at various times, research assistants on this project; we learned a lot from their work and their perceptive comments.

One of the real pleasures of teaching at the University of Sydney is the quality of the students. Our collaboration in this book stems from our joint teaching during the last decade and a half. Over the years approximately 1,500 students have enrolled in our Black Experience course, and many of the ideas in this book were first tried out on them. To be sure, the occasional student answering an exam question has managed to reduce African American culture to the wearing of a bandanna or a zoot suit, but in the scale of half-baked ideas held about blacks that is hardly of much moment. We have learned much from our students, which is just as it should be.

Australian scholars have produced a considerable body of writing about American history, arguably the most significant work done in any country outside of America itself. This scholarship is in part a product of the supportive environment fostered by a remarkably successful organization, the Australian and New Zealand American Studies Association. Every two years "old-timers" such as Elaine Barry, Peter Bastian, Roger Bell, Ian Bickerton, Paul Bourke, Bill Breen, Peter Coleman, Don Debats, Greg Dening, Warren Ellem, Renate Howe, Rhys Isaac, Allan Johnston, Neville Meaney, Donna Merwick, John Salmond, Chris Tomlins, Ian Tyrrell, and Tony Wood and more recent members such as Keith Beattie, Trevor Burnard, Doug Craig, Chris Dixon, David Goodman, Dolores Janiewski, and Ian Mylchreest gather together for the organization's conference, a function rather different from the usual run of such events. We would like to thank the members of ANZASA for their patient support of our various research efforts over the last two decades. We owe a particular debt to Rhys Isaac for his enthusiastic cheering on of this project and his penetrating comments on the material on slavery.

For years now, Richard Bosworth has been the first reader of all that we have produced. His impact comes not so much from his actual comments on the chapters, although they are always very helpful, as from our anticipation, while we are writing, of his inevitable reaction to our drafts.

Richard is none too keen on what he likes to call the Evil Empire, refuses to tolerate the sloppy, the romantic, or the sentimental in the writing of history, and has a habit of saying exactly what he thinks, a combination that has produced some fearsome critiques of our work. Though many pages will still make him cringe, we wish to assure him that he has had a significant influence on this book's arguments and that we are very grateful for his efforts and his friendship.

We would like to mention, too, a number of American institutions that helped us greatly. Not all of the funding for this book came from Australia. Shane White gratefully acknowledges the American Philosophical Society, which awarded him a grant, and the Library Company of Philadelphia, which made him a Barra International Fellow for 1995–96. Librarians and archivists at the Chicago Historical Society, Library Company of Philadelphia, Library of Congress, Municipal Archives of New York, New-York Historical Society, and New York Public Library were efficient and helpful. In particular, Phil Lapsansky at the Library Company fulfills the wildest dreams of researchers into African American history. The City of Philadelphia should slap a heritage order on him, or at least build a little sentry box outside the Library Company so he can enjoy a cigarette sheltered from the frigid winds that knife up Locust Street. Graham White expresses his particular appreciation to the staff of the South Carolina Historical Society, the Mississippi Department of Archives and History, the Amistad Research Center and William Ransom Hogan Jazz Archive at Tulane University (where Bruce Raeburn was particularly helpful), The Historic New Orleans Collection and the New Orleans Public Library's Louisiana Division, the Wilson and Davis Libraries and the Southern Historical Collection at the University of North Carolina, Chapel Hill. We also thank the Crisis Publishing Co., Inc., publishers of *Crisis,* the magazine of the National Association for the Advancement of Colored People, for authorizing the use of Figures 33, 34, and 53. Figures 35, 42, and 45 are reprinted by permission of GRM Associates, Inc., agents for *The Pittsburgh Courier;* copyright © 1925 by The Pittsburgh Courier; copyright renewed 1953. Figures 57, 58, 59, and 60 are republished from the *Baltimore Afro-American* by permission of the Afro-American Newspapers Archives and Research Center.

Further, Shane White would like to thank Jim and Susan Gilbert; Deborah Kaplan and Roy Rosenzweig; Cornelia, Josh, and Larry Levine; and Leon and Rhoda Litwack for putting him up and putting up with him;

staying with them on various trips was another of the real pleasures of researching this book. Shan Holt and Mike Zuckerman's hospitality while he was staying in Philadelphia was also wonderful.

We are especially grateful to Peter Agree of Cornell University Press for his enthusiastic support of this project from its first glimmerings to its completion and his elastic understanding of the meaning of deadlines. We are also indebted to Kay Scheuer and Grey Osterud for their help in turning our manuscript into a book. Ridiculous as it may seem, the most frustrating aspect of this whole exercise was the securing of permissions to reproduce the sixty illustrations that accompany the text. We did what we could from Australia, but without the energetic efforts of Mike Keegan and Catherine Rice many of the most interesting images would never have appeared.

Chapter 1 is a revised version of "Slave Clothing and African-American Culture in the Eighteenth and Nineteenth Centuries," which first appeared in *Past and Present: A Journal of Historical Studies,* no. 148 (August 1995) (World copyright: The Past and Present Society, 175 Banbury Road, Oxford, England). Portions of Chapter 2 appeared as "Slave Hair and African American Culture in the Eighteenth and Nineteenth Centuries" in the *Journal of Southern History* 61 (February 1995). A version of Chapter 3 was published as "Reading the Slave Body: Demeanor, Gesture, and African-American Culture" in Bruce Clayton and John Salmond, eds., *Varieties of Southern History: New Essays on a Region and Its Peoples* (Westport, Conn.: Greenwood Press, 1996).

Fortunately most Americans have been rather more welcoming of us and our work than LAX's immigration officials. To be sure, there has been the occasional dismissive comment, the odd banal explanation of some supposed fine point of American history, spoken slowly and loudly so a foreigner could understand, but these have been the exception. Mostly, as the names mentioned below will attest, we have been fortunate enough to mix with a remarkably cosmopolitan and sophisticated bunch of people. American colleagues and friends have read bits and pieces of this manuscript, supplied references, and been supportive of the project. We would like to thank Roger Abrahams, Ira Berlin, Michael Fellman, Jim Gilbert, Samuel Kinser, Eric Lott, Nell Painter, Marcus Rediker, Roy Rosenzweig, John David Smith, Dell Upton, Clarence Walker, and Al Young. Kathy Peiss kindly answered for us a series of questions about the history of cosmetics

ꟼNTRODUCTION

At 8:16 on the morning of July 3, 1923, the *West Hesseltine* docked at Dakar in Senegal. Eager for his first look at Africa, a twenty-one-year-old American sailor hurriedly disembarked and, braving the ninety-degree heat, explored the town. He set down his first impressions in a letter to his mother:

> You should see the clothes they wear here, everything from over-coats to nothing. I have laughed until I can't. No two people dress alike. Some have on capes, some shawls, some pants, some wear blue clothes fastened around their necks and feet blowing out like sails behind. Some have on preachers' coats, others knee pants like bloomers, with halfhose and garters. It's a scream!

Such a culturally insensitive reaction, of course, was part and parcel of the way travelers had for centuries been responding to Africa. Even by the early years of the twentieth century, few Americans had visited what remained, for them, the Dark Continent, a land almost impossibly exotic and strange. What was notable about this case was not the content of the observation—although for all its gaucheness the passage still exhibits a nice eye for detail—but the identity of the author. The young American sailor was, in fact, Langston Hughes, perhaps the most famous African American poet of the twentieth century and one who, as Arnold Rampersad has pointed out in his brilliant biography, was known for his deft and sensitive portrayal of the lineaments of black life in American cities, particularly in Harlem.[1]

Though Hughes had depicted a West African scene, the tone of his observations and the sense of wonderment and cultural dislocation he conveyed jibe well with descriptions by white visitors of the appearance of some of the slaves they encountered in the American South. To Fanny Kemble, resident on her husband's Georgia plantation in the late 1830s, the Sunday

1

dress of the slaves constituted "the most ludicrous combination of incongruities that you can conceive." Frederick Law Olmsted registered a similar dissonance. In December 1852, at the start of the first of three expeditions that, by the end of the decade, would make him the best-known of the myriad travelers who crisscrossed the South in the years before the Civil War, Olmsted made an early-morning trip to the Washington market and there, for the first time, he found himself among a throng in which African Americans were in the majority. What immediately struck him was the differences between blacks and whites. Almost as much as skin pigment, differences in the ways in which the blacks had clothed their bodies, and in their "language, manner, [and] motions," set them noticeably apart.[2]

More than a century later another cultural commentator—this time one with an inside vantage point—writing of much the same phenomenon that had attracted Olmsted's attention called it a "Negro American style." Ralph Ellison recalled that he and his young Oklahoman friends had "recognized and were proud of our group's own style wherever we discerned it—in jazzmen and prizefighters, ballplayers and tap dancers; in gesture, inflection, intonation, timbre and phrasing"; indeed, Ellison declared, these African American youths had been able to detect that style "in all those nuances of expression and attitude which reveal a culture." Ellison went on to add that, although he and his companions "did not fully understand the cost of that style," they "recognized within it an affirmation of life beyond all question of our difficulties as Negroes."[3]

This book is about an important aspect of African American expressive culture, about the way in which, over more than two centuries, ordinary black men and women developed a style that did indeed affirm their lives. It is a story of the public presentation of the black body, a search for the cultural imperatives that have influenced the ways in which African Americans have clothed themselves, styled their hair, and communicated meaning through gesture, dance, and other forms of bodily display.[4] Partly by inclination and partly as a result of our remove from the sources, we have chosen to traverse a considerable part of African American history. *Stylin'* is not, as a consequence, an encyclopedic treatment, but more a series of linked essays designed to suggest the importance of our subject. We begin with three chapters on slavery in both the North and the South, chapters that examine respectively slave clothing, slave hairstyles, and slave kinesics, or communicative bodily movement. In Chapter 4, we look at the way in which the struggle over what freedom meant was played out on the

streets of northern cities in the early decades of the nineteenth century.
Chapters 5 and 6 reprise many of these themes, only this time the terrain
is the post-emancipation South. Chapters 7 and 8 contain an extended inquiry into what constituted black style in the urban North in the first four
decades of the twentieth century, and in the Epilogue we briefly reconsider
the importance of the zoot suit.

In seeking to uncover the nature of black style, our method has been
to collect, from sources as diverse as advertisements for runaway slaves,
travelers' accounts, interviews with former slaves, sociological surveys,
black autobiographies, paintings, photographs, caricatures, and newspaper
reports, a very large number of depictions of the ways in which African
Americans have presented their bodies to themselves and to others. Then,
drawing on the literature of folklore, anthropology, and semiotics, on the
study of visual images in painting, sketches, and photography, and on investigations of theatrical performance and dance, we have sought to identify that which is distinctive about the body language of African Americans
and about the ways in which they have constructed their appearance.

Inevitably, however, this book is about more than African American
culture; it makes little sense to examine that subject in a vacuum. Ralph Ellison's admonition regarding the cost of black style reminds us that blacks
have created that style in a white world, a world in which black bodies have
been regarded with a mixture of envy and contempt, as something to emulate but also as a target for violence. When Willie Morris, later a journalist
and a southern man of letters, was growing up in Yazoo City, Mississippi,
in the 1940s, he knew that for local whites the term "nigger" connoted all
that was slovenly and backward, but he also knew about "the ineluctable
attraction of niggertown," the "strange heart-pounding excitement that
Negroes in a group generated for me." At the age of thirteen, Morris and
his young friends "went Negro."

> We tried to broaden our accents to sound like Negroes, as if there
> were not enough similarity already. We consciously walked like
> young Negroes, mocking their swinging gait, moving our arms the
> way they did, cracking our knuckles and whistling between our
> teeth. We tried to use some of the same expressions, as closely as
> possible to the way they said them, like: "Hey, *ma-a-a-n,* whut you
> *do*in' theah!," the sounds rolled out and clipped sharply at the end
> for the hell of it.

Yet despite (perhaps because of) his desire to emulate the behavior of young blacks, Morris, by his own admission, continued to harass and physically assault them.[5] On reflection, and much the wiser for having observed the revolution wrought by the Civil Rights Movement, Morris was, two decades later, pained by his actions, but what he recorded of his youth in Yazoo City nicely illustrates the larger themes of the ambivalence of white attitudes to black culture and the impact black culture has had on American life.

As Morris's recollections suggest, blacks' control over the presentation of their bodies has been far from complete. The bodies of slaves (and later of free blacks) were contested terrain, the sites on which a struggle between racial groups was often destructively played out. Slaves' clothing was normally provided by the slaveowner, a circumstance that sharply constricted opportunities for culturally distinctive aesthetic display. Black kinesics was tightly constrained by the etiquette of Jim Crow, as Richard Wright and others have memorably demonstrated. Yet within the confines of an oppressive social system, African Americans have been able to develop and give visual expression to cultural preferences that were at variance with those of the dominant racial group. What follows is our account of those cultural preferences and of the creative ways in which they have found expression in the lives of ordinary African American people.

Looking Mighty Sprucy

In 1822 Daniel, a slave on George Swain's North Carolina plantation, ran away. Swain explained the circumstances surrounding the incident in a letter to his son. Daniel had applied for a weekend pass, but his recent impertinent behavior and neglect of duties had prompted Swain to instruct him to return on Sunday evening, rather than on Monday morning as was customary. Daniel had indeed returned as directed, but after the plantation's evening church service had left again, this time without authorization.

Swain was in no doubt as to the reasons for his slave's defiance. He had "discovered a long time ago that finery made a perfect fool of [Daniel]," and now surmised that "like all other Dandies who measure their importance by their Dress," his errant slave "had entirely forgotten who he was, or what grade and station he ought to fill." During the previous week,

Daniel's thoughts of the splendid clothes he would soon be wearing, so different in all respects from his shabby workaday attire, had "deranged his mind," and when on the Sunday, now actually garbed in those clothes, he had realized that his opportunity for sartorial display had been cut short it had been "more than his tiny soul could bear." Daniel had therefore absconded, and had proudly presented himself at neighboring plantations, traveling "as far along that road as he could possibly find black audiences to exhibit his finery to."[1]

Though Daniel's behavior was obviously unusual, Swain's assertion that his slave's immoderate love of fine clothing had caused him to forget his lowly station was a sentiment that many slaveholders would have found unexceptionable. They, too, would have had occasion to mark their slaves' liking for showy garments and the ease with which they managed to accumulate them, sensing in these things, perhaps, some unfortunate warping of the social fabric and a worrisome loss of control. It is with an examination of the significance slaves attached to what whites considered to be inappropriate clothing, of the manner in which they rearranged and adapted the garments given them by their owners, and of the cultural imperatives that underlay their sense of coordination, color and design, that our story of black style begins.

Between 1619 and 1808 approximately 400,000 Africans were forcibly removed to British Mainland North America or, as it later became, the United States of America.[2] For all the scholarly inquiry into seventeenth- and eighteenth-century slavery, remarkably little is known of the initial experiences of these men, women, and children as they attempted to reconcile themselves to their fate, not only as slaves, but as slaves within a strange and threatening Euro-American world. Historians have done wonders with such seemingly intractable sources as tax lists, inventories, and runaway advertisements, revealing much about the lives of colonial slaves, but at the point of initial contact the record is particularly spotty, even more opaque than usual. It is hardly surprising, then, that our understanding of this crucial moment in African American history has been formed largely by Olaudah Equiano's compelling account of his capture in Africa, transportation across the Atlantic, and experiences as a slave in the New World.[3]

What seems reasonably clear is that newly arrived African slaves were quickly clothed in European garb and made to conform to European concepts of decency. In the notices of the jailer in Charlestown, which for the most part described slaves who had escaped and been recaptured within days of their arrival in South Carolina, there are occasional descriptions of Africans who wore mere scraps of clothing (one man taken up in 1736 had "only an Arse-cloth"), wrapped themselves in blankets, or even went stark naked.[4] But this was relatively unusual. Generally, African slaves, even those only a few days off the slave ship, wore European apparel. An advertisement appearing in the *Virginia Gazette* in November 1751 stated that a "new Negroe Man . . . imported this Summer," and unable to tell "who he belongs to," had on, when he went away, "a new strong Oznabrig Shirt, a blue Pennystone Waistcoat, sew'd up the Sides, the whole Breadth of the Cloth, and a new Scotch Bonnet."[5] Similarly, Quamana, a very young slave with "Country Marks on each Cheek, and on his Forehead," who escaped from John Blair of Williamsburg in 1737, was garbed in "a Kersey Jacket, Oznabrigg Shirt, and a Pair of Hamel Breeches."[6] Though, for most of the eighteenth century, recently arrived African slaves were a more sizable proportion of the slave population in South Carolina than they were in the Chesapeake, much the same pattern seems to have emerged in the latter region as well. Six Angola-born slaves, who decamped from Francis Yonge's Tobodoo plantation in 1771, wore "blue negro cloth jackets and breeches, with the letters F.Y. in scarlet cloth sewed upon the forepart of their jackets," and "negro shoes, and hats."[7] It is possible that the "negro cloth gowns or wrappers" the runaways were said to be wearing over their other garments had African origins (from its sparse description, this item of apparel does not sound too European), perhaps reflecting the continuing importance of African culture in eighteenth-century South Carolina, but the basic point—that African slaves quickly assumed European attire—still stands.

Prompted by Equiano's account, we are inclined to assume that accustoming the African body to the wearing of European garb was just one more facet of a painful process of adjusting to an alien culture. That ordeal could still be recalled in the 1930s by Chaney Mack, who said of her father, "a full-blood African" brought to the United States of America at about age eighteen, that "it went purty hard wid him having to wear clothes, live in houses and work."[8] Like Equiano, Bonna, a "New Negro Fellow" who ran away in 1772, came from "Ibo Country, in Africa" (although, as a "Canoe Man" in his homeland, he must have been rather more familiar with expanses of water than Equiano, in his autobiography, claimed to be). At the time of his escape, Bonna wore "a new Felt Hat, new Cotton Waistcoat and

Breeches, and new Shoes and Stockings," the last-mentioned being "knit, and spotted black and white"—an outfit which, in its newness, sounds particularly uncomfortable.[9] Nonetheless, items of European clothing would not necessarily have been entirely strange to newly arrived Africans. For all the power of Equiano's account of his enslavement, his depiction of an Africa relatively unsullied by European influences does not accord well with recent scholarship. In the area of dress, for example, John Thornton has suggested that, in the wake of European penetration, Africans, particularly the elite, quickly adopted some European fabrics and clothing styles, and that by the mid-seventeenth century the possession of European-style clothing had become an established sign of status.[10]

But, of course, donning an individual item of European clothing in the context of a developed and known set of African values was one thing; wearing such a garment as a slave in the New World was quite another. African slaves were thrust into a society with its own set of ideas about the appropriateness of clothing for various social groups, ideas that, in the fineness of their discriminations between various forms of European apparel, bore little relation to those current in the slaves' native lands. Though by the eighteenth century the earlier elaborate dress codes, occasionally set out in various pieces of sumptuary legislation, were breaking down, it was still the case that a glance could generally distinguish members of the elite from those who made their living with their hands. As laid down in the so-called courtesy books, which were published in England, but to which, as Richard Bushman has shown, the higher social orders in America paid close attention from the eighteenth century, the clothing of the genteel had to be close- rather than ill-fitting, clean and brushed rather than soiled, and, above all, smooth in texture rather than coarse. Garments for the genteel were made from silk, chintz (a fine cotton cloth), and superfine wools, rather than from plain cottons or poorer quality wools or from osnaburg (a coarse, inexpensive linen), fustian (a cotton and linen mix), or linsey-woolsey (a blend of wool and flax), from which the clothing of those lower down the social scale was cut. Specific items of genteel apparel differed too, the tailored shirts, stylish coats, and velvet breeches of the gentry contrasting with the loose shirts (which freed the arms for the kind of physical labor that would have been inappropriate for the genteel), short jackets, and trousers, or leather or osnaburg breeches, worn by the lower orders. In the same way, the silk gowns and lace accessories of elite women were easily distinguishable from the coarse dresses and aprons of their social inferiors.[11]

In such a schema it was clearly intended that slaves would wear loose-fitting garments made of the coarsest available cloth. South Carolina's Negro Act of 1735 actually went so far as to prescribe the materials suitable for slave clothing, allowing only the cheapest fabrics: "negro cloth, duffelds, course kearsies, osnabrigs, blue linnen, checked linnen," and "course garlix or callicoes, checked cottons or scotch plaids," as long as the price of the scotch plaids did not exceed ten shillings a yard.[12] As newspaper advertisements make clear, during the colonial period, when most cloth and clothing was imported, the materials used for slaves' garments fell into a separate category: for example, the freshly imported "white welsh plains," which the Charlestown firm of Hill and Guerard was offering for sale in 1736, were said to be "for Negro cloathing."[13] A good proportion of the runaway slaves advertised as having been "Brought to the Work-House in Charlestown" were described as wearing clothes made of this sort of material. For example, a slave incarcerated there in 1765, who "calls himself Tom, but can't tell his master's name," and who had country marks on his face, shoulders and back, had on "an old white negro cloth jacket and trowsers," while a "new negro fellow of the Jalunka country, who speaks no English" wore an "old white negro cloth jacket and breeches."[14] Two Coromantee Africans, taken up by Joseph Adams on his Edisto Island plantation in 1766, were similarly described: Cuff was "dress'd in old white negro cloth," and Bathsheba "has on a blue negro cloth petticoat, and white negro cloth wrapper."[15] For the most part, slaves were either given ready-made clothes or used "negro cloth" to make trousers, petticoats, and the like, but the "negro cloth wrapper" worn by Bathsheba does suggest that some of them may have used European textiles to fashion items of African design. Attempting to locate African origins for the clothing styles that are tersely described in runaway advertisements or contemporary newspapers is an exercise fraught with difficulty, but occasionally the language used by slaveholders conveys a sense of cultural distance: a planter, who in 1734 took up two runaways swimming in the Combahee river, described them as wearing "long Frocks of white Plaines," which was hardly customary Euro-American garb.[16]

In a context in which most clothing had to be imported, garments doled out to slaves throughout the American colonies tended to be drab, uniform and limited to relatively few items. So basic was the apparel of many blacks, particularly that of ordinary field hands, that in many runaway notices the nature of the miscreant's clothing was not even the main

definition, stylistic infractions by those lower down the social scale must have been apparent. References in Jones's description of Bacchus's clothing to a "fine Cloth Pompadour Waistcoat" and a "fine Hat cut and cocked in the [highly fashionable] Macaroni Figure" suggest that, however smudged the boundary between elite and nonelite clothing may have become, Bacchus had transgressed it. Of course, his stylish waistcoat and hat may have been well-worn, but presumptuous intrusions of the kind he had made into the realm of the elite must still have constituted an affront.

Particularly among house slaves, Bacchus's case was far from unique. After commenting that his female slave Road, who ran away in North Carolina in 1775, "wears her hair combed over a large roll" and "affected gaiety in dress," Josiah Hall itemized her clothing thus: "a homespun striped jacket, a red quilted petticoat, a black silk hat, a pair of leather shoes, with wooden heals, a chintz gown, and a black cloak."[23] Two years later, Charles Alexander Warfield, of Ann Arundel County, Maryland, offered eighty silver dollars reward for the return of the runaways Dick and Lucy. Dick, Warfield noted, had taken with him "a green cloth coat, with a crimson velvet cape, a red plush do, with blue cuffs and cape, a deep blue camblet jacket, with gold lace at the sleeves, down the breast and round the collar, a pair of Russia drab overalls, a white shirt, two osnabrig do, a pair of pumps and buckles, with sundry other cloaths." Lucy "had with her two calico gowns, one purple and white, the other red and white, a deep blue moreens petticoat, two white country cotton do, a striped do, and jacket, and black silk bonnet, a variety of handkerchiefs and ruffles, two lawn aprons, two Irish linen do, a pair of high heel shoes, a pair of kid gloves and a pair of silk mitts, a blue sarsanet handkerchief, trim'd with gauze, with white ribbon sew'd to it, several white linen shirts, osnabrigs for two do, hempen rolles petticoat, with several other things that she probably will exchange for others if in her power."[24] Not only is the sheer quantity of clothes these slaves owned striking, but it is also clear that many of the items they had acquired, such as the "crimson velvet cape," the "blue sarsanet [fine silk] handkerchief," and the intriguing "high heel shoes," were recognizable insignia of gentility.

Slave artisans, too, could assemble impressive wardrobes. According to his owner, the "proper Dress" of Abraham, a bricklayer, who ran away in South Carolina in 1771, "consisted of a Coat, Waistcoat, and long Trowsers of blue Plains, good Stockings, Shoes, Silver Buckles, and an old Beaver

Hat." On special occasions demanding more extravagant display, Abraham would don a "dark Olive-coloured Coat, and blue Breeches, both of super-fine Cloth."[25] Jachne, a cooper, also of South Carolina, who absconded in that same year, wore, unremarkably, "a blue duffil great coat, a blue negro cloth jacket, a pair of white negro cloth breeches, and a pair of negro cloth boots," but also carried with him "a suit of scarlet camblet, faced with green, a scarlet cloth waistcoat, trimmed with gold lace, and a gold laced hat."[26] These slaves, too, had managed to incorporate items of elite costume into their dress.

It was not uncommon for slaveowners to remark on their slaves' great love of fine clothing. Anthony, a young slave "handy at most any kind of business," who ran away from his master in Talbot County, Maryland, in 1787, was "very fond of shewy dress."[27] George, "a likely fellow," who went missing in Richmond, Virginia, in 1778, was not only "very fond of dancing and playing of his antic tricks" but also "fond of dress." "His cloaths I can't recollect," Robert Rawlings, his owner, conceded, "as he has a great variety of them, and of the best kind."[28] The Virginia slave Peter Deadfoot, a shoemaker, butcher, plowman, sawyer, waterman, and "one of the best scythemen . . . in America," who went missing in 1768, was also "extremely fond of dress." Deadfoot's "holiday clothes" had been confiscated when he had attempted to run away on an earlier occasion, but his owner expected him quickly to replace them, since a man with his skills would readily find employment.[29] Not surprisingly, Jenny, who ran away in Philadelphia in 1782, taking with her "a bundle of cloaths, consisting of one light chintz gown, a small figure with red stripes, one dark ditto with a large flower and yellow stripes, seven yards of new stamped linen, a purple flower and stripe, a pink-coloured moreen petticoat, a new black peelong bonnet, a chip hat trimmed with gauze and feathers, four good shifts, two not made up, and two a little worn, four aprons, two white and two check, one pair of blue worsted shoes with white heels" and "had in her shoes a large pair of silver buckles," was said by her master to be "very fond of dress" and, more opaquely, "particularly of wearing queen's night-caps."[30]

For many whites, the sight of a well-dressed slave, particularly one displaying expensive items of apparel, aroused suspicion that the wearer might be involved in some sort of illicit activity. Framers of the South Carolina Negro Act of 1735 referred disapprovingly to the number of Negroes who wore "clothes much above the condition of slaves, for the procuring whereof they use sinister and evil methods."[31] There is ample evidence that many blacks did steal clothes. Sometimes they took garments belonging to other slaves; the owner of Cloe, who had run away in 1783, surmised that her "unwillingness to return now, is not less owing to the shame of seeing the negroes whom she deprived of their cloathes, than the dread of correction."[32] More usually, however, African Americans stole from whites. The runaway Robin, "of the Guinea country," briefly returned of his own accord, but only to steal from his master's house "a whitney jacket and plush breeches, both blue, which he may possibly wear."[33] Tom, who ran from Arthur Neil of Charlestown in 1765, wore his own clothes, but took with him "a dark coloured jacket with vellum button holes, a linen jacket" and several other items belonging to his master.[34]

More significant than theft as a means of acquiring additional clothing, was white complicity. In 1735, the South Carolina legislature had specifically forbidden slaves to wear the cast-off clothes of their owners,[35] but this section of the Negro Act became little more than a dead letter, ignored by whites who had something to gain by exploiting the sartorial desires of their human property. Clothing was embedded in the system of rewards and punishments designed to make the plantations and, indeed, the whole institution of slavery run smoothly. In the 1780s, the Rev. Henry Laurens told John Owens, his overseer, that "Sam, Scaramouche, or any other Negro who has behaved remarkably well" should be rewarded, and suggested that Owens "distinguish them in their cloathing by something better than white plains." The overseer then saw to it that Laurens's most faithful slaves received quantities of blue cloth and metal buttons.[36] Owners also allowed slaves to earn small amounts of money on the side, either through doing extra work on their own or adjoining plantations or by raising vegetables, poultry, and the like on small plots of land not needed for commercial production. Though this happened particularly often in the South Carolina low country where the task system was in operation, many slaves throughout the mainland colonies had similar, if more limited, opportunities. Slaves were able to spend much of this extra money on clothing, which, as far as owners were concerned, was certainly preferable to having them buy alcohol.[37]

The result was a quasi-licit trade in apparel that in many ways mirrored the colonial elite's and middling classes' concerns with consumption and fashion. Not only was clothing valued by slaves for its own sake, but also, since it could readily be exchanged, it could function as a form of currency. The Maryland owner of the twenty-one-year-old Jacob was unable to say which clothes his slave was wearing because Jacob had "lost his own at cards just before he went away."[38] It was pointless to describe his runaway slave Peter's clothing, Samuel Sherwin declared, because the last time Peter returned after a brief absence he "had not one article of the dress he went off in."[39] Jack's owner did not bother itemizing his runaway slave's clothes because he had doubtless disposed of all but those he needed. Indeed, he had "offered some for sale, a little before he went off, for hard money."[40] Slaves bought, sold, bartered, and traded garments in an underground economy that easily and quietly absorbed items of questionable origin.[41] Little wonder, then, that many slaves, as they departed, grabbed an armful of their owners' clothing in order to finance their flight, or that many of these often expensive items ended up on the backs of other slaves. Some of the clothes that Erskyne, a "Guiney Country" slave who ran away in South Carolina in 1773, took with him were, his master noted tartly, "really too good for any of his Colour."[42]

Opportunities for acquiring additional clothing were always more numerous in urban areas. Here, the scope for conspicuous display was larger, and the ability to earn extra money greater. Particularly was this true of Charlestown. In 1772, the "Stranger" perceived "a great Difference in Appearance as well as Behavior, between *the Negroes* of the Country, and *those* in Charles-Town." Although the former were "generally clad *suitable* to their Condition," the latter were "the very *Reverse*—abandonedly *rude, unmannerly, insolent* and *shameless*."[43] The concentration of several thousand African Americans, many of whom were allowed virtually to fend for themselves, hiring out their own time and hustling around the markets, contributed to the striking dress and demeanor of Charlestown blacks. Slaveowner John Garden recognized the link between hiring out slaves in the city and their consequent control of their own appearance. When he advertised for Amey, who ran away in 1773, Garden simply noted that she "had a variety of cloaths" as she had "been hired out in Charles-Town for some years past."[44]

In Charlestown, too, concerns about the connection between well-dressed African American women and the sexual depredations of white men that were often veiled elsewhere, were made explicit. In 1744, less than a decade after the passage of the colony's Negro Act, a Grand Jury complained that clothing restrictions were being ignored: "it is apparent, that Negro Women in particular do not restrain themselves in the Cloathing as the Law requires, but dress in Apparel quite gay and beyond their Condition." The source of this unseemly display, the Grand Jury suggested, was either theft or "other Practices equally vicious."[45] A quarter of a century later, the "Stranger" lamented that "many of the *Female* Slaves [are] by far more *elegantly* dressed, than the Generality of *White Women* below Affluence," a state of affairs which he attributed to "scandalous *Intimacy*" between the "*Sexes of different Colours.*"[46] In a later letter to the *South Carolina Gazette*, the "Stranger" again complained that no one seemed interested in enforcing the regulations about slave dress: indeed, this anonymous correspondent expostulated, "there is scarce a new mode [of fashion] which *favourite* black and mulatto *women slaves* are not immediately *enabled* to adopt."[47]

Any attempt to work out the significance of slaves' clothing forces us to grapple with an African American culture whose relationship with the dominant culture was necessarily characterized by ambiguities and ambivalences. Such an enterprise is daunting not only because we are trying to grasp at something that was seldom if ever consciously articulated at the time but also because the sources are fragmentary and one-sided. There were at least two different and competing value systems operating in eighteenth-century America, and while it appears that many slaves were well aware that their actions had meaning in both Euro-American and African American worlds, only a few whites even dimly perceived this to be the case. Most colonists, whose observations are the source of virtually all our knowledge of this aspect of the black past, were content to dismiss what we call African American culture as little more than unsuccessful attempts by an inferior group to imitate white ways.

Nevertheless, whites can hardly have welcomed slaves' arrogation of elements of elite dress. Such actions disturbed the nuanced social order that clothing was supposed to display, blurring the borderlines between black and white, slave and free. Mention has already been made of Bacchus's lavish and, to whites, clearly inappropriate apparel and of his owner's expectation that Bacchus was off to Great Britain to obtain his freedom, an audacious plan that would doubtless have confirmed slaveholders' worst fears. But generally the point of slaves wearing such clothes was not so much that they were adopting white values as that they were subverting white authority. Often, it seems, there was a light mocking touch to slaves' activities, a characteristic that is extremely difficult to pick up two hundred years later. On a Saturday night in 1772, the "Stranger" attended a gathering of about sixty slaves who had assembled a few miles outside of Charlestown for a dance. As the festivities commenced, he noticed "the men copying (or *taking off*) the manners of their masters, and the women those of their mistresses."[48] At least some slaves, we are suggesting, through the way they shaped the appearance of their bodies, were indulging intentionally in a similar activity. Like many other blacks, John Jackson, who ran away in New York in 1794, was fond of clothes, often dressing in "rather beauish" fashion and wearing his "wool turn'd up and a comb behind." According to a postscript to the advertisement seeking his return, Jackson had been seen on the Kingsbridge Road resplendent in a "dark blue coat, with a velvet collar and his wool powdered."[49] The "beauish" clothing of this slave, and his powdering of his hair to resemble a wig, must have created an effect dangerously close to parody. Such use of clothing and appearance might, as Jonathan Prude has perceptively noted, "reveal a further way deference came to be interrogated during the eighteenth century."[50]

Although it is likely that many slaves were aware of the import of their actions in the white world, they were also wearing such clothing in the context of another set of values. Just as the African elite happily appropriated items of European clothing, so eighteenth-century slaves on the American mainland may simply have added to their ensemble any garment that caught their fancy or that they managed to acquire. Among many blacks there appears to have been little if any sense that such an item should coordinate in style, color, or anything else with the rest of their garb; it was precisely this characteristic of wearing what appeared, to white eyes, to be odd combinations of clothing, of lumping together, say, an elegant jacket with a pair of trousers fashioned out of coarse, drab material, that whites found risible. Yet at the same time, whites were probably unable entirely to dismiss the suggestion that their own behavior was being held up to gentle (albeit often very public) ridicule.

Consider, for example, the hats that some slaves fashioned for themselves. Erskyne, the runaway from the "Guiney Country" mentioned as having clothes "really too good for any of his Colour," completed his ensemble with a handkerchief tied around his head and a hat on top of it.[51] Will, a twenty-year-old runaway who was, according to his owner, a "great thief and lyar," took with him "a bright brown coloured Kerseymire coattee, waistcoat and breeches, a drab coloured broad cloth ditto, with old spangled buttons," and a hat whose band was yellow and whose crown was "covered with the skin of a large bird." [52] Jerry, a Maryland runaway, created a similar if somewhat more subdued effect by covering the crown of his straw hat with hare's fur. [53] Consider also the way in which slaves incorporated items of military garb into their dress. Jack, a Maryland slave who went missing in 1781, had on a "blue regimental coat," and Abel, a Virginia runaway, wore a "brown regimental coat faced with green," which must have contrasted interestingly with his "buff cloth waistcoat edged with blue." [54] In part, slaves may have worn these items of military apparel because they were all that was available during periods of shortages—many of the descriptions date from the Revolutionary War—but it also seems likely that their color, cut, and cloth made such garments desirable at any time. Dick, "a stout elderly Angola fellow" who ran away in December 1771, had on a coat and trousers made of blue negro cloth but also wore, underneath his coat, a soldier's jacket that was colored red. [55]

This aspect of African American culture probably attained its most heightened expression in the garb of the principal characters in Pinkster, Negro Election Day, and General Training. These slave festivals, which occurred sporadically in the eighteenth century throughout New England, New York, and New Jersey, usually lasted for one or two days in May or June, although Pinkster could occupy a week. The rituals varied considerably from place to place and over time, but typically a slave—usually called a King or Governor and usually African-born—was in charge of proceedings and slaves from the surrounding area gathered to drink, eat, gamble, listen to music, and dance. Generally, all slaves attending attired themselves in their best clothes, but, inevitably, most attention was focused on the candidates for office and on the black Kings and Governors, who often borrowed items of clothing, and even swords and horses, from their owners in order to create a spectacular visual display. Cyrus Bruce, the slave of Governor John Langdon in Portsmouth, New Hampshire, was well known for appearing at Election flamboyantly dressed, wearing a massive gold chain, cherry-colored small-clothes, silk stockings, ruffles, and silver shoe-buckles. But few would have managed to cut a figure quite as striking as King Charles, who officiated over Pinkster in Albany, New York, in the 1790s and early 1800s. His ceremonial garb consisted of a British brigadier's broad-cloth scarlet jacket covered in bright gold lace and reaching almost to his heels, fresh and new yellow buckskin small-clothes, blue stockings, highly burnished silver buckles on well-blackened shoes, and a three-cornered cocked hat also trimmed with gold lace. This slave's carefully constructed appearance was an act of cultural *bricolage,* the imaginative mediation of an African-born slave in a new, European-dominated environment.[56] But it was also an extravagant example—deliberately exaggerated for festival and, because of that, obvious even to us—of the way in which individual slaves throughout the American colonies managed to incorporate items of clothing into a "look" that whites found strange and occasionally even unsettling.

During the colonial period, slaves were sometimes involved in the fashioning of their clothing. In 1770, the Georgia planter John Channing offered ready-made clothing to his slaves, only to find that they "chose to have the Cloth given them and their Wives or Sisters to cut it out and make them up for them."[57] We have already noted that some slaves may have been using Negro Cloth to create their own garments, particularly the "wrappers" that covered their normal attire. Others used dyes to relieve the drabness of their appearance. Slaves performed most of the skilled tasks involved in the manufacture of indigo, and some put the knowledge acquired in this way to more personal use. In appealing for the return of London, his Gambia-born slave, in 1758, Daniel Legare pointed out that the runaway's clothes were "dyed with indico."[58] Jupiter, who went missing in 1779, wore a pair of osnaburg trousers "dyed with indigo."[59] African Americans' developing knowledge of properties of local flora gave them access to stronger colors. Sam, who escaped from his South Carolina owner, Alexander Moon, in 1741, had on when he went away "a Negro Cloth Jacket died with red Oak Bark," and both Harry and Yanki, who ran away from a plantation on John's Island in 1747, had colored their clothes with the same substance.[60] However, although instances of African American involvement in the styling and coloring of their dress did occur, they were not common and certainly did not reflect the situation that obtained on most plantations.

As far as we can tell from the occasional glimpses of slaves the sources allow, it appears that in the eighteenth century the creativity of Africans and African Americans in shaping their appearance lay not so much in their manufacturing and coloring their own garments as in the way they combined in their clothing ensembles items made elsewhere. Strange as it may seem, slaves too were consumers in the new and wondrous "empire of goods," an empire that, as T. H. Breen has shown, was by the middle of the eighteenth century besotting free whites.[61] Since most of the cloth and clothing in which slaves dressed was imported, slaves' as well as slaveowners' normal patterns of consumption were considerably disturbed by the non-importation movements of the 1760s and 1770s and by the Revolution itself. In 1774 Ralph Izard cautioned Henry Laurens that should "our disputes with England continue, which I am inclined to think, they will," it would become "very necessary for us to think of the means of clothing our negroes." Izard's fears proved to be well-founded. During an exchange of correspondence with Laurens the following year, he confessed that "no part of your last letter . . . affects me so much, as the want of clothing for the negroes."[62]

The pragmatic solution to this problem, as Joyce Chaplin has convincingly shown, was a move away from monoculture and commercial production toward a more diversified plantation economy. Driven by the political crises of the 1770s, planters turned to cotton, flax, and wool for the raw materials that would enable them to clothe their slaves. They also scrambled for the equipment necessary to process these raw materials and for slaves capable of operating it. During the Revolutionary War, overseas markets for rice and indigo closed, and, as Chaplin has noted, many planters in the South Carolina and Georgia low country simply allowed slaves to raise crops for their own subsistence in an attempt to keep them on the plantation, a development with important implications for the degree of autonomy the region's slaves enjoyed. Commercial production rapidly resumed at the end of the war, but the changes wrought by its disruptive influence could not be undone.[63] Increasingly, from this time, plantation slaves were given the job of making their own cloth and clothing, a trend that received renewed impetus during the Napoleonic Wars and culminated in the emergence of the Cotton Kingdom. Surrounded by the raw stuff of clothing, cotton planters in particular saw little sense in parting with hard cash for textiles and apparel that they could easily compel their slaves to produce.

By the 1840s and 1850s, a time when our knowledge of the details of plantation life increases exponentially because of the Works Progress Administration interviews with ex-slaves, the manufacture of slave clothing had, to a significant extent, passed into the hands of female slaves.[64] White women had some involvement in textile production; however, as Elizabeth Fox-Genovese has pointed out, "mistresses might supervise or even participate in making the slaves' clothing, but their efforts, which figure as such a burden in their accounts, seem diminished when viewed from the perspective of the slaves' work."[65] Lizzie Norfleet, a young slave on a Mississippi plantation during the Civil War, remembered that "all of our clothes was made on the place," a refrain that echoes through interview after interview conducted in the 1930s with former slaves.[66] A large number of interviewees commented on the amount of time that her or his mother and other female slaves spent weaving cloth, a task they often did communally. Jake McLeod from South Carolina remembered that "de women had to weave five cuts a week, one cut a night."[67] Tempie Durham from North Carolina told how "de cardin' an' spinnin' room was full of niggers. I can hear dem spinnin' wheels now turnin' roun' an' sayin' hum-m-m-m, hum-m-m-m, an' hear de slaves singin' while dey spin."[68]

Drawing on a rich botanical lore, much of it probably derived from Africa and adapted to local circumstances in the American South, these women also manufactured and used the dyes that gave slave clothing a distinctive appearance. Tempie Durham remembered the skill of Mammy Rachel with a sense of awe: "dey wuzn' nothin' she didn' know 'bout dyein'. She knew every kind of root, bark, leaf an' berry dat made red, blue, green, or whatever color she wanted."[69] Some of the W.P.A. interviews resemble nothing so much as a pharmacopoeia of the American South. Millie Evans, born in 1849, took the opportunity presented by her interview to educate her questioner:

> I'll tell yo' how to dye. A little beech bark dyes slate color set with copperas. Hickory bark and bay leaves dye yellow set with chamber lye; bamboo dyes turkey red, set color wid copperas. Pine straw dyes purple, set color with chamber lye. To dye cloth brown we would take de cloth and put it in the water where leather had been tanned an let it soak then set the color with apple vinegar. An we dyed blue wid indigo an set the color wid alum.[70]

Other slaves swore by walnut bark to make brown, a mixture of cedar and sweet gum to make purple, shumake to produce black, and cedar moss out of the canebrake to make yellow. Over seventy years later, Tempie Durham could still vividly recall Mammy Rachel hunched over steaming pots of "roots, bark an' stuff," using a stick to stir around hanks of wool or cotton in the boiling liquid. "An' when she hang dem up on de line in de sun," this former slave added proudly, "dey was every color of de rainbow."[71]

Slave women used this dyed thread to enhance the look of the cloth they made. Julia Woodberry, formerly a slave in South Carolina, remembered that "dey would take dat colored yarn en weave all kinds of pretty streaks in de cloth."[72] Bettie Bell, emancipated in Alabama at about the age of eight, told how her mother was particularly adept at "makin' two an' three color'd cloth by putting diff'rent color'd thread on de shuttles"; Hagar Lewis, another former slave, recollected that her mother put colored thread in the woven material that was used to make Hagar's "pretty" Sunday dresses.[73] Lizzie Norfleet, too, remembered that the dresses slave women made for themselves out of this cloth were "beautiful," with "one dark stripe and one bright stripe." "Folks them days," she averred, "knowed how to mix pretty colors."[74]

The role of slave women in fashioning the appearance of the slave community did not end there. Benjamin Johnson, an ex-slave from Georgia, told his interviewer that, although slaves' clothes were just "ol' plain white cloth," they "wus patched fum de legs to de waist," and that "some wus patched so till dey looked like a quilt."[75] This mending was in part a matter of necessity, but something more was involved. Hattie Thompson recalled that as soon "as the washing was brung in the clothes had to be sorted out and every snag place patched nice"; but, significantly, she also added that during her childhood, in the final stages of the Civil War and the early years of Reconstruction, "patching and darning was *stylish*."[76] Such testimony hints at the existence of an underlying aesthetic at some remove from that of the slaves' owners.

This aesthetic comes more clearly into focus if we look at the way these women remade second-hand items of clothing. It was not uncommon for favored slaves, often those working as servants, to receive discarded garments. Gabe Emanuel remembered:

> Course, all de time us gits han'-me-downs from de white folkes in de Big House. Us what was a-servin' in de Big House wore de marster's old dress suits. Now dat was somep'n. Mos' o' de time dey didn' fit—maybe de pants hung a little loose an' de tails o' de coat hung a little long. Me bein' de house boy, I used to look mighty sprucy when I put on my frock tail.[77]

In the slaves' eyes, such clothes often needed adjusting, and not only because they did not fit very well. A good example of the process of adaptation appears in Elizabeth Botume's *First Days amongst the Contrabands,* an account of this northern school teacher's experiences as she ministered to South Carolina ex-slaves during the closing stages of the Civil War and the beginning of Reconstruction. To the delight of her African American pupils, thirty new plaid worsted dresses, already cut and basted, arrived at Botume's sewing school, but when the young black women took the dresses home their mothers looked askance at them. The new garments, Botume soon learned, were considered far too short, it being "highly indecorous to have the feet and ankles show below the dress." So the pupils "pieced them out, often with the most unsuitable material, putting old cloth with the new, and a cotton frill to a worsted skirt." In one case, the mother obtained some new material, "which she inlaid to widen and lengthen and enlarge her child's gown," creating an effect "like a modern 'crazy quilt.'" [78]

What lay behind these differences was an African American aesthetic, the use not only of varied materials and patterns but also of contrasting colors in a manner that jangled white sensibilities. [79] Reflecting on the cultural gap between black and white, the northern traveler Frederick Law Olmsted astutely pointed out that the slaves took "a real pleasure, for instance, such as it is a rare thing for a white man to be able to feel, in bright and strongly contrasting colours, and in music, in which nearly all are proficient to some extent." [80] This juxtaposition of color sense and music was not accidental; Olmsted intuitively understood the way in which both expressive forms were linked by an underlying rhythm that was alien to Euro-American cultural forms. The more sensitive of observers often reacted to the manner in which slaves were clothed in much the same way as they reacted to African American music, dance, or other forms of cultural display, disdaining the individual elements but being impressed, in spite of themselves, by the total performance. For example, Mary Chesnut, the famed southern diarist, concluded that an African American sermon she heard was devoid of content. "There was literally nothing in what he said. The words had no meaning at all." Yet the manner of its delivery moved her to tears and excited her to the point where she "would very much have liked to shout, too," just as the black worshippers were doing. [81] Similarly, Elizabeth Botume, confronted by the young contraband woman's quilt-like dress, thought that it looked very odd but almost grudgingly had to concede that it was "really not ugly." [82]

It was African textile traditions, handed down and adapted by African American women, that helped to shape the appearance of the antebellum slave community. As Robert Farris Thompson has pointed out, in the widely influential Mande culture of West Africa "visual aliveness" and vibrancy are achieved in textile production by the deliberate clash not only between colors but also between the variously patterned and unpatterned narrow strips of which the material is made.[83] Thompson calls these "rhythmized textiles," writing that, "as multiple meter distinguishes the traditional music of black Africa, emphatic multistrip composition distinguishes the cloth of West Africa and culturally related Afro-American sites."[84] Although West African narrow-strip looms were not available in the slave South (they would hardly have been suited to the kind of textile production slaveholders required), it seems likely that on occasions African American women, by weaving irregular patterns into the broad-strip cloth they made, incorporated West African principles of design. The former South Carolina slave Mary Scott told a W.P.A. interviewer that she "could weave it [cloth] with stripes and put one check one way and nother strip nother way."[85] In relation specifically to color, Thompson writes that "African cloth has for centuries, as it is today, been distinguishable by deliberate clashing of 'high affect colors,' . . . in willful, percussively contrastive, bold arrangements." He quotes Ma Apina, whom he interviewed in the Djuka maroon capital in Suriname in 1981, as saying that "when Djuka paint something, the colors must clash [*kengi,* literally, 'argue'], and where you stop, there must be another color not looking like the one you end with but far away from it."[86]

Folklorists, students of material culture and, more recently, historians have recognized that such principles were at work in the making of African-American quilts. Maude Southwell Wahlman and John Scully suggest that, in ways that differ markedly from those of Euro-American quiltmakers, these black craftswomen played with colors in order to "to create unpredictability and movement." "A strong color may be juxtaposed with another strong color, or with a weak one; light colors can be used next to dark ones, or put together once and never again. Comparisons are made between similar and opposing colors at the same time in the same quilt. . . . Contrast is used to structure or organize."[87]

Elsa Barkley Brown, impressed by the pervasiveness of these principles, has even suggested that quilting may provide a framework for conceptualizing African-American women's history.[88] It is hardly surprising, then, that African American clothing was sometimes described as looking like a quilt. The same people were involved in both quilting and clothing manufacture and were using much the same materials. As one female ex-slave from Kentucky remembered: "I been knitting socks and sewing and piecing quilts every since I was eight years old." [89] Almost inevitably the aesthetic principles that animated African American quilts carried over into the making of clothing. Martha King, a former Alabama slave, remembered that "we made fancy cloth. We could stripe the cloth or check it or leave it plain." [90] It was this aesthetic that created the striking effect remarked by whites and often fondly remembered by ex-slaves. Another young woman, who was also a child when she was freed, recollected that "my mother used to quilt my skirts from way up here 'round the thigh down to the bottom." Although such a garment, she conceded, now seemed "funny," her "nice warm quilted skirt" had once protected her against the cold. [91]

The involvement of African Americans, during the last decades of slavery, in the making of their clothes allowed them the scope to fashion a distinctive appearance, which was most evident in their Sunday dress. It is possible to find an occasional eighteenth-century slave wearing garments that fit this later pattern: Cyrus, who ran away in Maryland in 1780, took with him "a very remarkable coat, having a great number of patches of different colours." [92] But if not quite unique, Cyrus's coat was extremely atypical, its design and multicolored, quilt-like appearance a harbinger of some nineteenth-century slave clothing but not at all representative of eighteenth-century garb.

It seems clear from the W.P.A. interviews with ex-slaves that the whole process of clothes-making—the fashioning from cast-off clothing and scraps of material of something that was of cultural importance to the slaves, the spinning, weaving, dyeing, and sewing typically completed in poorly lit cabins after a day's work in the fields or around the Big House, and the infusing of all this with an African American aesthetic sensibility—was almost entirely the achievement of slave women. The only part of slaves' apparel that was made by the male slaves was the shoes; and they, it was almost universally agreed, were a disaster. Fashioned from cowhide and usually clumsily fitted with a wooden sole, plantation-made shoes were tough, unforgiving encumbrances burdening black feet. Over seventy years later, the former Texas slave John Ellis still vividly remembered his shoes: "Lawdy ! Dey was so hard we would have to warm dem by de fire and grease dem wid tallow to ever wear dem 'tall." [93]

Joyce Chaplin has eloquently pointed out that a "terrible irony" lay at the heart of the South Carolina and Georgia planters' response to the crisis of the Revolution. Cotton, the crop that "briefly characterized slaves' wartime liberation from planters' full authority," became the staple that "would characterize the bondage of their children and grandchildren."[94] In the response to this crisis, too, lay the seeds of slaves' involvement in the production of their clothing. While that involvement considerably increased the burden borne by slave women, it also allowed slaves greater scope to fashion their appearance, to shape the visual impact of their bodies in ways that differentiated them from eighteenth-century African Americans and nineteenth-century whites. Thus the movement away from reliance on the "empire of goods" toward dependence on slave-made textiles for slave clothing supports Rhys Isaac's perceptive suggestion that in late eighteenth-century Virginia the cultural rift between black and white was widening.[95]

The clothes of children and the ordinary work clothes of adult slaves on antebellum plantations would not necessarily have displayed the irregular patterns and clashing colors of Sunday go-to-meeting clothes. Until young slaves reached the age of twelve or even fifteen, their clothing was androgynous; both males and females wore only a long shirt or smock, which prompted the expression "shirt-tail nigger" often used by ex-slaves in the W.P.A. interviews. At some time in their teens (not necessarily at puberty), males began to wear a shirt and trousers and females a dress. Yach Stringfellow from Texas remembered that "I wore shirt tail till I's fourteen, den de homespun britches and shirt."[96] According to Caroline Wright, in summer she and the ten other female slaves on her Texas plantation "wore cotton stripe and in de winter, linsey dresses."[97] On his travels through South Carolina, Frederick Law Olmsted came across a gang of about thirty slaves, most of whom were female, repairing a road. They were dressed in "coarse gray gowns" that were "very dirty" and "were reefed up with a cord drawn tightly around the body, a little above the hips" in order to enable the women to work relatively unencumbered.[98]

The material used for everyday work clothes was, as it had been in the eighteenth century, coarse, tough, and, if bought, cheap. Felix Haygood, an ex-slave interviewed in the 1930s, remembered, doubtless with only slight exaggeration, that if someone got "caught by his shirt on a limb of a tree, he had to die there if he weren't cut down."[99] Garments were also often uncomfortable. In the part of Virginia where the late-nineteenth-century black leader Booker T. Washington was raised, slave clothing was often made from flax. Washington states in his autobiography, *Up from Slavery,* that the "most trying ordeal" he had to endure as a slave was "the wearing of a flax shirt," an experience which he likened to having "a hun-

dred small pinpoints, in contact with his flesh." "One of the most generous acts that I ever heard of one slave relative doing for another," he said,
was when his elder brother John wore his new flax shirt for him for several
days until it was "broken in." [100]

Whites continued to use clothing, and their slaves' liking for it, in an
attempt to create a clear-cut slave hierarchy. Favorite slaves, black slave-
drivers, domestic slaves, and those who had been particularly productive
picking cotton, for example, were encouraged by a system of rewards that
often included items of clothing, both hand-me-downs and new garments.
Writing in the *Southern Agriculturalist* in 1836, "an overseer" claimed that
he always made the black driver "dress himself better than the other negroes," encouraging him in this way "to maintain a pride of character before them, which was highly beneficial." [101] The black driver, whom Basil
Hall used his camera lucida to depict in 1829, is garbed in an outfit that,
particularly in the case of the cutaway coat, a field hand would hardly have
worn to work (see Figure 2). Although the photograph of a group of blacks
on Woodlands plantation returning from the fields (see Figure 3) was probably taken around 1870, after the end of slavery, it is noticeable that the
driver is wearing an outfit remarkably similar to one Hall portrayed and is
clearly differentiated from the laborers he leads.

The major differentiation in African American dress in the antebellum
South, though, was not between different slaves but between what individual slaves wore Monday through Saturday and what they wore on Sundays. No matter how poorly they were treated, most southern slaves had a
few special items of clothing with which to dress up, and it was here that
slave women's handicraft skills with cloth and dyes were displayed to full
effect. One South Carolina bondsman told Olmsted that, although the local slaves were "a'mos' naked, wen deys at work," it was a different case on
the sabbath. With some pride the old man remarked that "Sundays dey is
mighty well clothed, dis country; 'pears like dere an't nobody looks better
Sundays dan dey do." [102] Julia Larken was only a young girl when freedom
came, but she could clearly remember the grown-up slaves heading off for
church from the Georgia plantation where she was raised: "dey was dressed
in deir best Sunday go-to-meetin' clothes and deir shoes, all shined up, was
tied together and hung over deir shoulders to keep 'em from gittin' dust on
'em." The men wore "plain homespun shirts and jeans pants," and while
some of the women wore homespun dresses, "most of 'em had a calico dress
what was saved special for Sunday meetin' wear." [103]

In many cases this Sunday go-to-meeting apparel was sufficiently striking to provoke in white observers feelings of bemusement or contempt. Fanny Kemble, resident on her husband's Georgia plantation in the late 1830s, pronounced the "sabbath toilet" of the slaves to be "the most ludicrous combination of incongruities that you can conceive . . . every color in the rainbow, and the deepest possible shades blended in fierce companionship."[104] In 1859, a visitor to the rice lands of the South labeled the Sunday clothing of a group of blacks waiting to enter a church as "a rainbow pot pourri."[105] The most spectacular effects, though, were found not on the plantations but in the urban centers of the South. In 1845 a Canadian visitor to Charleston, witnessing a Sunday congregation emerging from a "fashionable" African American church, reacted with incredulity: "such exquisite dandies, such gorgeously dressed women, I never saw before— howling swells, all of them! All slaves!"[106] Even during the Civil War, Arthur James Lyon Fremantle, a Sandhurst graduate and Southern sympathizer, out for a drive in Houston on a Sunday afternoon, found "innumerable negroes and negresses parading about the streets in the most outrageously grand costumes," apparel which he contrasted, doubtless with a certain amount of hyperbole, with the "simple dresses" of their mistresses.[107]

Olmsted observed the same phenomenon. After spending several hours in Richmond on a Sunday, he noted that a considerable number of the blacks were "dressed with foppish extravagance, and many in the latest style of fashion." On the better streets "there were many more well-dressed and highly-dressed coloured people than white; and among this dark gentry the finest French cloths, embroidered waistcoats, patent-leather shoes, resplendent brooches, silk hats,

Figure 2: *Two Slave-Drivers and a Backwoodsman with His Rifle* (detail). Basil Hall, *Forty Etchings, from Sketches Made with the Camera Lucida, in North America, in 1827 and 1828* (Edinburgh, 1829), sketch no. 20.

Figure 3: G. N. Barnard, *View of Laborers Returning from Picking Cotton at Sunset on Alexander Knox's [Woodlands] Plantation, Mount Pleasant* (stereograph c. 1870). Collection of The New-York Historical Society

kid gloves, and *eau de mille fleurs,* were quite common."[108] Nor was it only outsiders who commented on this feature of African American life. Mary Chesnut overheard a Southern lady in a Columbia hotel in 1862 declare that it was "one of our sins as a nation, the way we indulged them [the slaves] in sinful finery. We let them dress too much. It led them astray. We will be punished for it."[109]

Rather than "indulging" their slaves, as this lady suggested, slaveowners used clothing as a means of reinforcing paternalism. Olmsted speculated correctly that many of the garments he had seen in Richmond were the "cast-off fine clothes of the white people," and he also surmised that many slaves were buying clothing from shops in Richmond.[110] The internal economy that had existed in the eighteenth century was flourishing even more strongly in the antebellum years, and it was common for slaves to spend the money they managed to accumulate on clothing or other accessories. Shade Richards, born a slave in Georgia in 1846, remembered that slaves' Sunday clothes "were bought with the money they made off the little 'patches' the master let them work for themselves."[111] Tom Singleton's master allowed him to work at night time, cutting wood and mending fences for local, non-slaveholding whites. With the cash he earned Singleton "bought Sunday shoes and a Sunday coat and sich lak, cause I wuz a Nigger what always did lak to look good on Sunday."[112] In the sugar-growing regions of Louisiana, a correspondent of *Harper's Magazine* reported in 1853, local peddlers grew rich at Christmas time by selling to the slaves "ribbons and nick-nacks, that have no other recommendation than the possession of staring colors in the most glaring contrasts."[113]

Whatever the origin of individual items may have been, and however disdainfully whites such as this *Harper's* correspondent may have viewed black apparel, clothing constituted an important element in the remembered life of slavery, a point that is made abundantly clear in the W.P.A. interviews and other sources. At times it is the language the former slaves used to describe their appearance—one Alabama ex-slave claimed that he was "'bout the mos' dudish nigger in them parts," and Silvia Dubois, who had been enslaved in New Jersey, told C. W. Larison of her desire "to look pretty sniptious"[114]—but more commonly it is the way in which fond references to clothing are embedded in the mosaic of little incidents they recall, fragments of their lives given in answer to the interviewers' questions about slavery, that underlines the generality of this characteristic.

Jack Maddox, recollecting the first time he ever saw his future wife at a Louisiana party in 1869, commented that "she was a good dresser but not as fine a dresser as me."[115] Other ex-slaves readily supplied their questioners with very detailed descriptions of the clothes they wore when they got married. Addie Vinson explained that:

> My weddin' dress was jus' de purtiest thing; it was made out of parade cloth, and it had a full skirt wid ruffles from de knees to de hem. De waist fitted tight and it was cut lowneck wid three ruffles 'round de shoulder. Dem puff sleeves was full from de elbow to de hand, all dem ruffles was aidged wid lace and, 'round my waist I wore a wide pink sash. De underskirt was trimmed wid lace, and dere was lace on de bottom of de drawers laigs. Dat was sho one purty outfit dat I wore to marry dat no 'count man in.[116]

Although African American testimony makes clear to us the importance of clothing in the life of slaves, white reactions, principally those of outsiders such as Kemble and Olmsted, emphasize what was distinctive about the slaves' appearance. Their comments, which fall into three broad and overlapping categories, amplify points made earlier in this discussion. First, and most important, whites noted that slaves wore colors that were not merely bright and vivid but that, in Euro-American terms, clashed violently. Second, they observed that slaves combined not only different pieces of material in one garment but also various items of clothing within one ensemble in what they regarded as odd, even bizarre, ways. For example, when Fanny Kemble declared that the Sunday clothing of the slaves on her husband's plantation displayed "the most ludicrous combination of incongruities," she had more than startling color contrasts in mind. She was particularly taken by a young black man, the son of her washerwoman, who "came to pay his respects to me in a magnificent black satin waistcoat, shirt gills which absolutely engulfed his black visage, and neither shoes nor stockings on his feet."[117] To Kemble, the outfit seemed strange, but to the black youth the items of elite clothing he had appropriated signified differently. Finally, travelers and other commentators often complained about slaves' propensity to dress "above themselves," to engage in forms of conspicuous display inappropriate to their lowly station in life.

On any Sunday throughout the antebellum South these characteristics could be observed to varying degrees. The variation or exact mixture de-

Carnival (see Figure 4).[122] The painting may have been completed in 1877, but in its depiction of a "rag man" clothed in an outfit of brilliant and clashing colors, and even in the way the African American woman wielding a needle and thread administers a last-minute touch or two, it evokes both the Jonkonnu of slavery times (then the very recent past) and the role of women in fashioning slaves' appearance. Like the garb of King Charles on Pinkster days, the clothing of the "rag man" was a deliberate, festive exaggeration of the African American cultural principles that animated slaves' apparel, particularly on Sundays.

What then was the significance of the way in which antebellum slaves clothed themselves? Occasionally, slaves made the meaning of their garb so clear that no one could have been in any doubt as to their intentions. During the Civil War, Madison Bruin's mother, a Kentucky slave, displayed the "Yankee flag" on top of her dress, although a modicum of discretion did dictate that when "de 'federates come raidin'" she wore it "under her dress

Figure 4: Winslow Homer, *Dressing for Carnival* (1877). All rights reserved, The Metropolitan Museum of Art, Lazarus Fund, 1922. (22.220)

like a petticoat." [123] More usually, however, meaning is elusive, blurred and ambiguous rather than certain. James Washington, an ex-slave born in Mississippi in 1854, clearly remembered a dress worn by his mother: "it wus blue en had picturs uf gourds in it en mammy sed I wus 3 years old when she hed dat dress." [124] Washington's mother was wearing a dress of Euro-American cut, but the combination of the color (blue was a frequently used element in the African palette) and the motif of the gourd (an emblematic African and African American utensil) suggests that the design and the overall effect displayed an African American sensibility. Washington's mistress would never have worn such a dress.

At times slaves felt impelled to conceal their choice items of clothing from whites. Evelyn Jones's grandmother told her that when she went to church she carried her go-to-meeting outfit in a bundle, changed near the church, and hid her old clothes under a rock. After the service she changed back for the journey home. As Evelyn Jones remembered, "she didn't dare let the white folks see her in good clothes." [125] But this was relatively un-usual. Generally, as numerous commentators attest, slaves were only too keen to display, even to flaunt, their finery both to other slaves and to whites. This was particularly the case in the cities, where the Sunday promenade of well-dressed slaves attracted whites' rapt, almost voyeuristic, gaze. There can be little doubt that blacks intended to create such an effect. The vivid, visual presence they established was an emphatic repudiation of their al-lotted social role. By not merely appropriating valued items of white cloth-ing but also reassembling them according to a different aesthetic code, slaves garbed in their Sunday go-to-meeting clothes blurred racial and so-cial boundaries and intruded, in a disconcerting fashion, into the world and consciousness of their supposed betters. Some whites ridiculed such "over-dressed" slaves as little more than imitators; others, predictably, were outraged at the slaves' presumption; but, especially among more sensitive and acute observers like Mary Chesnut, there was an edginess underlying the white response to this black style, a sense that white control was, at least obliquely, being challenged.

The contours of the African American aesthetic that helped to fashion slave clothing are certainly difficult for us, at this remove, to work out; in-deed, at times those contours seem almost chimerical. But that is more a function of the paucity of evidence and the difficulties historians face in trying to construe its meaning than of anything else. Slaves on plantations and in cities had no such difficulties. If the intention of slaveholders was, as one of them asserted, to forbid their slaves "to do anything for themselves in order to cultivate attitudes of absolute dependence,"[126] then clothing proved to be a lapse of some significance. This was the case throughout the history of the institution of slavery in America, but it was particularly true in the three-quarters of a century leading up to the Civil War. Slaveholders may have forced slaves to fashion their clothes, originally because of shortages during the Revolutionary era, and later, when most plantations were abundantly supplied with cotton and wool, in order to save money, but slaves made the most of this extra burden and created something that a surprising number remembered many years later with pride and a sense of achievement. The way in which slaves combined both colors and individual items of clothing in the eighteenth and nineteenth centuries revealed the polyrhythmic nature of their culture, a characteristic that also infused other expressive forms, ranging from quilting, dance, and music to speech, and that was illustrative of a particular way of seeing and ordering the world. This understanding derived from African cultures, but, by the antebellum years, American-born slaves had adapted it to life in the New World. It is properly labeled "African American." In short, clothing was a vital and integral part of a culture that, fashioned out of adversity, made the lives of African Americans during the time of their enslavement bearable. But with the coming of freedom and the consequent dispersal of the slave community, African Americans were increasingly drawn into an economic system that left them with neither the time nor the facilities to fashion their own cloth and clothing and forced them to buy cheaply manufactured goods. This engagement with the market and consumption represented not novelty but a return to the patterns of the colonial past, an irony that was doubtless lost on African American sharecroppers and laborers as they struggled to find a secure place in a hostile, post-slavery world.

Done Up in the Tastiest Manner

Describing his sojourn in the region near Natchez, Mississippi, in the early 1830s, Joseph Ingraham paused briefly to reflect on the nature of plantation life. "No scene," the New-England-born traveler intoned, "can be livelier or more interesting to a Northerner, than that which the negro quarters of a well regulated plantation present, on a Sabbath morning, just before church hour." What Ingraham had warmed to, in particular, was the domestic busyness of the slaves as they spent their free time on the Lord's Day in a refreshing and suitably self-improving fashion. "In every cabin the men are shaving and dressing—the women, arrayed in their gay muslins, are arranging their frizzy hair, in which they take no little pride, or investigating the condition of their children's heads—the old people neatly clothed are quietly conversing or smoking about their doors."[1] This vignette may be suffused with an implacable sense of the rightness of the plantation order—indeed, such seemingly contented minions could only make the heart of any patriarch beat a little faster as he recognized an idyll usually confined to his dreams—but, nevertheless, Ingraham still observed and recorded an aspect of slave culture the significance of which historians have now, for the most part, lost. The way African American slaves styled their hair was important to them as individuals, and it also played a substantial role in their communal life.

Nearly forty years earlier, in March 1797, the architect Benjamin Latrobe stopped for a while on his trip through Virginia and painted a scene he observed through a window of the upper story of Drynane's tavern. He entitled the watercolor "Preparations for the enjoyment of a fine Sunday among the Blacks, Norfolk" (see Figure 5). The African American sitting on the barrel, Latrobe recorded in his sketchbook, "has taken his hair out of twist, and spread his tail," and a black man, with impressively sculpted hair himself, "begins combing and pulling the wool of the Man on the tub till he has compleated the Coiffure." At the same time, the black wearing the cap was shaving another male. Latrobe noted that the men styling and

Figure 5: Benjamin Henry Latrobe, *Preparations for the Enjoyment of a Fine Sunday among the Blacks, Norfolk.* Maryland Historical Society, Baltimore

shaving their friends then ended "the scene by mutually shaving and dressing each other."[2] In the 1850s, Frederick Law Olmsted, traveling through South Carolina, came across a campsite where "an old negro [sat] with his head bowed down over a meal sack, while a negro boy was combing his wool with a common horse-card." Throughout a conversation that took Olmsted three pages to recount, the boy (who turned out to be the old man's son) continued to card his father's hair. For African American slaves there was a decided, and often necessary, communal aspect to such toiletries.[3] On many nineteenth-century plantations the climax of the corn-shucking festival occurred when the slaves seized the master, carried him around the Big House, sometimes tossed him in the air, and took him inside where, as the ex-slave George Woods remembered, they would "place him in the chair; comb his head; cross his knees for him and leave him alone."[4] Along with manhandling their supposed better, the (at first glance) curious ritual of combing his hair was a way of suggesting a rough-and-ready, if temporary, equality between master and slave; after all, only a few hours earlier the young African American men involved had been doing precisely the same thing among themselves as they prepared for the festival.

Today it is difficult not to see negative overtones in slaves' hair styling. The testimony of various African Americans has made it clear to us that some of the communal aspects of hair care survived into the twentieth century, but these tend to be associated with processes that attempted to make African American hair resemble that of whites. The account of Shorty's induction of the boy who would later become Malcolm X into the world of the conk, with a home-made and extremely painful mixture of potatoes, eggs, and lye, is now well-known, and Malcolm X was hardly the only one to undergo this type of ordeal.[5] From the time Roger Wilkins, later Assistant Attorney General of the United States and a Pulitzer Prize-winning journalist, was two or three years old, his grandmother would put vaseline in his hair each night, brush each side of his head 100 times, and then tightly secure on his head a stocking, which stayed there until the morning. Even when he was in college, Wilkins, desirous of not being known as a "woolly head," still wore the stocking cap.[6] But in the years before the Civil War, when the vast majority of African Americans was enslaved, the styling of hair, far from having negative connotations, was one of the few areas of which it could be said that whites allowed blacks a relatively unhindered scope for cultural expression.

the heads of people, creating a stunning effect." In 1602, the Dutch explorer Pieter de Marees "published a plate . . . showing sixteen different hairstyles of various classes and genders in Benin alone." [15] (See Figure 6). Descriptions of hair arrangements contained in eighteenth-century runaway advertisements indicate that, within the obvious limits imposed by an oppressive system, African American slaves were engaged in the same cultural activity. The challenge is to discover what meanings, what shared understandings, were being conveyed.

The idea that the hair of one's head is a medium through which social messages can be conveyed and aesthetic standards of the dominant culture can be contested should not, nowadays, seem strange. Unevenly cropped and garishly colored hair flaunted on the head of a punk and the shaven crown of the skinhead encode statements of protest and alienation. Hippies' long hair signified freedom and nonconformity. Afro hairstyles of the 1960s and seventies were easily decipherable statements of black pride, bold challenges to a white aesthetic that had long made curly and kinky hair a symbol of inferiority. The dreadlocks of black West Indians also spoke of pride, since that hair arrangement required and celebrated the very texture of black hair, which white racism had devalorized. Afro and dreadlocks styles also signified political empowerment, through the association with the black power movement on the one hand and the radical Rastafarian movement on the other. Styling of hair, as Kobener Mercer has pointed out, is a universal cultural practice. The hair of one's head "is never a straightforward biological 'fact'," for it will "almost always [be] . . . 'worked upon' by human hands." Such procedures "socialize hair, making it the medium of significant 'statements' about self and society." [16] Whether in African or in New World societies, and in whatever period we attempt to see them, blacks engaged in this kind of cultural activity. The problem lies not so much in showing that enslaved Africans and African Americans were involved in this form visual communication as in understanding what their hair arrangements signified.

Reading these messages can be extremely difficult. Specific African influences are almost impossible to assess, since the cultures of the West African tribal groups from which most New World slaves came are numerous and diverse, and anthropological investigations of them tend to focus on the relatively recent past. Moreover, for much of the period covered by this study, the only verbal and visual representations of African Americans that

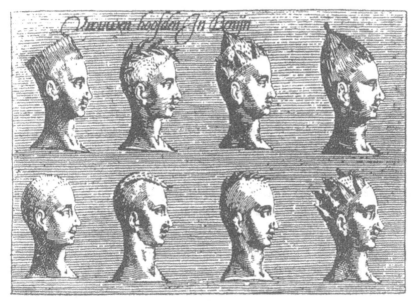

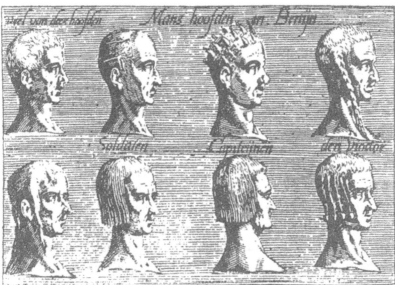

Figure 6: *Women's Heads in Benyn and Men's Heads in Benyn (Soldiers; Captains, the Viador)*. Plate taken from Pieter de Marees, *Description and Historical Account of the Gold Kingdom of Guinea* (1602: Oxford, 1987). By permission of the British Library, shelfmark YC 1988 B7796

style of wig are also relevant to our consideration of African American hair-styles. Sometimes the hair at the sides of the toupee, or on the bob wig, for instance, was frizzed, that is, curled tightly and combed to produce a bushy effect. Also, after about 1740, queues, that is, columns of hair, whether the wearer's own or false hair attached to a wig, which hung down at the back of the neck, became popular and remained so for many decades.[33]

Broadly speaking, wigs in the American colonies resembled those worn in Britain, and, as in Britain, they were an easily recognized sign of social status: the more elaborate and expensive the wig, the higher on the social scale its wearer was presumed to be. Clear evidence of this value system comes from the memoirs of Devereux Jarratt, who, though born in comparatively humble circumstances in Virginia in 1733, rose to become an Anglican clergyman of some note. As he looked back over his life from the perspective of the 1790s, Jarratt recalled the awe he had felt when in the presence of gentlemen whose "distinguishing badge," Jarratt noted, was the periwig. "When I saw a man riding the road, near our house, with a wig on, it would so alarm my fears . . . that . . . I would run off, as for my life." Offered the chance to improve his prospects by becoming a schoolmaster, Jarratt had dressed as well as he could, and, "that I might appear something more than common, in a strange place, and be counted somebody, I got me an old wig, which, perhaps being cast off by the master, had become the property of his slave, and from the slave it was conveyed to me. But people were not obliged, you know, to ask how I came by it, and, I suppose, I was wise enough not to tell them."[34] Even a cheap or well-worn wig, that is to say, could confer status in some degree.

The practice of wearing wigs extended well down the social scale. One study has shown that, during the twenty-year period from 1732 to 1752, of 182 notices appearing in the *South Carolina Gazette* seeking the return of white male indentured servants, nineteen, or 10.5 percent, mentioned that the absconders wore wigs.[35] Occasionally, advertisements for runaway slaves mentioned African Americans wearing or possessing wigs; those who did so were probably slaves of the elite, house slaves, skilled tradesmen, seamen, and the like. David Gratenread, who ran away in King William County, Virginia, "carried with him . . . [a] brown cut wig" (which he may have stolen); Exeter, who absconded in Dorchester County, Maryland, "had on a brown Wig"; Tom, also from Maryland, wore "an old black Wig." Joe, a mulatto sailor who ran away from his Norfolk master, "had on when he went away, a blue Fear-nothing Jacket, Trousers, an old Hat and Wig, Yarn stockings, and Shoes."[36]

What appears to have happened quite often, however, was that slaves styled their own hair to resemble the wigs worn by members of the dominant caste. Some runaway advertisements are quite specific on this point. John Van Dyke of New York noted that his slave Hamilton sometimes craped (that is, frizzed) his hair and that "when craped, it appears like a cut wig." Pompey, a Maryland runaway, was said to wear "his wool combed back on the top of his head, forming a toupee." The owner of Frank, a South Carolina "waiting lad," hoped that his slave would soon be recognized since Frank "would feign dress . . . the wool of his head in the macaroni taste, the which being that of a mustee, he has teazed into side locks, and a queue."[37] Hair combed upwards from the forehead or bunched at the front of the head must have resembled the pompadour worn by the elite. Hair that was combed high in front and shorn on the crown, or that was shorn on the crown and grown long at the back, or that combined all of these features could have looked very similar to the toupee. We could recall here the Maryland runaway James, who had "the top of his head . . . cut short, and all the other part of the wool . . . left pretty long, [and] turned up before in the fashion."[38] "The fashion" referred to here can only have been a Euro-American one. The meaning of such hair arrangments for whites must have been highly ambiguous and not a little disconcerting. Given that African Americans' hair, being black, was the "wrong" color, most varieties of wigs being white or light brown, and given the association between wig wearing and social status, the effect of such hair stylings must have been close to parody, especially when augmented by the common slave practice of wearing the hair tied behind in a queue, sometimes even a false one. African Americans who styled their hair to resemble fashionable wigs may well have been contesting the idea of how a slave ought to look.

Blacks, here, were doing more than imitating white hair arrangements. They were functioning as *bricoleurs,* drawing from both their African past and their American present to create a style that was new.[39] Consider, for instance, the Mulatto waiting man Jem, who "[wore] his own black Hair, which [was] commonly tied in a Cue behind, or platted, and [arranged in] curls on each Side of his Face"; Road, a North Carolina slave, who wore her hair "combed over a large roll"; and Jack, "a likely Virginia born Negro," whose hair was "trimmed to a roll and by frequent combing [had] grown to a prodigious length." Picture also Elleck, a Baltimore runaway, who had "bushy hair, or rather wool, which he combs and dresses neat by frizing &c.," and Peter, who "lets his Hair grow from his Temples Half Way down his Face, very long and frizzed." When the owner of the Maryland runaway Lot described his slave's hair as being "done up in the tastiest manner for his colour," he was, in effect, acknowledging the existence, at least among some blacks, of a distinctively African American style.[40]

Admittedly the evidence is fragmentary, but it appears that some groups of blacks were more likely than others to partake of this style. Although a few of the older African Americans had their heads completely shaved, for the most part, the more elaborate hair arrangements were worn by younger males, aged roughly between fifteen and twenty-five. If this was indeed the case, then such hairstyles may well have had their origins in the peculiar position in which male slaves of this age group found themselves. Although "country marks," or ritual scarifications, were quite common on African-born slaves, to our knowledge at least, no one has found evidence of them on American-born slaves. The reason for this may well be relatively straightforward. African culture was based on an integrated view of the world, a view that the slave trade and enslavement in the New World turned upside down. Subjected to slavery, with the consequent loss of control of their lives and the mixing up of the complex mosaic of African tribal groups, it is likely that Africans and African Americans would have seen initiation ceremonies and ritual scarification signaling the rite of passage to manhood as wildly inappropriate. In such a situation, the elaborate and distinctive styling of male hair may well have served as a form of substitute bodily decoration that still marked these young men off but seemed rather more attuned to their new circumstances as American slaves.[41] At the end of the eighteenth and in the early years of the nineteenth century, as the African-born proportion of the slave population shrank and Africa increasingly was a place remembered by a dwindling group of aging men and women, these hairstyles quietly disappeared.

At times, too, the sources suggest that there were regional variations in hairstyles. In late eighteenth- and early nineteenth-century New York City, for example, Thomas De Voe, an antiquarian, described the different groups of African Americans who came to the breakdown (or dancing) contests staged at Catharine Slip. According to De Voe, the New Jersey blacks, mostly from Tappan, wore their forelocks plaited with tea leads, while the

Long Island blacks had their hair in a queue tied with a dried eel skin.[42]
Similar geographic differences may have occurred in the eighteenth-century
South, but the evidence is simply not good enough to pick up this sort of
variation. As so often happens with the fragmentary and incomplete sources
left for historians interested in these sorts of issues, there is enough material to tantalize but not enough to allow us to draw more than speculative
and tentative conclusions.

Whites seemed to have approved of some black hair arrangements, especially those that were neat and orderly. Joe, a gentleman's waiting man
from Maryland, was said by his master to have his hair "comb'd very
nicely," and Jemmy's Virginia master noted that his slave wore his hair
"comb'd and parted."[43] We should remember, however, that neatness and
good grooming could be African as well as Euro-American cultural imperatives; unkempt hair had strongly negative connotations in some African
societies, especially for women. Thus the "much Delight" that the Maryland slave Daniel was said by his master to take in his very neatly arranged
hair may not have resulted merely from a recognition that he was satisfying
white expectations. The same could have been true of Blair, who, according to his Virginia master, took "great pride in keeping his wool combed."[44]
But if some African American hair arrangements won praise from whites
for their neatness, many others must have been confusing, disturbing in
their odd combinations of length and shape and in their mixture of African and Euro-American influences. John Evans, for example, described his
runaway slave Gilbert as having "the Top of his head Shaved, and he combs
it back like a Woman"; whatever this hair style may have meant to Gilbert,
Evans was confounded by it. Even styles that copied whites' hair arrangements must have appeared odd when crafted out of African Americans'
hair, with its different texture and color. If unkempt hair seemed vaguely
offensive to whites, hair that was groomed and elaborately arranged must
also have seemed out of place, suggesting, as Gwendolyn Robinson has
pointed out, "an attention to cosmetic detail only permitted by the enjoyment of a free and independent status."[45] Our impression is that blacks'
hair styles constituted, for whites, unreadable signs with ambiguous meanings, creating a semiotic confusion whites found disconcerting. Blacks' thick
hair and dark skin must have seemed to clash discordantly with the items
of formerly expensive clothing and cast-off military apparel that slaves were
sometimes able to acquire. Hair shaped like a fashionable wig must have

looked even more out of place when combined with an ensemble of shabby, nondescript garments and a vocabulary of gesture and bodily movement whose meanings whites could not easily decipher.

Whites' confusion at the appearance of blacks could easily be displaced into ridicule, a patronizing mockery of black pretensions and lack of "taste." What whites failed to detect were the signs of an emerging African American culture, a series of borrowings and blendings which, always changing over time, at least obliquely challenged the hegemony of blacks' oppressors.

Toward the end of the eighteenth century, wigs lost popularity, and in the 1790s hair began to be worn short, a trend which continued into the nineteenth century and which African Americans appear to have followed.[46] Advertisements for escaped slaves reflect this change.

In eighteenth-century runaway notices, the expressions most commonly used by slaveowners to describe the hair of their slaves emphasize its abundance and length. Male slaves are said to have "a large bushy head of hair" worn "remarkably high," "a large Quantity of long Wool," "remarkable long hair"; female slaves to have "long black Hair," "remarkable long hair, or wool," a "remarkable bushy head of hair."[47] Such phrases are rarely found in nineteenth-century notices. Moreover, where descriptions of hair are included in these notices, they are usually meager. Among South Carolina slaves who absconded in 1830, Peter possessed "straight black hair," Isaac "some grey hairs," Leah "short hair," and Rachel "reddish hair." Sye, a male slave who ran away that same year, was merely said by his owner to have "rather short" hair; this despite an otherwise precise description of such physical characteristics as the size of Sye's chest and arms, the structure of his legs and cheek bones, the mole on his face, his general demeanor, and his clothing. Though occasionally owners were a little more forthcoming (Hager, "a dark mulatto, or mestezo," who escaped in 1810, had "a bushy head of hair when out of plait"), they often did not mention hair at all, even when they supplied a very full and precise description of the runaway. In seeking the return of Lizzie, who ran off in 1810, the owner provided information about her appearance, demeanor, clothing, and previous owners. Lizzie was "about 30 to 35 years of age, rather tall and thin," and possessed of "a sedate, hypocritical countenance." She "pretend[ed] to be very religious," was "well informed" and "artful," and had taken with her "several calico wrappers, a black bombazet petticoat, as well as dimity, blue woollen, &c." Lizzie had been owned by Dr. Joseph Johnson for several years and "at one time had nursed Mrs. Lopez's children." What is missing, here, is any mention of Lizzie's hair. A "mulatto Boy named John," who ran off in 1830, was "about 29 or 30 years of age, of a pale yellow complexion, 5 feet 3 or 4 inches high," wore "a suit of domestic mixed cloth, but carried other clothing, a blue coat in particular," was "plausible when spoken to, though sulky," bore "visible marks from infancy on the shoulders and throat, the color of port wine," and had "a grandmother . . . in the village of Sumter," towards whom he was likely to be heading, and "a relative residing in Charleston, where more than probable he may endeavor to reach, and make an attempt to leave the State."[48] But of his hair we learn nothing.

Although arguing for the absence of something seldom sounds convincing, it is significant that there is no sign in these nineteenth-century advertisements of the elaborate and striking hair arrangements that eighteenth-century slaveholders strove to describe. Nor do travelers' accounts, which proliferate in the nineteenth century, yield much information about African American hairstyles, even though the authors of those accounts often essay quite lengthy descriptions of blacks. This absence of detail suggests that hair was generally shorter and therefore less amenable to the prominent or distinctive arrangements often displayed by eighteenth-century African Americans.

Because of these virtual "silences," it is not easy to discover how black hairstyles changed in the early decades of the nineteenth century. However, the appearance of photographic studies of slaves in the 1850s confirms that there had been a shift to shorter hair among African American males, and at least among those females who appear in photographs with heads uncovered.[49] Also, from mid-century, African American voices become audible, providing information about black hair arrangements.

Former slaves interviewed by W.P.A. employees make it clear, for example, that shaving the head of a slave was a not uncommon form of punishment. It seems, however, that during the last years of slavery, unlike the situation in the eighteenth century, it was, for the most part, African American women who were treated in this fashion; furthermore, it was almost invariably white women who meted out the punishment. James Brittian remembered that his grandmother, an African-born slave, had hair that was "fine as silk and hung down below her waist," hair that made the "Old Miss" jealous of her and the "Old Master." The result was that the Old

Miss, who was "mighty fractious," had Brittian's grandmother whipped and her hair cut off. "From that day on," he recalled, " my grandma had to wear her hair shaved to the scalp." When Judge Maddox, owner of a Texas plantation, brought home "a pretty mulatto girl" with "long black straight hair," his wife was skeptical that the slave had been purchased for doing fine needlework. As Jack Maddox, then a young slave, later remembered, the wife waited until the Judge was away, "got the scissors and cropped that gal's head to the skull." [50] Interestingly, in most of these incidents it was the similarity of these slaves' hair to whites' hair that was particularly unnerving to white women, a similarity that either provided circumstantial proof that husbands, brothers or sons had been illicitly visiting the slave quarters or suggested that, if something were not done soon, the temptation for them would be too great. As a result of the warped sexual dynamics of antebellum plantations, the mutilation of an African-American woman's hair was usually an action directed at white men rather than at the victim herself, although doubtless its import was not lost on the slaves in the quarter. Whatever the motivations for these incidents may have been, they occurred frequently enough to become part of the remembered fabric of slavery, passed on from generation to generation. In her autobiography Sarah Rice recalled her mother telling her about Sarah Rice's great-grandmother. As a slave, she had had "gorgeous hair," which she had styled into ringlets, "but her mistress didn't like it and took her and cut it all off." [51]

Interviews with former slaves also frequently describe African American hair-styling practices and reveal something of what those practices meant. African-American women's hair, though probably shorter than in the previous century, could soon become tangled and unmanageable if uncared for. This problem must have particularly affected field slaves, whose typical labor regime, stretching each day from "can see" to "can't see" and often involving cooking and mending duties as well, made adequate care of the hair difficult, if not impossible. Only on Sundays, their day off, could slaves find the time for grooming and styling, with whatever implements they could locate. Former slave James Williams recalled for his W.P.A. interviewer how the "old folks" used continually to talk about how much harder the life had been before freedom came. "Said the onlies time the slaves had to comb their hair was on Sunday. They would comb and roll each others hair and the men cut each others hair. That all the time they got. They would roll the childerns hair or keep it cut short." Removing tangles must have been a painful process. Jane Morgan explained that "we carded our hair caze we never had no combs, but de cards dey worked better. We used de cards to card wool wid also, and we jes wet our hair and den card hit. De cards dey had wooden handles and strong steel wire teeth." (The cards referred to here were implements used to prepare washed fleece for spinning, to make the fibers lie evenly in one direction.) Recalling his childhood on a large South Carolina plantation, Jacob Stroyer told how, before each inspection of the slave children by the plantation owner and his wife, attempts were made "to straighten out our unruly wools with some small cards, or Jim-crows," as they were called. On one such occasion, an old woman had attempted to comb his hair straight, but "as she hitched the teeth of the instrument in my unyielding wool with her great masculine hand, of course I was jerked flat on my back. This was the common fate of most of my associates." Aunt Tildy Collins's account of the preparation of slave children for Sunday school is equally graphic: "Us chilluns hate to see Sunday come, 'caze Mammy an' Granmammy dey wash us an' near 'bout rub de skin off gittin' us clean for Sunday school, an' dey comb our heads wid a jimcrow. You ain't neber seed a jimcrow? Hit mos' lak a cyard what you cyard wool wid. What a cyard look lack? Humph! Missy, whar you been raise—ain't neber seed a cyard? Dat jimcrow sho' did hurt, but us hadder stan' hit, an' sometimes after all dat, mammy she wrap our kinky hair wid thread an' twis' so tight us's eyes couldn't hardly shet." [52]

The "wrapping" (or "threading," as it has more recently been called) referred to here was a process by which, once the hair had been brushed free of tangles, small clusters of it were bound with cotton or some other material to keep it from knotting and also to cause it, when released, to curl. Having prepared their hair in this fashion, slave women would then wrap a head rag or bandanna around their head in order to preserve whatever hair arrangement the threading had achieved. On Sundays or other important occasions, the bandanna would be removed, the threading undone, and the hair brushed into the desired shape. Later, the hair would again be wrapped and covered with a bandanna. Obviously procedures were not uniform, but this general sequence seems to have applied. Gus Fester, a former slave who had been born in 1840, told how slave women "took dey hair down out'n de strings fer de meeting. In dem days all de darky wimmens wore dey hair in string 'cep' when dey 'tended church or a wedding. At de camp meetings de wimmens pulled off de head rags, 'cept de mammies. On dis occasion de mammies wore linen head rags fresh laundered." Amos Lincoln explained the purpose of threading thus: "d' gals uster dress up come Sunday. All week dey wear dey hair all roll up wid cotton dat dey unfol' off d' cotton boll. Sunday come dey comb out dey hair fine. . . . Dey want it nice an' nat'ral curly. Monday dey put d' cotton string back so it hab all week t' git curly ag'in." Olivier Blanchard concurred: "I think it eel fish they strip the skin off and wrap round the hair and make it curly." Some slave women preferred to plait their hair, sometimes in such a way as to form patterns on the scalp (a procedure known as "corn-rowing"). The interviewer of Ma Eppes described how "proudly the old woman unwrapped her 'head rag' to display a thick mop, woolly white but neatly parted into squares. Dozens of little plaits, wrapped with yards of twine, just as her hair had been dressed in the slave quarters before the War, adorned her head." Other women, to simplify the difficult business of hair management, straightened their hair by greasing it and then applying a heated cloth.[53]

Braiding and threading are traditional techniques in African hair design. The origin of the bandanna, on the other hand, is more problematic. Although the bandanna is now widely worn in West Africa and widely regarded as a traditional African garment, the first Europeans to encounter Africans found among them a "nearly universal bareheadedness," to use John Thornton's phrase. Thornton suspects that the bandanna emerged from the mixing of aesthetic traditions that occurred in the community of Africans and Europeans which developed along the Atlantic coast in Africa and in slaveholding societies in the New World. He suggests that this form of headwear may have originated in the Christian requirement that the head be covered during mass.[54]

Whatever its origins, among female slaves in North America the bandanna had strongly utilitarian functions. It afforded some protection from the sun, kept the hair clean, helped preserve patterns of braiding and wrapping, or even — especially, perhaps, in the case of runaways — concealed telltale scars or African country marks. Phebe, who escaped from Chester County, Pennsylvania, in 1763, had "three or four large Negroe Scars up and down her Forehead, but [was] apt to wear a Handkerchief round her Head to hide them."[55] The bandanna could also conceal dishevelled or dirty hair, which, especially for African American women, may have been a particular cause of shame. In her study of the Mende people of West Africa, anthropologist Sylvia Ardyn Boon stresses the preeminent cultural significance of women's hair. "West African communities, including Mende," she writes, "admire a fine head of long, thick hair on a woman." In Mende culture, such hair is intimately associated with the ideal of beauty. "Great hair is praised as *kpotongo*—literally, 'it is much, abundant, plentiful'." Beyond this, however, certain cultural imperatives exist. Mende women's hair "must be well-groomed; merely to be presentable, a woman's hair must be clean, oiled, and plaited. For the sake of elegance and sexual appeal, hair must be shaped into beautiful and complicated styles. . . . disheveled, neglected hair is anathema to Mende. It signifies insanity. . . . Mende culture finds it morally unfitting to leave the hair unarranged and equates wild hair with wild behavior." Loose, unplaited hair is associated with loose morals.[56] These insights suggest both the humiliation slave women may have felt in being prevented from grooming and styling their hair as they wished and the importance they are likely to have attached to whatever hair stylings they were able, during the time of their enslavement and after, to achieve.

The bandanna had a more positive significance. For African American women who lacked the implements and the leisure to create intricate coiffures, the often brilliantly colored bandanna or headkerchief offered an alternative means of self-adornment and aesthetic display.

As advertisements for escaped slaves show, head-wrappings were quite common among the female slave population in the eighteenth century. A "NEW-NEGRO WENCH . . . of the Guiney country," who ran away from a plantation at Goose Creek, South Carolina, in 1769, wore "a new oznabrug coat and wrapper, and a black striped silk handkerchief round her head." Sarah, a South Carolina runaway who escaped in 1784, covered her hair with "a spotted red and white handkerchief." Nanny, a Georgia slave who absconded in 1787, had on when she went away "an oznabrig coat and wrapper, and . . . a check handkerchief on her head."[57] There are no direct references in these eighteenth-century advertisements to the threading and braiding techniques that former slaves later described, but neither is there any reason why slaveholders, concerned, after all, with the appearance of slaves at the time of their escape, should have included such information. Female slaves who hoped to avoid detection and possibly to pass as free would probably have combed out or covered their hair before fleeing. It would be surprising, however, if the traditional techniques of threading and braiding were not being used in the eighteenth century and earlier, given the importance of hair styling in West African cultures and the confirmation, once direct black testimony becomes available, that such practices were common in the mid-nineteenth century slave community. Indeed, an eighteenth-century silhouette of an enslaved woman, Flora, appears to show such a hair arrangement. (See Figure 8).

By the middle of the nineteenth century, as the photographic record and other evidence shows, bandannas had become nearly ubiquitous among the female slave population.[58] African American women acquired these items of apparel through routine distribution, as gifts, or through purchases with money they were able to accumulate by farming small plots or hiring themselves out. Frederick Law Olmsted recorded that the slaves on one large Mississippi plantation he visited "were furnished with two suits of summer, and one of winter clothing each year. Besides which, most of them

Figure 8: Unsigned silhouette ca. 1796. Accompanied by *Bill of Sale, Margaret Dwight of New Haven County, Connecticut, sold Flora, a nineteen-year-old slave to Asa Benajmin of Fairfield County, Connecticut, for the sum of twenty-five pounds sterling.* Courtesy of The Stratford Historical Society, Stratford, Connecticut

got presents of holiday finery (calico dresses, handkerchiefs, etc.), and purchased more for themselves, at Christmas." A former South Carolinian female slave told how, each Christmas "every woman got a handkerchief to tie up her hair."[59] It is likely, too, that the greater involvement of nineteenth-century slave women in plantation textile manufacture meant that they were able to make headkerchiefs themselves, incorporating in the cloth their distinctive color combinations and designs.

In an era when hair was generally shorter, these bandannas attracted the gaze, and sometimes the admiration, of whites. A New England school teacher who witnessed a number of church services in Charleston in the late 1840s commented favorably on the "various colored turbans" that the African American women wore, which, she said, made the women "a very attractive part of the audience." Frederick Law Olmsted, attending church in rural Georgia, spoke admiringly of the black women's "handkerchiefs, generally of gay patterns, and becomingly arranged." In the same way, a guest inspecting the slave quarters of a large South Carolina plantation one Christmas day in the early 1860s was struck by the slave women's "gaily-colored handkerchiefs arranged in turban fashion upon their heads." Northerners who came into contact with recently freed blacks made similar comments. A white woman who saw African Americans performing a ring shout on Port Royal in 1862 wrote that "the women generally [had] gay handkerchiefs twisted about their heads," and Whitelaw Reid, who reported on a meeting for newly freed blacks in Charleston just after the war, found himself confronted by "a motley, but brilliant army of bright-colored turbans, wound around wooly heads."[60]

Whites' evident interest in the headkerchief signals a shift in the focus of black bodily display. In the eighteenth century, whites' indifference to African American hair arrangements had left an expressive space that blacks were able to exploit. In the nineteenth century, partly as a result of their greater involvement in textile manufacture, slave women were able to explore the creative possibilities of color and design, and, as we have seen, the seemingly odd combinations of garments, discordant color combinations, and irregular patterns that slave clothing sometimes displayed encoded a cultural aesthetic that was different from that of the dominant white society.

The early years of freedom opened relatively few opportunities for aesthetic expression, and ahead lay a racial climate so oppressive that any sign of ostentation would have been perilous, and an era of hair-straightening in which the potential of African American hair for stylistic innovation was largely denied. Though the subtleties of oppositional black hairstyling were undoubtedly still there—one thinks, for example, of Kobena Mercer's suggestion that the so-called "conk," rather than slavishly copying prevailing white hair styles, deftly "played" with and subverted them—it would not be until the black power movement of the 1960s and 1970s that the hair of African Americans would again become a primary visual medium for exuberant display.[61]

I'd Rather Dance
Den Eat

On May 24, 1854, the runaway Virginia slave Anthony Burns was recaptured in Boston. Within hours, Richard Henry Dana, best known to us as the author of *Two Years before the Mast* (1840) but also a prominent lawyer, had volunteered to defend him. The fugitive was a solidly built man, about six feet in height, and possessing a considerable presence, but he did not make a favorable impression on his putative advocate; Dana thought him "a piteous object, rather weak in mind & body," who "seemed completely cowed & dispirited," and who, when questioned by the presiding judge, had "looked round bewildered, like a child." The lawyer left the Court House convinced that his services were not wanted, that the slave runaway, fearing retribution from his master and having no wish to delay proceedings, was willing to return meekly to a life of bondage. That night, however, Burns was visited by friends, who convinced him that Dana was trustworthy and would prove a powerful ally, and when the two men met the following day the prisoner's demeanor had entirely altered. Burns now seemed, as Dana expressed it, "a very different man"—"self possessed, intelligent," and imbued with "considerable force both of mind & body."[1]

This incident, although of little importance in the larger scheme of things, does serve to show the way in which kinesics, that is, communicative bodily movement, formed a crucial, if generally neglected, element in the social interactions of the past. Undoubtedly Burns had been intimidated by his predicament, and when brought face-to-face with Dana, who must have been marked as a gentleman by everything from his clothing and demeanor to the deference accorded him by court officials, Burns had drawn on the gestural vocabulary of slavery to guide him in his dealings with the lawyer, creating an impression of resignation and abject docility. Once Dana's antislavery credentials had been established, however, not only the words Burns used but also his body language—his bearing, gestures, facial expressions—combined to create, in the lawyer, a radically different impression. Much the same kind of reclamation of the body, a shucking off of the vestiges of a hated institution, would often occur as slavery ended. Elizabeth Barker, a black hairdresser born in 1900 and interviewed in the 1970s, recalled hearing of the determined efforts former slaves had made to stamp out all reminders of their bondage. To that end they had "insisted their children stand ramrod straight so they could look any man in the eye, as contrasting to the way slaves had to look at masters, with heads bowed and eyes cast down."[2]

The crucial role of gestures and bodily movements takes on a particular clarity at the point of transition between slavery and freedom, either in individual cases, such as that of Anthony Burns, or collectively, at the time of emancipation. But such non-verbal language also formed an indispensable part of the myriad transactions that occurred on plantations every day. This chapter is an exploratory and necessarily speculative attempt to recover something of black kinesics and to show what the repertoire of black gesture and bodily movement can reveal about the cultural codes that existed within sections of the African American slave population. We begin with the gestures used in the most constrained of situations—face-to-face interactions between blacks and whites—and then move on to a consideration of black dance, an expressive realm in which slaves enjoyed considerable liberty in the use of their bodies and in which cultural differences were often dramatically displayed.

There was always a tension in the slave South between the "ideal" master/slave relationship imagined by planters and the often recalcitrant behavior of their "troublesome property," but generally the realities of power and control on the plantation allowed little scope for direct verbal resistance. Examples of such open defiance do occasionally appear in contemporary sources. Quamina, a skilled carver and chair maker who ran away at the age of seventeen, and whom his master described as "well known in and about Charlestown by his impudent behaviour," told his master to his face that he intended to go where he pleased and that his master could "do nothing to him, nor . . . ever get a copper for him." The aggrieved owner of Limus, a slave "well known in Charles-Town from his saucy and impudent Tongue," invited anyone who discovered Limus "out of my Habitation without a Ticket" to administer a severe thrashing, "for though he is my Property, he has the audacity to tell me, he will be free, that he will serve no Man, and that he will be conquered or governed by no Man."[3] These stark verbal challenges to their authority had clearly made a considerable impression on the owners who placed these advertisements, but incidents of this kind must have been rare.

In her superb explication of Aztec culture, Inga Clendinnen has suggested that when speech is "curbed there might well be an equivalent expansion of a vocabulary of demeanor and gesture, where understanding must be sought through an analysis of observed action." We cannot, of course, directly observe the repertoire of demeanor and gesture of African American slaves, but we can examine contemporary descriptions of such nonverbal communication, in order to determine whether it was culturally distinctive in any sense. Frederick Law Olmsted certainly thought that it was. As he watched the day-to-day activities of African Americans in the Washington market place, he concluded that not only "in their dress," but in their "language, *manner, motions*—all were distinguishable almost as much [as] by their colour, from the white people who were distributed among them, and engaged in the same occupations—chiefly selling poultry, vegetables and small country produce."[4] But Olmsted did not elaborate upon this typically acute observation.

Though travelers' accounts contain occasional comments on blacks' gestures, facial expressions, eye movements, and so on, by far the richest source of such descriptions is the thousands of notices slaveowners placed in the contemporary press appealing for the return of slaves who had run away. Such advertisements described not merely the runaway's clothing, hairstyle, visible signs of mutilation, and so on, but also any physical mannerisms that could aid identification. Thus we can learn, from the Maryland slaveholder William Colyer's description of his slave Warwick, that "the balls of [Warwick's] eyes are uncommonly white, and, when talked to, he rolls them unusually." We discover that Clem, another runaway, had "a swaggering Air with him in his Walk," and that "when spoken to," the Virginia runaway Samuel "often turns his head on one side, and shuts one of his eyes." [5] Were the eye movements, mode of walking, and manner of inclining the head described here different from those of whites and, if they were, what did those differences signify?

The distinctive nature of black kinesics begins to emerge when we compare contemporary descriptions of African Americans with the informal codes that operated to regulate social interaction. Earlier we have shown that the codes relating to dress were often reasonably precise, even, on occasion, being written into law. But ideas of how slaves ought to look embraced not merely notions as to how they should be clothed but expectations relating to demeanor and posture, to the way slaves held their heads, directed their gaze, moved their bodies, and so on. Just as there was opposition to slaves who dressed too grandly, so, too, was there resistance to slaves (and free blacks) who stood too proudly, approached too nearly, gazed too directly, walked too confidently. If slaves were not supposed to appropriate the garb of the elite, neither were they expected to adopt their manners or bearing. Slaves, in short, were expected to look the part.

The so-called courtesy manuals, English publications to which, as Richard Bushman has shown, white Americans in the higher social orders paid close attention from the eighteenth century on, attempted to impose social standards governing interaction between various groups in society. Those aspiring to gentility were advised to "remain erect" and to "keep the line from the base of the spine through the neck to the back of the head as straight as possible." But if a proud, upright carriage was appropriate in the elite, signifying, as Jonathan Prude has pointed out, not merely gentility but power, it was hardly so for those further down the social scale, and most emphatically not for slaves, whose bearing was expected to be deferential, not to say servile. In much the same way, members of the lower orders were instructed, for instance, that, "in Speaking to men of Quality," they ought neither to "lean nore Look them full in the Face, nor approach too near them."[6] The personal space of the elite was to be respected.

Unwritten rules governing African Americans' lives emerge, too, in the testimony of former slaves. One man recalled being whipped for his "sullen, dogged countenance." Another told how, though in agony from a flogging, he had had to temper his response to a sympathetic inquiry as to his condition: "A slave must not manifest feelings of resentment," Charles Ball explained, "and I answered with humility."[7] "We have been taught a cringing servility," the former slave Edward Wilmot Blyden declared. "We have been drilled into contentment with the most undignified circumstances." Ex-slaves' recollections of their first experience of freedom also reveal the rules that had formerly bound them but that no longer applied. One black soldier remembered how, having gained his freedom, he had "walked fearlessly and boldly through the streets of a southern city" without being "required to take off his cap at every step" or move off the sidewalks for planters' sons. "Now we sogers are men—men de first time in our lives," an exultant Sergeant Prince Rivers of the First South Carolina Volunteers, United States Colored Troops, told an interviewer during the Civil War. "Now we can look our old masters in de face."[8]

Slaves' eyes may or may not have been windows to their souls, but they do provide a number of clues to what we now call African American culture. Some contemporaries certainly thought that this was so. When Frederick Law Olmsted discussed with a number of Mississippi overseers the problem of identifying a very light-skinned person as a slave, one of them "thought there would be no difficulty; you could always see a slave girl quail when you looked in her eyes." For other white southerners—and without prejudging the issue too much we would suggest that they were the more perceptive ones—the eyes of slaves were rather more opaque; these observers were certainly less sure of their ability to read facial features than the chillingly confident overseer Olmsted had memorialized. Prompted by the Civil War, the murder of a nearby slaveowner by her slaves, and her own considerable doubts about the morality of the slave system, Mary Boykin Chesnut started to look at the surrounding sea of black faces in a fresh way, trying to decipher their meaning in what seemed an almost surreal semiotics of survival, but she quickly realized that they "are as unreadable as the sphinx." Although Chesnut was "always studying these creatures," the slaves were "inscrutable," indeed "past finding out," and that recognition of slaves' unknowability, in spite of all her years of close contact with them, became an anxious refrain in her diary. Decades later W. J. Cash, echoing Chesnut, distanced himself from the easy conclusion of the white South that it "knew the black man through and through," suggesting that "even the most unreflecting" must feel, when dealing with a black, "that they were looking at a blank wall," and that "a veil was drawn which no white man might certainly know he had penetrated."[9] Cash's metaphor of the veil, alluding to Du Bois before him, with its suggestion of the partly concealed, conveys well the difficulties of discerning meaning from the descriptions and words of slaveowners. But for all that, slaveowners' often scrupulous and fascinated attention to detail, their search for precision as they attempted to represent slave gestures and eye movements that were at once everyday and familiar yet still disconcertingly strange, indicates that they recognized that slaves' actions were different. That the slaveowners were also frequently unable to understand what they saw was partly caused by the misunderstandings and clumsy translations which inevitably ensue whenever cultures come in contact, but mostly it was the result of the reasonable and sensible desire of slaves to conceal their feelings from whites. Nowhere are the resulting ambiguities and ambivalences more clearly seen than in the eye movements of slaves.

Consider the so-called "down look," the practice among blacks when in the presence of whites of inclining their heads and directing their gaze toward the ground. As Jonathan Prude has pointed out, this gesture "fit the polite conviction that plebeian types should neither stand erect nor stare back," and this may be part of the reason why so many references to it appear in the runaway advertisements.[10] There is little doubt, however, that the phrase "down look" did accurately describe one aspect of the appearance of many slaves. Advertising for the return of a young slave, his Georgia owner noted that Isaac "has a down look when any white person speaks to him." Likewise Quash, a young Virginia slave who ran away in 1776, had "a down Look when spoken to," and Kate, aged about twenty, also of Virginia, was said by her master to have "a down look when she talks." Expressing the matter rather differently, the owner of Frank, a young Maryland slave who escaped in 1789, stated that "when confronted his eye falls and discovers an uncommon wide space between the lid and the brow."[11]

Not all slaves, however, were prepared to display this outward sign of deference, particularly when the slave's well-being was under threat. One former slave reported that he had disconcerted buyers at a slave auction and avoided being sold by aggressively meeting the gaze of prospective bidders as they cast their eyes over him.[12] Other slaves habitually held their heads erect, meeting their masters' eyes with a direct stare, an assertive, even troubling characteristic that their owners were sure to remember when composing a runaway slave advertisement. Thus we read that, "when speaking," the North Carolina slave John "looks you full in the face," that "when spoke to" and "if sober," the Maryland slave Bacchus "generally looks you full in the face," and that the bondsman Peter, who escaped from his Maryland owner in 1783, was in "no ways bashful" but was prepared to "look a person stedfast though guilty."[13]

Even slaves who assumed the seemingly submissive down look could invest this gesture with ambiguous meanings. Dick, who made his escape from Baltimore in 1764, was described as having a "roguish down look," Peter, who ran from his Maryland owner in 1784, as having a "sneaking down look," and Sam, who absconded in 1785, as displaying a "down impudent look." A Pennsylvania slave, described by his master as "a very bragging fellow, given much to flattery," had "a down designing look."[14] The down look, then, was no guarantee of easy compliance with planters' authority. As many slaveowners realized, this gesture could mask a slave's true nature and intentions. John, who ran away in 1779 at about the age of thirty, may have had a "down look," but his master Robert Daniel also described him as "very artful." Tom, a "young well set Negro Man" who went missing in 1778, had "a down look" but "when spoke to, leers with his eyes which are large and full," a disconcerting gestural combination. There is a sense of dissonance, too, in the descriptions of the runaways Moses, who had "a very swanky walk, with a down look, and sour countenance," and Abel, who displayed "a down look, unless when spoken to, and then has a smile on his countenance," and who had "but little to say, and is inclinable to be sulky and sullen, when angry." When captured, the Louisiana runaway William "had around his neck an iron collar with three prongs extending upwards" and "many scars on his back and shoulders from the whip," yet the rebellious William, too, was described as having "a down look."[15] Even where slaveholders recognized the down look as an ambiguous sign, they may not have suspected that averting the head and eyes, constituent elements of the down look, could possess, for African Americans, an added cultural significance.

The difficulties slaveholders had in interpreting blacks' intentions must have been increased by the existence among slaves of gestural codes of which they were largely ignorant. In his discussion of Kongo influences on African American artistic culture, Robert Farris Thompson states that *nunsa,* a "standing or seated pose with head averted, . . . is present in black America" and that the turning of the head to one side "signals denial and negation." Thompson continues:

> In 1977 I saw a black man from New Orleans counter accusations by turning his head to one side, with lips firmly pursed. . . . There are countless mirrors of this pose in Gullah country, especially when a black mother sharply rebukes her child. Steward writes that "the child purses the lips, turns his head to one side, and it stays there." A cognate expression was observed in colonial times [in the West Indies] by Charles William Day: "when Negroes quarrel they seldom look each other in the face." . . . Annette Powell Williams summarizes an extension of this fundamental gesture in black United States: "an indication of total rejection is shown by turning one's head away from the speaker with eyes closed." [16]

Close examination of the runaway advertisements turns up examples of what may well have been similar instances of black resistance or contempt. The owner of Samuel, a Virginia slave who escaped in 1786, noted that "when spoken to, [he] often turns his head on one side, and shuts one of his eyes." The Virginia slave Jack, who ran away in 1766, "speaks plain for an African born, but avoids looking in the Face of them he is speaking to as much as possible." Osym, a "new Negro" about eighteen years of age who absconded in 1766, was "inclin'd to squint or looking side-ways." And if, as suggested above, the closing of the eyes was also a sign of dismissal, the gestures of other slaves may take on added meaning. Of Phill, a Virginia slave, his owner remarked that "when he speaks, or discourses with any person, [it] appears as if his eyes were almost shut," while Dinah, another Virginia slave, "keeps her eyes rather closed when speaking." [17]

Slaveholders and other white observers drew attention not merely to the way slaves directed their gaze but also to the manner in which they moved their eyes. Caesar, a South Carolinia slave from the Ibo Country, was described as having "remarkably large rolling eyes," and, according to her master, "when spoke to," the "negro wench, Scisley" became "very huffy, and remarkable in shewing the white of her eyes." Billy, who escaped in Virginia in 1776, exhibited "a remarkable turning of his eyes and winking, with some hesitation before he replies upon being spoken to," and of Warwick, who escaped in 1790, his Maryland owner remarked that "the balls of his eyes are uncommonly white, and, when talked to, he rolls them unusually." [18]

It is important to remember that runaway slave advertisements typically described the eye movements of slaves in a carefully circumscribed and very constrained series of situations. Slaveowners' comments were based on observations of slaves' behavior while they were conversing with, or, perhaps more correctly, listening to the instructions of, their owners. (Because of the limited nature of the surviving evidence, we have virtually no idea what sort of gestures or eye movements occurred when African Americans talked among themselves.) Judging by slaveowners' language, many masters were never as aware as were their slaves of the dramaturgical nature of these everyday interactions, but the slaves themselves, and any knowing audience of their compatriots who happened to be nearby, certainly realized that they were engaged in a performance, in which the slightest misjudgment about how transparently they could display their attitude to whites could have the direst of consequences. The range of behavior detailed here indicates, perhaps, some ways in which slaves tested the limits of bondage—ways that allowed them to register what the owners would have labeled impudence but is more correctly characterized as dissent, frustration, and even contempt for white authority—and to do so with a minimal chance of retribution. And we suggest that the gesture these white slaveowners were observing was the lineal ancestor of a social signal which, in the second half of the twentieth century, would come to be called "rolling the eyes." [19] Of course, the power of slaveowners, a power which many were remarkably uninhibited about exhibiting in all its visceral rawness, ensured that there were clear limits to slaves' actions. In most cases, whites compelled their slaves to obey their instructions, however grudgingly and incompletely. Nevertheless, this type of bodily language was important in allowing slaves to fashion a psychic space within which African American culture flourished.

If these eye movements directed at whites were intended to be difficult to read, the advertisements also depict bodily movements that were much less opaque. Such behavior clearly transgressed codes supposedly governing slaves' demeanor. Rather than appearing submissive, some slaves evidently adopted a prideful bearing, standing erect and walking in a forthright, confident manner. According to his Maryland owner, Sam, who ran away in 1779, had "a proud bold lofty carriage." Likewise, Renah, a young Virginia slave woman who absconded in 1781, had "a brisk walk and lively carriage"; Betty, a Virginia runaway, was said by her owner to be "proud in her Carriage"; Peter, who escaped in Maryland in 1783, "walk[ed] with a great air"; Clem, who fled in 1771, also in Maryland, had "a Swaggering Air with him in his Walk"; and John, a South Carolina runaway, had "a strutting walk."[20] As with blacks who dressed in expensive clothing, those so described may have been testing society's boundaries, contesting white notions of how a slave should look.

But as well as registering concerns which slaveholders would have regarded as legitimate, the runaway advertisements demonstrate a fascination on the part of the owners with the ways in which slaves' behavior differed from their own: indeed, it is possible to see whites grappling with the limitations of their language as they tried to capture the elusive physical movements of their missing human property. As we hope to have shown above, we can learn something from their attempts, but a more vivid and dramatic demonstration of kinesic differences between blacks and whites can be achieved if we turn to a different set of sources and examine the ways in which African Americans moved their bodies during musical performance, especially in black dance. Given the importance of dance in African cultures, it is hardly surprising to find blacks continuing with this activity in the New World societies into which they were forcibly incorporated, but since whites' descriptions tend to be meagre, it is hard to tell what forms such dancing took. Our concern, however, is not to identify various African and European dances, or syncretic blendings between them, but to identify an "otherness" in the way blacks used their bodies in dance, and, beyond that, to understand its cultural significance.

One difference white observers sometimes noted related to the angular movement of major joints—elbows, knees, ankles. Peter Wood links this phenomenon to West African dance forms, particularly those associated with the Bakongo culture of the Congo River, and points out that such movements persisted in the dance motions of African Americans in the Sea Islands, a region to which many slaves from the Angola region were originally brought. One slave song called on dancers to "Gimme de knee-bone bent," an instruction which whites probably associated with the Christian requirement to bend the knee in prayer, but which probably related to the West African belief that "straightened knees, hips, and elbows epitomized death and rigidity, while flexed joints embodied energy and life."[21] Writing from the Sea Islands in 1862, schoolteacher Laura Towne described how blacks performing the religious dance known as the shout shuffled in a circle, "turning round occasionally and bending the knees" (a shuffling motion would, of itself, require that knees and ankles were bent). Folklorist Benjamin Botkin noted that "one might shout acceptably by standing in one place, the feet either shuffling, or rocking backward of forward, tapping alternately with heel and toe, the knees bending." Lydia Parrish, who studied the music of the Sea Islands, pictured one shouter as giving "a stylized, angular performance," with "arms held close to her body, elbows bent at right angles."[22]

Another characteristic of black dance that often attracted comment from whites was its emphasis on the lower body or pelvis. In his classic study of African "survivals" in African American culture, Melville J. Herskovits noted that the European practice of men and women dancing close, with their arms around each other, was regarded by Africans and relatively unacculturated West Indian blacks as "nothing short of immoral," while "the manipulation of the muscles of hips and buttocks that are marks of good African dancing" evoked, in whites, a similarly disdainful response.[23] Evidence gathered by Lynne Fawley Emery and Dena J. Epstein on the nature of black dance in the African diaspora supports Herskovits's contention that whites considered black dances obscene. Describing the Calenda, a dance that was very popular with West Indian blacks around the turn of the eighteenth century, Père Labat noted how, in response to the drum beat, the lines of dancers would alternately "approach each other [and] strike their thighs together, . . . the men's against the women's" and then

"withdraw with a pirouette," all the while using "absolutely lascivious gestures."[24] George Pinckard, who saw Barbadian slaves performing what was
probably the Calenda early in the nineteenth century, protested that the
dancers' "approaches" to each other, and "the attitudes and inflexions in
which they are made," were "highly indecent."[25] Similar comments were
made about the Chica, another dance favored by West Indian blacks. In
the late eighteenth century, Moreau de St.-Méry, after noting the same al-
ternating forward and backward movement by pairs of dancers, wrote that
"when the Chica reaches its most expressive stage, there is in the gestures
and in the movements of the two dancers a harmony which is more easily
imagined than described."[26]

What whites apparently found alienating was the emphasis in black
dancing on the lower body, or pelvis, as the axis and originator of movement. In this respect, black dance seemed to de-emphasize those aspects of
the body that Europeans took as communicative, namely the arms and the
legs (as, for example, in classical European ballet, which thinks of all movements in terms of the arrangement of limbs around an unchanging torso).
Conversely, black modes of dancing seemed to emphasize those aspects of
the body that Europeans preferred to repress or deny.[27] Of course, during
black dance the arms, legs and feet were moved in some degree, but these
motions seemed subsidiary, and were less highly esteemed. The Englishman Edward Long, having observed a female slave dancing in Jamaica in
1774, concluded that "in her paces she exhibits a wonderful address, particularly in the movement of her hips, and steady position of the upper
part of her person." Long commented further that "the execution of this
wriggle . . . is esteemed among them [Jamaican blacks] a particular excel-
lence."[28] In 1790, J. B. Moreton, also describing black Jamaican dancers,
considered it "very amazing to think with what agility they twist and move
their joints," so that it seemed as though the dancers "were on springs or
hinges, from the hips downward." "Whoever is most active and expert at
wriggling," Moreton went on to say, "is reputed the best dancer."[29]

On the mainland, the most spectacular and most obviously "African"
dances performed during the nineteenth century were those that took
place at Congo Square in New Orleans. There, on Sundays, hundreds of
African Americans, both slave and free, assembled to watch extravagantly
dressed dancers perform to the accompaniment of drums, banjos, violins,
and other instruments. Observing this spectacle in 1819, Benjamin Latrobe,

who had been attracted to the Square by "the most extraordinary noise, which I supposed to proceed from some horsemill, the horses trampling on a wooden floor," experienced only a profound sense of cultural alienation, his description of the festivities highlighting such things as the "incredible quickness" of the drumming, the "curious" African-style instruments, and the "uncouth" singing, which he assumed to be "in some African language." "I have never," Latrobe declared, "seen anything more brutally savage and at the same time dull and stupid."[30] Others, more observant of the dancers themselves, have left accounts which suggest a strong West Indian influence, a predictable enough development given the cultural links between New Orleans and the Caribbean and the fact that the Haitian Revolution of the 1790s and early 1800s had prompted many Haitian planters to migrate to the city, bringing their slaves with them. Recalling a Congo Square dance, Henry Castellanos wrote of "the ludicrous contortions and gyrations of the Bamboula" and "the vibratory motions of the by-standers, who . . . contributed to the lascivious effect of the scene."[31] Later, a correspondent from the *New York World* described a Congo Square dance in which "[the]women did not move their feet from the ground [but] only writhed their bodies and swayed in undulatory motions from ankles to waist [while the] men leaped and performed feats of gymnastic dancing."[32]

The influence of Catholicism and New Orleans's French and Spanish background made the city somewhat tolerant of black cultural display, but elsewhere on the mainland a more restrictive attitude prevailed. Religious opposition to slave dancing increased from the early nineteenth century, particularly in the wake of the evangelical revivals of those years. Partly in response to this opposition, there grew up, within the slave community, a seemingly curious distinction between "dancing," which was considered sinful, and what Alan Lomax has called "holy dancing," which was not. Many white preachers condemned dancing of all kinds and did their best to persuade slaves to give it up. But, perhaps recognizing the virtual impossibility of forcing African Americans to remain quiescent in a musical setting, black ministers disallowed only certain European practices, specifically couples embracing while dancing, and crossing the feet while executing dance steps.[33] "Us 'longed to de church, all right," former Louisiana slave Wash Wilson explained, "but dancin' ain't sinful iffen de foots ain's crossed. Us danced at de arbor meetin's but us sho' didn't have us foots crossed!"[34]

The most famous of the holy dances was the Ring Shout, in which slaves shuffled counter-clockwise in a circle, to the accompaniment of hand-clapping, foot-stamping, and the rhythmic chanting of snatches of protestant hymns. The description of "M.R.S.," who visited a school in Beaufort, South Carolina, in 1866, is typical:

> After school the teachers gave their children permission to have a "shout." This is a favorite religious exercise of these people, old and young. In the infant schoolroom, the benches were first put aside, and the children ranged along the wall. Then began a wild droning chant in a minor key, marked with clapping of hands and stamping of feet. A dozen or twenty rose, formed a ring in the centre of the room, and began an odd shuffling dance. Keeping time to the weird chant they circled round, one following the other, changing their step to quicker and wilder motions, with louder clappings of the hands as the fervor of the singers reached a climax.[35]

Though whites generally associated the shout with Christian religious observances, there was some skepticism on this point, as M. R. S.'s reference to the "wild droning chant" suggests. Laura Towne saw in the shout "the remains of some old idol worship" and declared that she had never seen "anything so savage." "They call it a religious ceremony," she told her parents in 1862, "but it seems more like a regular frolic to me." William Francis Allen, also a schoolteacher, seems nearer the mark. "Perhaps," he wrote in 1863, the shout was "of African origin, with Christianity engrafted upon it. . . . These people are very strict about dancing, but will keep up the shout all night. It has a religious significance, and apparently a very sincere one, but it is evidently their recreation—just as prayer meetings are the only recreation of some people in the North."[36] As performed by slaves in the antebellum period, the Shout seems like a typical African American adaptation, which retained the ring formation, foot-stamping, polyrhythmic clapping, and shuffling of African dance forms but blended them with elements from a religion to which many had by then been converted or encouraged to adhere.

The shout may have eliminated "sinful" foot-crossing, but it is not at all clear that the emphasis on the lower body as the axis of movement had disappeared. Sea Islands schoolteacher Harriet Ware told how her pupils moved round in a circular fashion, with their arms and feet maintaining the beat, and "their whole bodies undergoing most extraordinary contortions." Though there is no direct reference to hip movements here, it is possible that this observer considered that subject too indelicate to mention. The South Carolina rice planter D. E. Huger Smith, who had frequently attended both "shoutings" and slave dances and declared himself "competent to describe" both, was more explicit. Huger Smith was not at all sure that his carpenter John, appointed religious "leader" by the visiting Methodist minister, had been able to persuade the other slaves "entirely to accept 'shoutings' as a substitute for dances." In time with the "inspiring" religious music supplied by the onlookers, this slaveholder wrote, the shouters "dance without any fancy steps, *but with an indescribable motion of the hips.*" [37]

By Huger Smith's account, secular dances were "quite different." To the music of the fiddle, accompanied by sticks (beaten on the floor) and bones, black dancers performed their jigs. "The dusky swain would grip the hand of the darksome belle. One swirl of both bodies under the arch of their arms and then they fell apart and made their 'steps' face to face." [38] Despite religious constraints, such secular dancing continued among the slave population and, as the recollections of former slaves show, was greatly enjoyed. "We used to git back in de end cabin an' sing an' dance by de fiddle till day break," Sally Ashton told her interviewer. "Sho' had one time, swingin' dem one piece dresses back an' foth, an' de boys crackin' dey coat-tails in de wind." Sometimes slaves would attend larger dances on a nearby plantation: "Musta been hundred slaves over thar," Fannie Berry recalled, "an' they always had de bes' dances." But "wasn't none of this sinful dancin' where yo' partner off wid man an woman squeezed up close to one another. Danced 'spectable, de slaves did, shiftin' 'round fum one partner to 'nother an' holdin' one 'nother out at arm's length." Nancy Williams told how courting couples would slip away to a cabin far out in the woods to dance to the music of fiddles, tambourines, banjos, and bones. "Whoops!" she declared, "Dem dances was somepin." She would be "out dere in de middle o' de flo' jes' a-dancin'; me and Jennie, an' de devil. Dancin' wid a glass o' water on my head an' three boys a-bettin' on me. I . . . didn't wase a drap o' water on neider. Jes' danced old Jennie down. Me'n de debil won dat night. One boy won five dollars off'n me." "I was ve'y wicked when I was young," Martha Showvely, another former slave confided; "I'd rather dance den eat."[39]

The general impression we get from such descriptions is of complex movements rapidly executed. This impression is confirmed by the testimony of Silvia Dubois, a former slave who was interviewed in the 1880s. She had attended a dance recently only to find that levels of skill had seriously declined. "They had a fiddle and they tried to dance," she averred, "but they couldn't—not a damned one of 'em." The problem was that these present-day dancers knew no steps. "You can't dance unless you have the step," Silvia Dubois declared, "and they were as awkward as the devil; and then they were so damned clumsy. Why, if they went to cross their legs, they'd fall down." In her own youth, she explained, "I'd cross my feet ninety-nine times in a minute and never miss the time, strike heel or toe with equal ease, and go through the figures as nimble as a witch."[40]

In Charles Dickens's famous description of the great black dancer Mr. Juba, performing in the 1840s in a cellar in the Five Points district in New York, the impression we gain is, once again, of a general vigor of bodily movements, of complex steps performed at lightning speed, but also of great physical flexibility and suppleness. Several couples had taken the floor, Dickens wrote, where they had been "marshalled by a lively young negro, . . . the greatest dancer known." The account continues:

> But the dance commences. Every gentleman sets as long as he likes to the opposite lady, and the opposite lady to him, and all are so long about it that the sport begins to languish, when suddenly the lively hero dashes in to the rescue. Instantly the fiddler grins, and goes at it tooth and nail; . . . Single shuffle, double shuffle, cut and cross-cut: snapping his fingers, rolling his eyes, turning in his knees, presenting the backs of his legs in front, spinning about on his toes and heels like nothing but the man's fingers on the tambourine; dancing with two left legs, two right legs, two wooden legs, two wire legs, two spring legs—all sorts of legs and no legs— what is this to him? And in what walk of life, or dance of life, does man ever get such stimulating applause as thunders about him, when, having danced his partner off her feet, and himself too, he finishes by leaping gloriously on the barcounter, and calling for

something to drink, with the chuckle of a million of counterfeit
Jim Crows, in one inimitable sound![41]

As Lynne Fawley Emery has revealed, when Juba danced in London his extraordinary physical virtuosity provoked incredulity. One eyewitness wrote
that he had never seen such "mobility of muscles, such flexibility of joints,
such boundings, such slidings, such gyrations, . . . such mutation of movement." Another critic wished to know how Juba could "tie his legs into
such knots, and fling them about so recklessly, or make his feet twinkle until you lose sight of them altogether in his energy."[42]

Juba (William Henry Lane), of course, was an internationally famous
dancer, quite exceptionally talented, but broadly similar descriptions by
whites of other African Caribbean or African American dancers—descriptions emphasising suppleness, flexibility and rapidity of movement—can
be found in contemporary accounts assembled by Emery and Epstein.
Describing Jamaican dancers in 1790, J. B. Moreton thought it "very amazing to think with what agility they twist and move their joints:—I sometimes imagined they were on springs or hinges, from the hips downwards."
Mainland slaves performing the Juba dance, William Smith wrote in 1838,
displayed "the most ludicrous twists, wry jerks, and flexible contortions of
the body and limbs, that human imagination can devine." The suppleness
of blacks' bodies was associated with the free movement of the pelvis, the
fluidity of black dancers' bodies contrasting with what Lawrence Levine
refers to as the "stiffly erect" bodily position commonly assumed in European dance forms, but more was involved than this.[43]

A sense of cultural difference pervades whites' descriptions of African
American dance. Even if the steps black dancers were using were familiar
to whites, those steps were being performed at different speeds, combined
in different ways, and executed with different movements of the torso and
limbs.[44] Even if slaves were performing European dances such as the
quadrille, the cotillion, and the schottische, differences in style—the rhythmic complexity, the persistent improvisation, and unusual body movements—suggested that different cultural values underlay the performance.

In their classic article on African American dance, John Szwed and
Morton Marks point out that attempts to investigate this phenomenon are
made difficult by the lack of visual or literary sources.[45] However, they go

on to suggest that, because the relationship between black dance and music is so intimate, an examination of the latter may throw considerable light on the former. The performance known as "patting Juba" lends itself to this approach.

According to the description given by ex-slave Solomon Northup, "Patting Juba" was performed "by striking the hands on the knees, then striking the hands together, then striking the right shoulder with one hand, the left with the other—all the while keeping time with the feet." After noting that African Americans set much greater store than do whites on "the acquisition of a sophisticated rhythmic sensibility," Frank Kofsky has asserted that patting "initiated the young into the complex rhythmic patterns necessary for the creation not only of music but also of dance," a function which the Hambone game of more recent times also performs. Like "Patting Juba," from which it is derived, the Hambone game "teaches 'independence'—that is, the ability to execute simultaneous cross-rhythms with both arms, both legs, the head and the torso," which is not only a necessary precondition for the creation of jazz, for instance, but "an integral and fundamental aspect of Black dance." To suggest the difficulty of attaining "independence," James Lincoln Collier has written: "You can learn to pat your head and rub your stomach at the same time, but try doing it to different tempos, especially when somebody is beating a drum at yet a third tempo." [46] Within the characteristic circle formation associated with black performance style, a basic or ground beat might be laid down by the rhythmic stamping of feet, but against this beat singers, clappers, drummers, other instrumentalists, or a dancer (through the use of his or her body) may set up counter rhythms, which play against the basic beat. It is this rhythmic complexity that the black dancer manages somehow to express.

Studies of African performance style throw light on how this is done. After noting that West African dance, like West African music, is characterized by "multiple meter," Robert Farris Thompson cites Waterman's observation that "the [West African] dancer picks up each rhythm of the polyrhythmic whole with different parts of his body." Thompson quotes Bertonoff's finding that, when the Ewe of Ghana dance, "the various limbs and members, head, shoulders, and legs are all moving simultaneously but each in a rhythm of its own." Alan Lomax has uncovered the same connection, concluding, on the basis of his cross-cultural study of dance forms, that "African cultures lead all the rest in emphasis on bodily polyrhythm, where the shoulders and the pelvis erotically rotate and twist, often to two separate and conflicting meters."[47] Dances in which the performer simultaneously expressed, through the movement of hips, shoulders, arms, knees and feet, the multiple rhythms provided by other members of the group were bound to appear alien and complex to white observers. The African American cultural preference for constant rhythmic variation must have served further to disorient white onlookers.

Though whites did not fully understand what they were seeing, one can discover in their writings descriptions of slave dancers or singers picking up the various rhythms of a polyrhythmic structure with different parts of the body. Describing dancers in Congo Square, Colonel James Creecy noted that "the most perfect time is kept, making the beats with the feet, heads, or hand, or all, as correctly as a well-regulated metronome." Frederika Bremer, who attended an evening service in an African American church in South Carolina in 1850, described how the congregation "sang . . . with all their souls and with all their bodies in unison; for their bodies wagged, their heads nodded, their feet stamped, their knees shook, their elbows and their hands beat time to the tune." Alan Lomax has recently shown that this tradition survived in the Delta and is visible elsewhere in twentieth-century musical and dance performance. Describing the performance style of G. D. Young's fife and drum band, Lomax writes that "they capered without lifting their feet; their shoulders, belly, and buttocks separately twitched to the beat." Napoleon Strickland, another of the black folk musicians whose performances Lomax observed, was able to create "multipart rhythms" from a diddley bow, "play[ing] a different beat pattern with each hand—two against three, or six against eight—and lay[ing] in the melody on top of these." This is a complex and difficult process, but the black musician "manages with ease, since from childhood he has practiced patting games like *juba* to make himself perfectly bilateral, as well as multileveled, so that he can do different things with his right and left sides, meanwhile moving his feet and middle body and shoulders to other beat patterns."[48] In black dance, the same kind of rhythmic dexterity is displayed.

As suggested above, the polyrhythmic, improvisatory, and physically vivacious nature of black dance does indeed reflect a more general cultural aesthetic. We argued earlier that as slave women became heavily involved in the production of cloth and clothing on nineteenth-century plantations,

the design of these items began to display a different aesthetic, whose clashing colors and irregular patterning also informed the artistic design of African American slave quilts. Maude Southwell Wahlman and others have
shown that this aesthetic is still found among twentieth-century black quil-
ters. "If I have red," Leola Pettway, an Alabama quiltmaker, explained to
Wahlman, "I put a different color next to it. If I am scraping a quilt, I put
different materials together." The quilts of Plummer T. Pettway, of Boykin,
Alabama, Wahlman writes, conveyed a sense of "variety and movement."
Colors were "place[d] . . . at uneven intervals, so that her patterns appear
to be constantly shifting." The effect produced by differences in patterns,
color strengths, and placements was one of "constant surprise."[49] This aesthetic also underlies some African Americans' apparent preference for what
seemed, to whites, odd combinations of clothes, garments that "clashed"
with each other and whose color combinations seemed incongruous. As
the African American quilter Sarah Mary Taylor explained to Wahlman, "I
tries to match pieces like I'd wear clothes."[50]

The same aesthetic characterizes African American music, as even
whites seem to have intuited. The metaphors they used to describe black
singing frequently evoked images of textile design or quiltmaking. In 1870,
Elizabeth Kilham, who had gone to the South as a teacher, pondered the
nature of hymns which, originally created by whites, had been reworked by
blacks to suit themselves. "Were they composed as a whole," she wondered,
"with deliberate arrangement and definite meaning, or are they fragments,
caught here and there, and pieced into a mosaic, haphazard as they
come?"—a question that might equally well have been asked about an African American quilt. To Texas schoolteacher William P. Stanton, his black
students' hymns "seem[ed] to be a sort of miscellaneous patchwork, made
up from the most striking parts of popular Methodist hymns." Endeavor-
ing to describe the singing of companies of black soldiers as they marched
along, Colonel Thomas Higginson, the white commander of the First Regiment, South Carolina Volunteers, wrote that "for all the songs, but especially for their own wild hymns, they constantly improvised simple verses,
with the same odd mingling—the little facts of to-day's march being inter-
woven with the depths of theological gloom, and the same jubilant chorus
annexed to all."[51]

Maude Southwell Wahlman has observed that "the unpredictable
rhythms and tensions of Plummer T's [Plummer T. Petway's] quilts" are

"similar to those found in . . . other African-based black American arts, such as jazz," a comment that recalls Frederick Law Olmsted's observation that both the slaves' color sense and their music were related to an underlying sense of rhythm, one that was alien to Euro-American cultural forms.[52] In similar vein, Robert Farris Thompson has pointed to the correspondence between the "emphatic multistrip composition" of "the cloth of West Africa and culturally related Afro-American sites" and the "multiple meter" of "the traditional music of black Africa." Thompson also sees a "visual resonance" between the "rich and vivid suspensions of the expected placement of the weft blocks" in Mande or Mande-influenced narrow strip cloth and "the famed off-beat phrasing of melodic accents in African and Afro-American music." For Thompson, the deliberate clash of colors and patterns gives Mande textiles their sense of vibrancy and "aliveness"; for John Miller Chernoff, the "clash and conflict of rhythms" produces in African music precisely these same characteristics.[53]

The remaining link, with black dance, is not hard to forge. The relationship of dance to both African and African American music is so intimate that these forms of cultural expression should probably be considered as one. Like African American music and textile design, black dance is characterized by rhythmic complexity. It, too, privileges improvisation over predetermined form. As with black music, whether from the slave period or after it, and as is also true of black quilts and clothing, African American dance conveys an impression of "aliveness" and "vibrancy," the "unpredictable rhythms and tensions" of the performer evoking a sense of "constant surprise." Just as the clashing colors and irregular patterning of slave textiles and the multiple rhythms and unreproducible sounds of slave music jangled white sensibilities, so the movements of the black body in dance often seemed alien and unaccountably strange.

Under slavery, the black body was a contested site, a surface on which the struggle for dominance between master and slave was often quite visibly played out. We have shown that blacks were sometimes able to exercise a surprising degree of control over the manner in which they clothed their bodies and styled their hair, but blacks' bodies could still be branded, mutilated, penetrated by the owner, or bought and sold like any other piece of property. "They 'zamine you just like they do a horse," a Mississippi slave woman complained. "They look at your teeth, pull your eyelids back and look at your eyes."[54] Some slaves may have managed to walk upright, presenting their bodies in a prideful manner, but many more were forced into awkwardness by injury or inadequate diet, by coarse, ill-fitting clothing or painful shoes. Runaway ads depict these men and women as shambling along, with bodies bent forward from years of unremitting toil. George, who absconded in Maryland in 1785, had a "very lubberly gait" and "stoop[ed] forward"; Bacchus, who ran away in Maryland in 1789, walked "inactively and awkwardly"; James Nicholas, who escaped in Virginia in 1772, walked "slow, and stoop[ed] in his shoulders"; Strephon, a South Carolina runaway, had "a slouching clumsy Gait."[55] To all such negative representations of the black body, the black dancer presented a powerful counterimage, a self-presentation in which African American slaves could feel deeply satisfying pride. Contrasting the festive dancing of the whites, before whom, as a skilled slave violinist, he had often played, with that of ordinary plantation blacks, ex-slave Solomon Northup was moved to exclaim: "Oh, ye pleasure-seeking sons and daughters of idleness, who move with measured step, listless and snail-like, through the slow winding cotillon, if ye wish to look upon the celerity, if not the 'poetry of motion'—upon genuine happiness, rampant and unrestrained—go down to Louisiana and see the slaves dancing in the starlight of a Christmas night."[56] If the prideful way in which some slaves presented their bodies tested the limits of the system's tolerance and the subtleties of their eye movements allowed the transmission of social signals that whites could not understand, black dance allowed slaves emphatically to refigure their construction within an oppressive system as pure physicality and utility. By aestheticizing the black body, by putting its vitality, suppleness and sensuality defiantly and joyously on display, the black dancer repudiated slavery's evaluation of the slave body as brute physical labor, and constructed, for a time, a world of difference, sharply at variance with that which blacks were normally compelled to inhabit.[57]

Dandies and Dandizettes

Just before 11 o'clock on the night of January 3, 1799, Elizabeth Drinker, a Philadelphia Quaker, sat down at her desk to pen an entry in her diary describing the day's events. Earlier that evening, she recorded, Jacob Turner and Sarah Needham, two of her black servants, had gone to a wedding. Drinker lingered a while in her narrative, detailing the garb in which the two young African Philadelphians had set out: Turner had worn a "light cloth coat, white casamer vest and britches," white silk stockings, and a new hat, while Needham, a bridesmaid at the ceremony, had dressed in white muslin, bedecked from head to toe with white ribbons, and "Yellow Morocco Shoes with white bows." The two had been picked up in Benjamin Oliver's Coachee, whose driver was white, and, even though the hour was late, had not yet returned. "They are both honest servants," Drinker noted in her diary, "but times is much altred with the black folk."

In Philadelphia, as elsewhere in the North, the ending of slavery fundamentally transformed relationships between blacks and whites. Like the vast majority of Philadelphia blacks at the turn of the nineteenth century, Jacob Turner and Sarah Needham were not slaves but servants, and, as Elizabeth Drinker's wryly detached account of the role reversals attendant on that difference makes clear, she was well aware of the distinction. So, too, were her black employees. A few months later, in early April 1799, Turner and Needham were married in a ceremony conducted by Absalom Jones, himself a former slave, in Jones's newly established African Church of Philadelphia. Elizabeth Drinker had offered to hold a wedding supper for her two servants "if they would have it here in a sober way," but the offer had been promptly though politely turned down, the couple preferring to make their own arrangements. "A wedding without a frolick," Drinker observed in her diary, "would be no wedding, I believe, in their view."[1]

This small, almost inconsequential, incident, uncustomary in its gentleness—not all blacks would be as polite as were this couple, and very few whites would have bothered to try to consider things from the perspective of their black servants, as Drinker had done (that "in their view" is unusual)—but it is a pointer to many of the issues that would confront both blacks and whites as African Americans set out to discover what freedom meant. For blacks, the fact that they were no longer slaves had to mean less interference in their lives: in this case, the ability to attend a black church or to celebrate a wedding with their compatriots away from disapproving white eyes. On the other hand, many whites clearly desired blacks' status to remain much as it had been when they were slaves and often felt, at the very least, an abiding sense of uneasiness at the spectacle of newly freed slaves choosing to assert a greater measure of autonomy.

The ending of slavery in the North was a long, drawn-out process, taking over half a century from the time of the Revolution. Most northern legislatures and courts, loathe to interfere with the property rights of slaveowners, instituted only the most gradual of measures. The legislation in New York (1799) and New Jersey (1804), the northern states with the largest numbers of slaves, freed only the as-yet-unborn children of slaves; owners of slaves born before the passage of the New York law were not compelled to free them until July 4, 1827, and in New Jersey slavery lasted even longer. But once it became clear that the institution was to end, many bondsmen and bondswomen managed to negotiate an early release by buying their own freedom, or by promising faithful service for a certain number of years, or by some combination of these measures. For blacks, this was a messy and capricious process; it was not at all uncommon for some family members to gain their freedom while others were compelled to spend years more in bondage. Only slaves' determination to be free and the individual initiative they exercised enabled them to overcome such obstacles and hasten the dilatory timetable set in place by whites for slavery's demise in the North. The grudging process of abolition—some obdurate owners retained their human property until the bitter end—hardly augured well for the state of relations between newly freed African Americans and their fellow citizens.[2]

The degree of tolerance Elizabeth Drinker displayed toward free blacks was unusual. Far more common was the mixture of condescension and disdain demonstrated by John Fanning Watson, Philadelphia patrician and annalist of his city. Almost half a century after Drinker had observed that "times is much altred with the black folks," Watson lamented the state to which African Philadelphians had sunk since, as he put it, they "received their entire exemption from slavery." What particularly offended Watson was the presumptuous and flamboyant clothing worn by many of the freed blacks. "In the olden time," he began, "dressy blacks and dandy *coloured* beaux and belles, as we now see them issuing from their proper churches, were quite unknown." The reasons for this unwelcome development were clear enough to Watson: "their aspirings and little vanities have been rapidly growing since they got those separate churches" and since they had been granted their freedom. No longer, moreover, would former slaves allow themselves to be addressed as "servants, blacks, or negroes, but now they require to be called coloured people" and, furthermore, "among themselves, their common call of salutation is—gentlemen and ladies." In short, the city's blacks were demonstrating "an overweening fondness for display and vainglory—fondly imitating the whites in processions and banners, and in the pomp and pageantry of masonic and Washingtonian societies," ostentatious displays which made "judicious men wish them wiser conduct, and a better use of the benevolent feelings which induced their emancipation among us." For Watson, African Americans had been passive ciphers in the process of abolition, and he clearly wished, now that they had received their freedom, that they would demonstrate their gratitude to the "judicious men" who had conferred it on them by being a bit more passive, and certainly less conspicuous about town.[3]

Whites' feelings of disquiet about free blacks coalesced around the perceived lack of self-control African Americans exercised in the presentation of their bodies. Drinker and Watson responded to this differently, but their fascination with the appearance of the free blacks was typical of a wide range of white opinion: for many, the changed look of African Americans was the most visible and obvious result of emancipation. This concern was not limited to the appearance of especially "well dressed" individuals, but broadened out to include unease at black collective behavior, such as that displayed at churches and in the African American parades that, by the 1820s and 1830s, were criss-crossing northern cities.

What is particularly intriguing about this concern over the presence and behavior of African Americans is that it occurred at a time when blacks formed a very small and declining proportion of urban populations. In 1830, there were 1,875 black persons in Boston, 13,977 in New York, and 9,807 in Philadelphia, these numbers constituting, respectively, 3.05 percent, 6.90 percent, and 12.19 percent of the inhabitants of those cities. New York's black population was still increasing (it had more than doubled since 1800) but blacks' share of the population was decreasing (from 10.53 percent at the turn of century), indicating that blacks had failed to match the city's exponential rate of demographic growth, an increase spurred by an influx of migrants from Europe. Though New York was the extreme case, much the same was happening elsewhere in the North. The exception was Philadelphia, whose black population, expanding at about the same rate as New York's, marginally increased its share of the total population of that city.[4]

Not only were blacks a small and, for the most part, diminishing minority of northern urban populations, but, increasingly, their lives were segregated from those of the vast majority of whites. Blacks became free and entered the housing market in the years which saw the old mixed neighborhoods of the "walking city" give way to the more specialized spatial arrangements of the emerging industrial one. Workers were paid now in cash rather than receiving board and lodging from an employer as part of their remuneration—and had to find their own accommodation. Mostly, they did so in areas that were rapidly developing into distinctively working-class wards.[5] For African Americans, the result was a clustering of black households in the relatively limited sections of the city in which they could get access to scarce housing. In Boston, most of the city's blacks were concentrated in the West End, behind Beacon Hill; in Philadelphia, most lived in the southern part of the city in a 34-block area bounded by Cedar, Fourth, Spruce, Walnut and Twelfth streets. In early nineteenth-century New York, a majority of African Americans was clustered around Bancker Street and, on the lower west side, around Chapel and Anthony streets, although by mid-century most black households had moved further up the west side, to an area around Canal Street. To be sure, there were still many whites residing in these locations—in Philadelphia, blacks tended to live in alleys, courts, or at the rear of other buildings; in New York, they often rented basement cellars, frequently with whites literally living on top of them in the rest of the building—but, even so, some of these areas increasingly took on the appearance of identifiably black neighborhoods.[6]

As slavery wound down in the North, the physical separation of blacks from whites, particularly that between blacks and the class of whites who had been slaveowners, increased. Only the poorer whites, especially Irish immigrants, lived in the same areas as African Americans. A concomitant development, as many observers noted, was that free northern blacks, particularly those living in the cities, bore the brunt of an increasingly virulent racism. In 1829, a visitor from Montreal remarked that in New York all blacks "indiscriminately are looked upon with aversion by the white population." After a stay in Philadelphia in 1841, Joseph Sturge concluded that "there is probably no city in the known world, where dislike, amounting to hatred of the coloured population, prevails more than in the city of brotherly love!" Similarly, Francis and Theresa Pulszky thought that, on the whole, "there is great prejudice in the North against colored people," but that, "strange to say, you find it more with the town folks and the higher classes than with the farmers." Things were never quite as extreme as they were in the twentieth-century South, but increasingly northern whites demanded segregated facilities and exhibited a distaste for any kind of physical contact with African Americans. Blacks may now have been free, the visitor from Montreal noted, but no one knew "how to talk or to act towards them," and, furthermore, any "known connection with them insures a degree of disgrace." Henry Fearon, an English traveler to New York in 1817, could scarcely conceal his amazement at the fact that any black hairdresser who wished to retain his white clientele could not service a perfectly respectable-looking black man. A few years later, J. S. Buckingham commented that, whereas in the South slaves would shake the hand of whites when they met, "at the North I do not remember to have witnessed this once." Not in "Boston, New York, or Philadelphia would white persons generally like to be seen shaking hands and talking familiarly with blacks in the streets."[7]

Northern whites, particularly members of the respectable classes, may have avoided interacting in any way with African Americans on the streets (where blacks and whites were most likely to meet), but they certainly gazed at them with a degree of intensity. Increasingly in the nineteenth century, as the cities became more segregated spatially, respectable whites developed a prurient interest in the way of life of the lower orders generally, and of African Americans in particular. Indignant letters in contemporary newspapers complained bitterly and endlessly about the appearance and behavior of lower-class urban-dwellers. In New York in 1817, "CIVIS" wrote to the *National Advocate* demanding that action be taken over the "numerous vagrants who literally inundate" Henry and Bancker streets. The "greatness of their number," "their idle and dissolute habits," and "their general appearance, which [was] extremely offensive to delicacy," greatly perturbed this New Yorker, as did the fact that "blacks and whites are there mingled together." A dozen years later, W. S. argued in the *New York Evening Post* that "every day gives us a new proof that there is great need of doing something for that famous place called Five Points," an area presently "inhabited by the vilest rabble, black & white, mixt together." No one, he continued, "can form any idea of this den, who has not seen the same after sunset."[8]

The wording of W. S.'s letter bears further examination, especially his admission that he had made at least one night-time visit to Five Points, this "famous place." Timothy Dwight was another white observer who, early in the nineteenth century, found his way to one of the less respectable parts of the city, in this case an embryonic slum near the East River. Dwight subsequently claimed that this neighborhood stood "aside from the walks of gentlemen who visit this city," but he was wrong: not only did he himself go there, but so also did virtually every other gentleman traveler and commentator on the northern cities, and through them their readers as well.[9] This voyeuristic impulse was heightened when its focus was ordinary African Americans; indeed, at times it seems that many whites, at least in part, lived vicariously through African Americans, projecting their own fantasies onto the bodies of black men and women.

Whites' fascination with observing the behavior of African Americans reached its most heightened form in the scrutiny of what were termed "dandies," the well-dressed black males and females who were a more obvious presence on the city streets after freedom. Travelers endlessly commented on these African Americans, describing them in rich detail. Partly this was the curiosity of the traveler in search of exotic material for subsequent publication, but we would suggest that it was also an attitude picked up from the respectable white milieu in which these travelers almost invariably moved. Such interest in the appearance and demeanor of flashily dressed blacks was hardly confined to travelers' narratives, however; it was common fare of newspaper and other accounts of city life.

From the late eighteenth century, European travelers to the United States who disembarked in New York were struck by the numbers of African Americans they encountered on the city's thoroughfares. Patrick M'Robert, who visited New York in 1774, felt compelled to record in his diary that "it rather hurts an Europian eye to see so many negro slaves upon the streets." Two decades later, in comparing New York with London, a recently arrived William Strickland emphasized the "greater number of the Blacks particularly of women and children in the streets who may be seen of all shades till the stain is entirely worne out." The stream of such comments carried on unabated into the nineteenth century, even while, as we have seen, the percentage of blacks in most northern cities was actually falling. To Henry Fearon, the "striking feature" of the New York of 1817 was "the number of blacks, many of whom are finely dressed, the females very ludicrously so, showing a partiality to white muslin dresses, artificial flowers, and pink shoes." Fifteen years later, James Stuart, engaged, as many travelers continued to be, in making comparisons between New York and London, wrote that "one of the great novelties to us" was the "immense number of people of colour,—many of them as well dressed as the whites." [10]

Increasingly, then, it was not just the numbers of blacks but their appearance that attracted the attention of newcomers to New York and to northern cities with smaller black populations. Stephen Davis, who visited New York in 1832, "repeatedly saw coloured females in the height of fashion in Broadway." Others, less interested in generalizing, recorded in detail the attire and demeanor of individual blacks who caught their eye. Lady Emmeline Stuart Wortley, sojourning in New Haven in 1849, "saw one very curious specimen of a dandy . . . lounging down the street." This African American was "a sable Count d'Orsay," whose "toilette was the most elaborately *recherché* you can imagine." "He seemed," Wortley continued, "intensely and harmlessly happy in his coat and waistcoat, of the finest possible materials; and the careful carelessness of the adjustment of the wool and hat was not readily to be surpassed." [11]

For many whites, a well-dressed black was an at least slightly comic figure, but there was also often, in whites' observations, an underlying sense of disquiet, a fretful complaint at the blurring of what had seemed relatively clear-cut racial boundaries. William Blane, an English gentlemen who visited Philadelphia in the early 1820s, recollected that "frequently," on being "desirous of ascertaining whether the beauty of some finely dressed female was equal to her attire," he had "perceived under a huge Leghorn bonnet and lace cap, the black face and great white eyes of a negress." Quite often he "could hardly help laughing, so ludicrous was this contrast." A decade later, the traveler S. A. Ferrall, while walking down Broadway in New York, "was struck with the figure of a fashionably dressed woman, who was sauntering before me." Having overtaken the woman, Ferrall turned around, only to be shocked by what he saw. "O angels and ministers of ugliness!" Ferrall later wrote, "I beheld a face, as black as soot—a mouth that reached from ear to ear—a nose, like nothing human—and lips a full inch in diameter!" Both of these men derided blacks for copying white behavior; Blane wrote of African Americans being "so eager to imitate the fashions of whites." But, unnerved by what, in their terms, could be called the success of these particular blacks in managing to look like whites, the two white men had marked themselves off by lampooning the blacks' facial features. [12] To be sure, there was a long history of the use of caricatures to demean Africans and African Americans, but, as the viciousness of Ferrall's description suggests, such negative portrayals of black people took on a new importance at a time when other barriers were crumbling.

Whites' descriptions of African Americans were usually set in a framework of failed imitation, of a clumsy, inept and inappropriate black translation of whites' mores into blacks' own lowly situation. Limited by both discrimination and meager finances, most African Americans had little choice but to spend their leisure hours on the city streets, a site that made their bodies and their actions easily visible targets for white ridicule or worse. Far from being cowed by this constant threat, however, African

Americans insisted on their right to the streets—they were, after all, citizens and entitled to be there—and continued to dress up and display themselves on prominent thoroughfares to their compatriots and to whites as well. In a development born, perhaps, of a cruel necessity and economic hardship, the early decades of the nineteenth century saw the sociability of the street, the importance of the leisurely stroll through the neighborhood, become established as one of the defining features of northern black urban life. This phenomenon was most obvious on Sundays; as one writer in New York's *National Advocate* in the early 1820s observed, African Americans' "modicum of pleasure was taken on Sunday evening, when black dandys and dandizettes, after attending meeting, occupied the sidewalks in Broadway, and slowly lounged towards their different homes." [13]

Attempts by African Americans to establish alternative venues for sociability, especially anything more upmarket than a tavern or a dancehall, met with white opposition and hostility. Blacks were, for example, excluded from all of the ice cream and tea gardens in New York. In 1821, however, a new venue, designed exclusively for an African American clientele, opened at the African Grove, behind the hospital on the west side, a development that the *National Advocate* attributed to the increase in the number of blacks in the city. The African Grove was a place where "ebony lads and lasses could obtain ice cream, ice punch, and hear music" and where "black fashionables saunter up and down the garden, in all the pride of liberty and unconscious of want." Again, the writer of this largely derisive commentary chose to highlight the appearance of the black patrons, focusing particularly on a courting couple: "the gentleman, with his wool nicely combed, and his face shining through a coat of sweet oil, borrowed from the castors; cravat tight to suffocation, having the double faculty of widening the mouth and giving a remarkable protuberance to the eyes; blue coat, fashionably cut; red ribbon and a bunch of pinch-beck seals; white pantaloons, shining boots, gloves, and a tippy rattan," and the lady wearing "pink kid slippers," a "fine Leghorn, cambric dress with open work," "well fitted" corsets, and a "reticule hanging on her arm." Outraged by "these sable fashionables," local whites complained to the police, and the place was quickly closed down. Some time later an African Theater was established on this spot—Ira Aldridge, the famous black actor, first went on stage there—but following police harassment and riotous behavior by whites it too was closed. [14]

More typically, then, African northerners were forced to compete with whites on the city streets and to carve out their own locale. In 1832, Carl Arfwedson, a Swedish traveler, landed near the southern tip of New York, close to a "fashionable promenade, called the Battery." According to Arfwedson, "on Sundays this public walk is filled with people of all classes, particularly those of the sable cast, making a profuse exhibition of their finery." For blacks, "this place of resort is, something like Hyde Park, near London, a place for show." The Swede was particularly taken with the dress of African New Yorkers, which, he declared, bordered on "extravagance": "the women wear bonnets decorated with ribbons, plumes, and flowers, of a thousand different colours, and their dresses are of the most showy description," while the men were attired in "coats so open that the shirt sticks out under the arm-pits; the waistcoats are of all colours of the rainbow; the hat is carelessly put on one side; the gloves are yellow, and every sable dandy carries a smart cane." Like local whites, Arfwedson found these blacks amusing in their incongruity, although his was a gentler, less vicious humor. Initially, the traveler wrote, "it was with difficulty I could refrain from laughing, on seeing these black *beaux* (the name by which they generally go) doing homage to the black housemaids or cooks, known as *belles*" [15] (see Figure 9).

Comments such as these reveal much about whites' fascination with black bodies; they also reveal something of the activities that attracted whites' gaze. Finding material, originating with African Americans and commenting on their own bodily display, was more difficult for this chapter than for any other in the book. Nevertheless, we would suggest that the attaining of freedom in the North sparked an exuberant cultural display, as newly liberated blacks deliberately, consciously, and publicly tested the boundaries of freedom. At an individual level the result was a venturing out onto the city streets by African Americans garbed in colorful and, what often seemed to whites, bizarre combinations of clothes—ensembles that reflected the existence of an African American aesthetic similar to that which we have identified earlier when dealing with slavery—and a prideful bearing of the blacks' bodies so adorned. The intention that animated such behavior becomes even clearer if we look at two organized and collective uses made by African Americans of the public spaces of northern cities, the street parade and the ball.

In the early years of the nineteenth century, newly freed slaves in northern cities established the African American parade as part of the civic calendar. If the burgeoning number of processions and parades staged by whites in the early years of the new republic constituted, to quote Clifford Geertz, "stories a people tell about themselves," then blacks were, to all intents and purposes, omitted from those stories, in much the same way that

Figure 9: Edward Clay, *Life In New York*. Clay's caricatures were the visual equivalent of the descriptions in the travelers' accounts. Whites were increasingly fascinated by the way African American lives, particularly their sex lives, were played out in public on the streets. Here the intended destination of at least one of the black males was the Battery, which Carl Arfwedson described in the text. The Library Company of Philadelphia

they were excluded from most other public aspects of northern life. To be sure, blacks occasionally found a place in some marches, but the integrative impulse was tepid at best. Parades and processions to mark Evacuation Day (celebrating the British retreat from New York during the Revolution), Washington's Birthday, the Fourth of July, and special events such as the ratification of the Constitution in 1788 or the opening of the Erie Canal in 1825 could be viewed by blacks, but only whites could participate.[16]

To contest this exclusion, free black associations—and the 1790s and early 1800s witnessed a burst of such organizational activity among African northerners[17]—stepped into the void and arranged their own parades. Groups such as the African Society in Salem, the African Society for Mutual Relief in New York, the Wilberforce Benevolent Society in New York, and many others usually marked their anniversaries with a highly visible procession through town. In 1797, for instance, the black Masons staged the first of many annual parades through the streets of Philadelphia (see Figure 10). But the most important and spectacular of these processions were those which, from 1808, were held in Boston each July 14th to mark the abolition of the slave trade, and those which, from 1827, were held in New York on July 5th to celebrate the end of slavery in the Empire State.

As one of the authors of this study has argued elsewhere, certain features of these parades—the presence of marshals and even the pace of the march—harked back to the northern slave festivals, but in the present context the most important element of continuity was the way the marchers dressed. In June 1827, an editorial in the *New York Morning Chronicle* anticipated that the forthcoming July 5th parade (this "jubilee nonsense," as the newspaper described it) would contribute to the increase of the city's "criminal calendar, pauper list and *dandy* register." The paper was right to emphasize the continued importance attached by the participants to clothing; other observers made the same point, though in less acerbic fashion. In 1827 the *New York Daily Advertiser* described the marchers as "remarkably well dressed," and in 1833 James Boardman, an English traveler, observed that the "extremely well dressed" marchers looked striking in their "sashes and ribands." The garb of the officers of various black societies, who led the march, attracted particular attention. Decades later, James McCune Smith, a prominent black doctor, recalled how "splendidly dressed in scarfs of silk with gold edgings" those in the vanguard of the 1827 New York march had been, and the *Mercantile Advertiser* declared the officers in the July 5, 1829, New York march to be "most extravagantly dressed, in cha-peaus, bands, sashes and gold lace &c.," many wearing "broad rich collars, and almost all carried canes." Several times a year, in New York and in other urban areas across the northeast, African Americans deliberately marched all over town—some of these parades took nearly three hours to complete—not only emphasizing differences in the way they looked and moved but also insisting that they had a right to the streets and that mile-stones in their collective past were a part of the city's history.[18]

The second organized event to stake a claim for public space was the African American ball. At least as early as the 1820s, African Americans in New York and Philadelphia began to stage formal balls for themselves dur-ing what constituted "the season," the period in late February and March leading up to Easter. As was the case with just about everything else free blacks managed to arrange, these events did not sit well with the local

Figure 10: David Claypoole Johnstone, *A Splendid Procession of Free Masons,* c. 1820. Here John-stone derides one of the numerous African American parades that occurred in northern cities. White onlookers responded to these events in much the same spirit by hurling abuse, mud, and stones at the black participants. Courtesy of the Boston Public Library, Print Department

whites; it is, in fact, from satirical and supposedly amusing pieces published in contemporary white newspapers and magazines that our knowledge of these affairs mostly derives (see Figure 11). Interestingly, the focus of most of the stories about the balls was not on the dancing itself but on the garb of the patrons and the manner of their arrival at the various venues, in other words, on how they looked and comported themselves on the street. A story in the *National Advocate* in March 1825 provides a good example. The African American ball that the writer described was held in "their grand saloon" in Mulberry street in New York. As the carriages arrived, one or two "masters of ceremonies [were] ready to hand the *ladies* out," and there was much yelling from managers, "ordering the white drivers to turn 'de horses head to Pump street,'" which created quite a "bustle." Indeed, as the writer noted, "the place was kept lively and interesting." About ten o'clock, the Police Magistrate and a dozen members of the watch broke the event up and escorted many of the black participants off to the Watch House. The following morning about forty were "brought forth for a hearing," the women among them (many with "*borrowed robes,*") being "dressed in tawdry elegance," displaying "coloured silk pantalets," "nodding plumes and spangled petticoats." Some had been "accused of using the liquid rouge." The manager of the ball defended the event—the newspaper account of his address was rendered in black dialect—but this hardly impressed the Magistrate, whom members of the Grand Jury had previously requested to break up such affairs, which, they asserted, created riots and nuisances, "decoyed" servants from their employers, and "led to bad habits." [19]

Much the same themes run through the coverage of a fancy-dress ball held in a Mr. August's rooms, on Fourth Street near Chesnut, in Philadelphia on February 28, 1828. Under the caption "High Life below Stairs.— Black Ball," the *Pennsylvania Gazette* labeled the whole affair a "joke of no ordinary magnitude." According to this paper, an unruly and jeering mob gathered in the street outside, insulting the ladies, tearing the dresses of a few, and frightening the horses. "It is worthy of remark," the *Gazette* continued, "that many of the coaches . . . were attended by white coachmen and *white footmen,*" a fact that made the paper wonder "how long it will be before servants and masters change places." The *Democratic Press* began its brief coverage of the affair by commenting that the blacks were "very

Figure 11: Edward Clay, *Life in Philadelphia*, Plate 5. The idea of African Philadelphians holding balls was preposterous to many white Philadelphians. Undoubtedly Clay had read the derisory newspaper accounts of these balls and picked up on the popular mood with this image. The Library Company of Philadelphia

stylishly dressed," the men wearing "superb uniforms, gold epaulets, sword &c. &c.," before acknowledging that there had been some chaos earlier "owing to the inattention of the hack drivers, in not always setting down their company with their horses heads to the north."[20]

The February 28, 1828, gathering prompted a four-page article, "The African Fancy Ball," in the recently established *Philadelphia Monthly Magazine.* This publication too lampooned the behavior of local blacks, but the writer also went into considerable detail about the ball itself. Having outlined the way in which a committee had organized the event, the author proceeded to an account of the preparations: in Little-Pine Street, "nothing was to be seen but belles and beaux bearing bundles of 'costumes'; second hand clothes rose fifty per cent., and the gentlemen of the Three Golden Balls, licensed and unlicensed, made most unlicensed profits." Late on the afternoon of the 28th, "showers of hair-powder began to fall in the vicinity of Shippen and Sixth-streets," and the streets echoed to the sound of the "creaking of whalebones, and the snapping of corset laces." That evening the "company began to assemble at half past seven." A while later, the band struck up and African Philadelphians danced cotillions until midnight, after which they switched to waltzes. At three, a supper was served and the dancing finally finished at five in the morning.

According to the *Monthly Magazine* correspondent, the African Philadelphians who attended, "excited by a laudable spirit of emulation," were copying, however comically and ineptly, functions staged by whites. Of course, there can be little doubt that the balls held by whites were the starting point for blacks' balls, but to follow the lead of the newspaper and magazine writers of the 1820s by quickly dismissing these events as risible clones of the practices of white society would be a mistake. In the case of the Philadelphia ball of 1828, the *Monthly Magazine's* detailed account includes material that undermines such a dismissive view. For a start, a large map of Africa had been rendered in charcoal on the dance floor and opposite the band there shone an imposing transparency, designed by a black, which depicted, among other things, the Abolition Society breaking the shackles of slaves, and a vessel about to sail for Liberia. As well, there were, during the evening, positive references to Haiti, the great black republic established after a successful revolution against the French colonial administration (a specter that haunted whites on the eastern seaboard of America in the early decades of the nineteenth century). Organizers of the ball had resolved "by acclamation" to invite any Haitian army or navy officers who happened to be in town, and one such notable who did attend became the star of the evening, "whose easy manners and fascinating address gave all the ladies and gentlemen present a favourable opinion of the state of society in that island." But, most importantly, the orchestra had been put together by Frank Johnson (1792–1844). Johnson, easily the most famous African American composer and bandleader in the antebellum period, was, in the words of one white observer, "inventor-general of cotillions; to which add, a remarkable taste in distorting a sentimental, simple, and beautiful song, into a reel, jig, or country-dance." Even where the scores of Johnson's music are extant, working out how that music was performed and, more importantly, how it sounded is virtually impossible. We suspect, however, that the word "distort" is of some importance here: it suggests that Johnson had a talent for syncretizing European forms and the rhythms of the African American dancing cellars, creating a sound that was distinctive and new.[21]

Both the African American parade and the African American ball were complex, multifaceted events that can be interpreted in more than one way. Both involved an element of "copying" white American practices, as blacks took from what they found around them in order to structure their lives now that they were free. But the process was more intricate than that. Even if the origins of the parade and the ball were to be found in white American culture, that was just a starting point: northern blacks infused these events with their own cultural imperatives, creating something fresh. Not only that, but even as they borrowed from whites, there was a conscious undercurrent of satirizing, or signifying on, that which they were appropriating. Participating in events that had cultural significance for themselves, they also, at least in part, parodied white Americans' behavior when marching on July 4th, or staging balls. It was this parodic element in African American culture, coupled with the impossibility of determining any precise meaning of black celebratory events, that made blacks such a good vehicle for whites who wished to criticize their own society. Thus James Boardman, who had closely watched white New Yorkers in their July 4th celebrations in 1833, had no doubt that the African Americans who paraded on July 5, particularly those wearing uniforms and dashing about on horseback, were "a parody upon the shopkeeper colonels of the previous day." In similar vein, the white author of the long account of the African Ball in

Philadelphia in 1828 had stated that the organizing committee had given instructions "to furnish no person with tickets who could not trace his pedigree as far back as his mother, at the least."[22] Undoubtedly the writer had made this story up; undoubtedly, too, the story denigrated blacks. But this white writer had also used the occasion of an African American ball to ridicule the aristocratic pretensions of white Philadelphia society.

Another factor adding to the complexity of these events was the considerable dissension among African Americans as to whether they should be held at all. At this point it is necessary to enter some caveats about the nature of African American society in northern cities. The frequent use by historians of the term "community" sometimes seems to suggest a unanimity of opinion, a charming niceness to the character of black life, that may occasionally have existed but most often did not. The vast majority of African northerners were very poor, much worse off than their white counterparts; in the hard and unforgiving urban environment they had to struggle merely to exist. Inevitably, these circumstances corroded most aspects of day-to-day life. Unscrupulous blacks preyed on unsuspecting compatriots: one sold fake lottery tickets to old African-American women; another, claiming to be a slave raising money to manumit himself, solicited contributions from the unwary.[23] Blacks also stole goods and money from each other as well as from whites, and violence between blacks, both domestic (unsurprisingly, poverty placed an enormous amount of pressure on the black family) and otherwise, saw a constant stream of cases brought before the courts.

There was also a gap of some importance between the ideas of various black leaders, concerned for what would later be called "the future of the race," and the behavior of ordinary African Americans. Since the 1790s, when large numbers of blacks began to attain their freedom, white and black leaders had implored free African Americans to lead exemplary lives. Only then could they avoid confirming whites' stereotypes about idle and dissolute blacks and prevent their behavior being used as an excuse to delay further the end of slavery. African Americans had probably debated these issues before, but the advent of black newspapers brought tensions into the open.

The editor of *Freedom's Journal,* the nation's first black newspaper, campaigned indefatigably against the holding of processions to celebrate the end of slavery in New York. Aside from crime, he railed, "nothing serves more to keep us in our present degraded condition, than these foolish exhibitions of ourselves," which rendered blacks "complete and appropriate laughing stocks for thousands of our citizens, and to the more considerate of our brethren, objects of compassion and shame." The editor was particularly annoyed by the profligacy of the whole affair: "has any man yet been held in estimation on account of his *fine dress?* is it the mark of *prudence* to put all our earnings upon our backs?" A decade later, writers to the *Colored American* were still hammering away at similar themes. AGNES declared that the "thousands of wretched females, who throng our streets, owe their degradation to a love of dress, and a desire to be fashionably arrayed," and urged readers to set an example "by dressing with simplicity, and ceasing to wear costly and useless ornaments." [24]

It was not only the way many blacks had begun to dress that aroused the ire of various black leaders; in the early decades of freedom, an explosion of dancing and music in northern cities also caused disquiet. Some groups, particularly the Methodists, opposed the mushrooming dance halls and cellars on religious grounds. Other critics were more concerned with waste and with the way such activities reinforced negative stereotypes most whites held of black people. In 1833, Maria Stewart, speaking at the African Masonic Hall in Boston, implored "our men, and especially our rising youth, to flee from the gambling board and the dance-hall; for we are poor and have no money to throw away." Though dancing was not "criminal in itself," it was a "frivolous amusement" that had "been carried on among us to such an unbecoming extent, that it has become absolutely disgusting." The editor of *Freedom's Journal* also opposed dancing: "the obloquy and contempt which have heretofore been heaped upon us, as a body, for our much and continual dancing, will, we hope, cause many who are persons of reflection to think some upon the propriety of spending so many valuable hours in this amusement." He particularly deplored the balls held by New York and Philadelphia blacks because of their impact on public opinion: "*ought twenty thousand innocent persons to be held up to public contempt, condemned unheard, for the folly of one or two hundred young persons who saw proper to amuse themselves with dancing for the evening?*" [25]

It was not merely whites, then, who decried the increased assertiveness of ordinary northern blacks, as manifested in what was seen as public displays of extravagant clothing and the unfettered use of the body in dance. There was, of course, good reason for the African American spokespersons' caution, for their insistent and repeated exhortations to blacks to behave in an exemplary fashion and, above all, to maintain a low profile. Even if whites living in northern cities were prepared to accept that African Americans were no longer slaves (and, as we have seen, many were not), most still recoiled in horror from any suggestion that blacks were in any way their social equals. In the early decades of the nineteenth century, two issues in particular brought these fears to the surface.

First and foremost was the vexed issue of sexual relations between blacks and whites. A horror of what was then known as racial amalgamation was, at the very least, implicit in virtually all discussions of the behavior of free African Americans. To be sure, a considerable amount of interracial sex between white men and black women, ranging from brief liaisons with prostitutes through more permanent relationships, did occur, particularly in the poorer areas of the cities where most African Americans lived. Such activities were an important element in respectable whites' prurient interest in Five Points and similar neighborhoods, and clearly there was at least some tolerance of white males' transgressions. In 1836 Henry Marine, a young white man, and a "genteel black young woman" were taken up by the watch early on a Sunday morning in a Philadelphia alley. According to Marine's testimony in the Mayor's Court, he had got drunk at a carpenter's "rasing frolic" and had no idea "how he came in contact with the sable damsel." His co-accused "listened to his story, as they stood side by side, with a most provoking air of incredulity, and had the mayor given her a chance, an *ecclairciesement* would no doubt have taken place." The court reporter's amused detachment was not shared by the Mayor, who, anxious to hurry the case through, suspended judgement, or by Henry Marine, who was obviously very embarrassed. More commonly, white voyeurism was cloaked in loud and strident condemnations of the repulsiveness of amalgamation. Another case brought before the Philadelphia Mayor's Court that year concerned a white man who, the *Public Ledger* declared, had been found "fondling and caressing in a most unequivocal situation a—faugh!—negro wench, of the most filthy and revolting appearance."[26]

Even more shocking were the few cases that came to light in which white women were shown to have been attracted to black males, occurrences apparently so horrible that newspapers seemed able to acquaint readers with their details only by borrowing from Shakespeare. In 1827, the *New*

York Evening Post reported that an "*Othello* has been recently married to a *Desdemona*, who it seems considered him 'comely although he was black.'" A Boston paper commented, in relation to this event, that "we have seldom known a more gross outrage on common decency, and the usages of society." In another instance in New York, a white woman was reported as having accosted her "better half," who was a "gentleman of color," and "thinking herself slighted for some more favored fair one, sought redress with a case knife, which she attempted to bury in the heart of her faithless Moor." In case anyone had missed the point, the story was run under the caption "*A Female Othello.*" A few years later, lurid rumors that African New Yorkers were about to "mullatoize" white neighborhoods played on white men's fear of their wives and daughters being raped by, or perhaps even worse, attracted to, black men, and were a factor in the explosive riot of 1834.[27]

Not only did the possible social equality of African Americans pose a sexual threat to whites that was constant and underpinned most of whites' commentary on blacks, but it also posed a political threat, although this became a matter of public discussion only sporadically. The best example of this perceived political threat occurred in New York City in the early 1820s. At the time of the 1820 state election, in which a number of blacks in the city did vote, newspaper stories explicitly linked black dandies with the franchise. For example, one described a meeting of black voters at which "to make their numbers look respectable their wools are to be combed and powdered, and they are to be scented and perfumed at Mr. Clinton's expense." At the State Convention of 1821, at which the Republicans succeeded in broadening the white and limiting the black franchise and debated the issue of whether African Americans should be able to vote, city newspapers again picked up on the subject.[28] After warning of an influx of emancipated blacks from the South and pointing out that, "organised and led by designing persons, they will give us great trouble," the *National Advocate* reported that the question of whether blacks should be allowed to vote "creates great sensation in this city." This newspaper lost no opportunity to remind its readers of the dangers of allowing African Americans to get ideas above their station. Unwelcome developments such as the African Grove were attributed to blacks' "high wages, high living and the elective franchise." A report of a court case between two blacks opened with the sentence: "One of the first benefits arising from permission to grant the elective franchise to people of colour, is a dash at the higher walks in life, and attempts to emulate their more fashionable neighbours." A notice ostensibly advertising an African American theater performance lamented that "since they have crept in favour with the convention" blacks "assemble in groups" and "are determined to have balls and quadrille parties" and "solicit a seat in the assembly or in the common council." Indeed, one "black gentleman respectfully insinuated, that he thought, 'as how he mout be put on the grand jury!'" Even more gratuitously, a report of a black man raping a white woman in Danbury, Connecticut, included the warning that such a "shocking instance of hardened villainy" demonstrated "the liberties they assume without the right of franchise."[29] Clearly, a considerable body of white opinion in the city saw any sign that blacks were attaining a degree of social equality as portending the end of civilization.

Attempts by African northerners to assert, or on occasions retain, what they saw as their rights, provoked white responses that fell into two broad and related categories: humor demeaning blacks, and physical violence against them. Obviously there had been a long history of derogatory jokes about blacks, but the quantity and intensity of the material circulating in the North in the early decades of the nineteenth century, and the particular targets against which such "humor" was directed, bespeak an edgy concern with the status of newly freed persons and the threat they posed to the established social hierarchy. Stories lampooning African Americans for their pretensions, their behavior, and just about any aspect of their culture were ubiquitous. One piece in the *National Advocate* began by pointing out that the "fashion of servants aping their masters and mistresses is becoming very prevalent," and that "they, like their betters, have their coteries and converzationes." It turned out that a "gentleman" living in Mercer Street had been awakened by a noise in the early hours of the morning, and, on investigating, had discovered in his kitchen "several strapping black gentlemen and ladies, together with the cook of the family, who was entertaining her guests." Wearing his white shirt and night cap, the irritated New Yorker had burst into the room, only to be "taken instantly for a ghost," whereupon "the guests set up a scream so loud and shrill, as to awaken the watch." In Albany, Mr. Charles, a celebrated ventriloquist, and an acquaintance had sought out a black fortune teller in the city directory. In the middle of her performance, Charles had thrown his voice into the desk drawer from which the woman had taken her tarot cards: a cry of *"hold! you d——d old hag—you're telling lies!"* boomed out, causing the fortune teller and her assistant to overturn the table and flee panic-stricken from the room "swearing the devil was in the house."[30]

Whites seemed to take particular delight in recording instances in which circumstances conspired to puncture the "pretensions" of African northerners. In its coverage of the city's July 5, 1827, parade celebrating the end of slavery in New York, the *New York American* could not resist including a "diverting" anecdote. On Greenwich Street a sudden downpour had caused the band and marchers to scramble for shelter under the awnings and stoops of the shops. As a result, the marshal and his aides were left out the front "without a single follower" until the marshal's appeal—"For shame gentlemen—for shame! you behave like boys! form, and move on!"—persuaded the marchers to reassemble. The newspaper's claim that in relating this incident "we by no means wish to throw ridicule on the ceremony" was anything but convincing. Similarly, Carl Arfwedson's account of the black beaux and belles strolling on the Battery ended with a mockingly patronizing description of the effects of a sudden downpour. As a few spots had fallen, one extravagantly dressed black man had felt "uneasy" and, "having already seen the effect on his straw-coloured gloves . . . prosaically addressed the fair: 'Had we better not retreat?—we shall be deluged with rain.'" He had then offered his female companion his arm, whereupon they had "wandered up Broadway in the midst of one of those sudden and drenching showers so frequent in America."[31]

This last story illustrates a central feature of much of this humor: a ridiculing of the way in which African northerners spoke. John Fanning Watson was hardly the only northern white to find it galling that African Americans gave one another titles; indeed, a considerable part of the derisory humor directed at urban blacks depended on the assumption that it was inappropriate for them to use such language. John Palmer, a traveler to America in 1817, recounted a conversation between two well-dressed blacks that he had supposedly overheard on a Philadelphia street:

Mr Quashi—Ah Mrs. Sambo, I hope I have the felicity of seeing you well this morning.
Mrs. Sambo—Oh, Sir, yes, thank you, Sir; I hope your family are in good health.
Mr. Quashi—Thank you, quite well; but how is your amiable

daughter Miss Sambo? has she quite recovered from her late alarming indisposition?

Palmer acknowledged that few blacks used "exactly such polished language," but he was certain that "they universally address each other by the titles of Mr. Mrs. Miss, Sir, and Madam," and for Palmer, as for many northern whites, this was in and of itself absurd [32] (see Figure 12).

More commonly, though, it was not polished language but unpolished, maladroit and malapropic black dialect that was featured in the satirical and humorous material circulating among whites in the cities. The use that could be made of a rendering of Black English was familiar enough to northerners; such "humor" had been ubiquitous in the almanacs and the newspapers of the 1790s. But from the early years of the nineteenth century, when more and more African northerners were achieving their freedom, the character of both the humor and the black dialect took on a harder, nastier edge. This change is most easily seen in the jokes and broadsides concerning "Bobalition" (abolition), a brand of humor which was associated most closely with Boston, and which constitutes perhaps the earliest extensive and regular seam of black caricature in America. [33]

Starting somewhere around 1815, the annual July 14th parade of Boston blacks celebrating the end of the slave trade prompted a series of broadsides labeling the event "Bobalition." These posters were plastered all over the city in advance of the procession. The broadside entitled "Grand Bobalition, or Great Annibersary Fussible" and dated "Bosson, Uly 14, 18021," provides a good example of the character and tone of these posters (see Figure 13). It takes the form of a set of instructions for the parade, supposedly written by Cesar Crappo, president of "De African Shocietee," to Cato Cudjoe, "de sheef Marsal," and begins: "Most superfluous Sir, It hab once more become my duty to deform you dat dis be fourteent day of de mont, spose you hab no almanack to find out the time of day by youruself." [34] For all their derogatory nature, however, the Bobalition broadsides contain a closely observed view of Boston life. Embedded in them are numerous textual references, most of which are now obscure, but some of which are still clear, to the history of the July 14th parade and other local events. In the 1821 broadside, a reference to the previous year's parade (at which there was "some little sturbance . . . bout de Moosic," a problem since solved as "we hab make derangement to prebent all sort of combomblification on dat account") related to the refusal by the band to turn out unless its members

"Is Miss Dina at home?

"Yes Sir but she petickly engaged in washing de dishes."

"Ah! I am sorry I cant have the honour to pay my devours to her, Give her my card."

Figure 12: Edward Clay, *Life In Philadelphia.* The use of titles—"Miss" and "Sir"—and the fact that the African American man had a visiting card, as well as the use of malapropism, were all designed to show that African Philadelphians were getting absurd ideas well beyond their station in life. The Library Company of Philadelphia

Figure 13: *Grand Bobalition, or "Great Annibersary Fussible,"* caricatured the annual celebration of the abolition of the slave trade held by African Americans in Boston, Massachusetts, July 14, 1821. Courtesy of the American Antiquarian Society

received what many blacks considered to be the exorbitant fee of forty-five dollars.[35] At the end of the instructions for the 1821 event was printed a series of toasts to be made after the dinner, and here the point of reference went beyond the African Bostonians. Satirical barbs were directed at such contemporary concerns as the Mill Dam, the actor Edward Kean, and the sea serpent that had been appearing with suspicious regularity off the coast near Gloucester.[36]

These broadsides demeaned Boston blacks, deflecting attention from the serious purpose of their celebration and depicting them as a bunch of pompous, intellectually inferior incompetents. Underlying these posters and other material published in the newspapers was an almost palpable resentment not only at the fact that Boston blacks had freed themselves from slavery but also at the organized and visible way in which they seemed to flaunt their freedom by marching all over town. On at least one occasion, however, a broadside was published which disputed the accuracy and fairness of these derogatory images. A "Reply to Bobalition" (see Figure 14) conforms to the genre of "Bobalition" posters, using black "dialect" and malapropisms (though in a more muted form), but it also signifies on the genre and contains a pointed critique of the behavior of white Bostonians during the city's African American celebration. Thus, Scipio Smilax tells Mungo Meanwell that "De folks no let us alone to joy ourself peaceably, but dey muss do juss as dey do for number year pass—dey disrepresent all our proceedum, and publish such a set of tose as de old boy heself wouldent be consider de autor of." Mungo had difficulty working out why whites could not leave blacks alone; after all, blacks did not interfere in white festivals. He continued: "But no sooner dey get well sober arter deir Independence, den dey begin to brackguard our Independent Day fore we sellybrate him.—Spose now we write Bobalition bout dem on the fourt of July, and scatter him bout town all day, why dey would take us up for salt and batterum direckly." The African American duo went on to ask why newspapers gave saturation coverage to the July 4th celebrations but virtually ignored those of July 14th., and to give a scathing account of the way whites had behaved at the opening ceremony for the Mill Dam.[37]

"Bobalition" may have started in Boston, but it tapped into the prevalent mood elsewhere in the North and was easily translated to other locales. Material from Boston was reprinted in other city newspapers: for example, in 1822 the *New York Evening Post* listed a series of nine toasts allegedly given at the July 14th celebration, including ones for "*Masser Wilberforce*

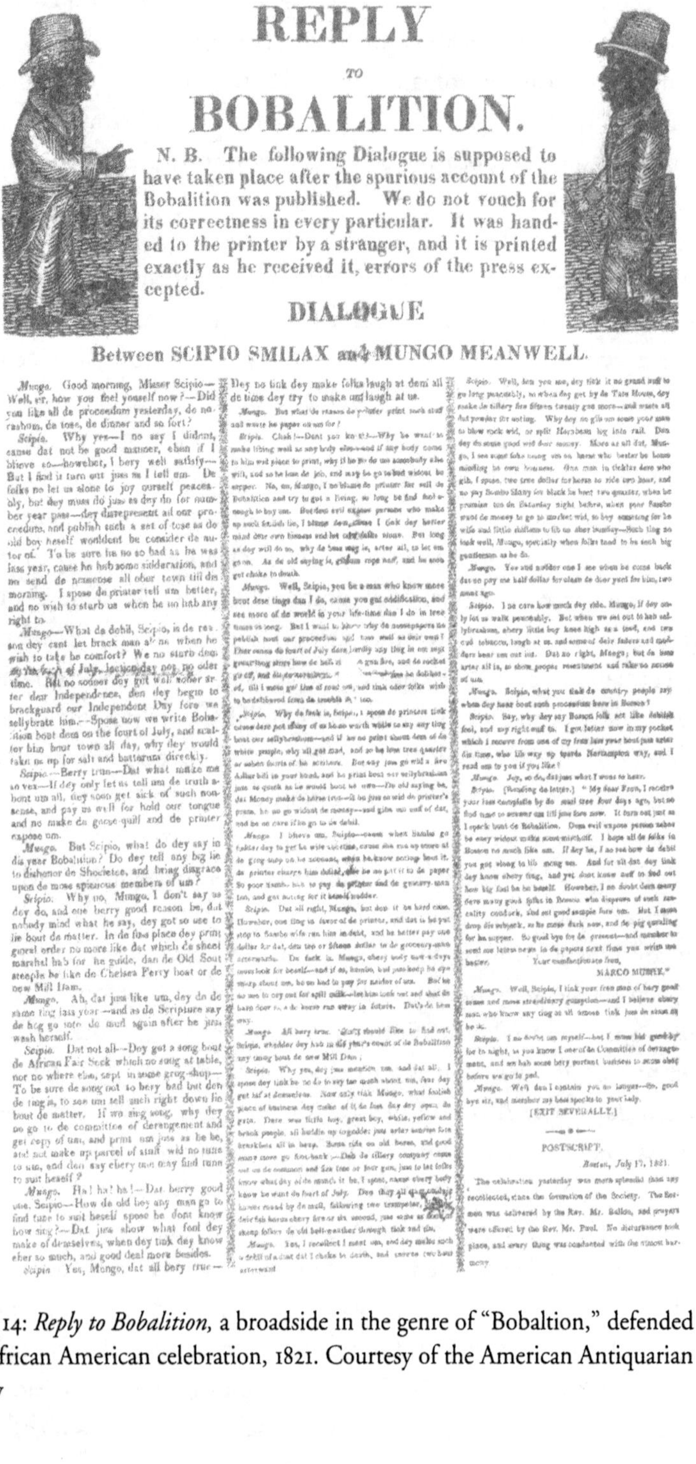

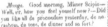

Figure 14: *Reply to Bobalition,* a broadside in the genre of "Bobaltion," defended Boston's African American celebration, 1821. Courtesy of the American Antiquarian Society

and the other survivors of the bobalition," "De minister of de African Church" and *"Misser Thomas Jefferson."* More interestingly, people from outside Boston began using the term. A caricature entitled "Grand Celebration ob de bobalition," a part of the *Life in Philadelphia* series but printed in London, satirized the passage of measures in 1833 abolishing slavery in the West Indies (see Figure 15). In 1823 the *National Advocate* ran a piece entitled "GRAND CONCERT OF DE BOB-LINK SOCIETY" in the format of a musical program, which pitilessly savaged those involved in the African Theater in particular (*"great couragement* bin had at skunk point for *dramtick* beformance") and African New Yorkers in general:

Figure 15: *Grand Celebration Ob De Bobalition Ob African Slabery.* The Library Company of Philadelphia

Finale by big *Parrot,* companied on de organs of *insult,* base lungs of *curses* and *well toned* pianos of *squizit vulgarity,* wid a *general shout of murder* and watch by de *hole,* during which the following *trio* will be sung:

> Who de debil cares for him?
> He no *officer,* knock him down.   Woodcock
> Shout aloud de *riot* hymn,
> We no be in *soudern town.*   Whip-poor-will
> *Go H-ll mam,* what is't to you?
> Spose he gib you dat new gown.   Jackdaw[38]

Even in this short extract from quite a long item, the references to the garishly plumed parrot (although conceivably this also plays on the name of Russell Parrott [1790–1824], a prominent African Philadelphia leader), *squizit vulgarity,* and the suggestion that blacks released from the discipline of slavery had become an aggressive and riotous menace on the streets of New York are clear enough. By the 1820s Bobalition, or bob-link as it was also often known, had become a catch-all term that embodied a churlish and spiteful response to the new-found status of free blacks, and that was instantly recognizable in Boston, Philadelphia, New York, and even in London.

Although the Bobalition broadsides usually included some visual elements, they relied primarily on black dialect to convey their message. This relationship, however, was reversed in a flood of satirical etchings produced in Philadelphia in the late 1810s, 1820s and 1830s that denigrated the activities of that city's black citizens. In a note in his sketchbook accompanying an image from 1819 (see Figure 16), James Thackera wrote: "The Black gentry aping their masters, dress quite as extravagantly, and frequently wear their clothes, long before they are cast off. They not only ape the dress of their masters, but also their cant terms, being well versed in the fashionable vocabulary." At about the same time, David Claypoole Johnston, scion of one of Philadelphia's prominent Quaker families, produced a derisory caricature of the city's annual march of black masons (see Figure 10). The most famous images belonging to this genre, however, were those contained in Edward W. Clay's *Life In Philadelphia* series, produced in 1828 (see Figures 11, 12, & 17). These publications were very popular, running through at least three editions by 1830 (and were reprinted in London).

They also spawned a less successful *Life in New York* series (see Figure 9). Clay's images of flamboyantly dressed African Americans engaged in various activities about town were the visual equivalent of the verbal descriptions of elaborately dressed blacks that appeared in travelers' accounts and newspapers. To be sure, these representations were demeaning caricatures, but they were also recognizable, if somewhat exaggerated, versions of what many whites claimed to see on the streets of Philadelphia and other northern cities every day, and that, undoubtedly, was part of the reason for their enthusiastic reception. Time did nothing to lighten Clay's mood: caricatures in *Life In Philadelphia* appear almost benign compared with some of his work from later in the 1830s. *Practical Amalgamation*, for example, pan-

Figure 16: James Thackera, *A New mode of Perfuming & Preserveing Clothes from Moths* (Philadelphia, 1819). The Historical Society of Pennsylvania

dered in a deliberately grotesque fashion to the fear of what would later be called miscegenation, a fear inextricably entangled in the social imagination of the anti-abolitionists (see Figure 18).[39]

All of these strands—the use of a version of black dialect, an exaggerated rendering of the clothing, hairstyles, and body movements of black

Figure 17: Edward Clay, *Life in Philadelphia*. The Library Company of Philadelphia

dandies, and the exploitation of blacks as a vehicle for criticizing aspects of white society—culminated in the minstrel show, achieving a three-dimensional apotheosis in the figure of Zip Coon. Beginning in the 1830s and reaching its fully developed structure in the early 1840s, the minstrel show, which centered on whites in blackface, enjoyed enormous popularity with the white working classes of northern cities. Zip Coon, the ludicrously fashionable Broadway swell replete with malapropic black dialect, was instantly recognizable to this audience, and was, along with Jim Crow, a key character in early minstrel performances (see Figure 19).[40] Similarly caricatured figures featured in some of the playlets that minstrel performers staged in the 1830s: for example, T. D. Rice, originator of "Jim Crow," wrote *Bone Squash* and *O Hush! or, The Virginny Cupids,* both of which were set in New York, and in both of which the focus was once again on the contrast between, as Hans Nathan has put it, "the colored dandy and

PRACTICAL AMALGAMATION.

Figure 18: Edward Clay, *Practical Amalgamation* (New York, 1839). By the end of the decade, Clay produced even more nasty images of blacks. Here he panders to the fear among the anti-abolitionists of what would later be called miscegenation. The Library Company of Philadelphia

the colored workman, or, to say it in style, between 'Nigga Gemmen and Common Niggas.'"[41]

The struggle of African northerners to work out what freedom meant, a struggle that took place on the streets of New York and other cities, provided much of the material that ended up in minstrel performances. In-

Figure 19: George Washington Dixon, *Zip Coon* [1830s]. Bequest of Evert Jansen Wendell, The Harvard Theatre Collection, Houghton Library

deed, the contents of the minstrel show's "humorous" sketches and the show itself—arguably one of the most important cultural developments of the nineteenth century—were largely inspired by what many whites perceived as the newly freed blacks' socially transgressive behavior in the public spaces of northern cities, behavior that whites in blackface appropriated and did their best to ridicule out of existence. It was this immensely entertaining, rambunctious and potent mixture of voyeurism and contempt for black life (and of, in Eric Lott's terms, love and theft) that struck such a chord in the predominantly white working-class audiences flocking to performances. Through its distortions of and popular commentary on black life, the minstrel show became an influential factor in the messy and piecemeal negotiations that resolved in the negative the question of whether newly freed blacks were to be treated as American citizens and relegated them to a lesser category.

The other white response to the behavior, indeed the very presence, of free blacks on northern city streets, a response that was probably inevitable given the flood of derogatory material asserting that African Americans were lesser beings, was violence. Partly this manifested itself as a continual, low-level harassment of African Americans who ventured into public spaces. As early as the 1790s the French traveler Moreau de St. Méry noted that in Philadelphia white children would without provocation "strike" black children and, further, that when "it snows, any colored man who passes is sure to be showered with snowballs by white children." By the antebellum period such behavior, and not only from children, had become a commonplace in all of the northern cities. As one angry African American recorded, if a black passed a group of whites on the street, "ten chances to one" there would be a "sneer or snigger, with characteristic accompanying remarks."[42] But all too often verbal abuse escalated into physical violence. In 1827 in New York, for example, Jacob Simmons, a black who resided at 106 Chapple Street, was returning to his home along Anthony Street, proceeding, as he noted, "in the middle of the Street to keep clear of the Irish as the walk was full." For no reason at all, "one man came up to him & asked where he was going and immediately tripped him up & several Irish fell upon him & beat him [and] one struck him with a stick." Only the quick response of the watch to his cries for help saved Simmons's life. Most of the victims of such attacks were African Americans, but in some areas of the cities white pedestrians were fair game for young blacks, particularly late at night. In 1836 in the Philadelphia Mayor's Court, the watchman responsible for the area around South Street and Lombard complained bitterly of a "set of drunken vicious black scoundrels, who go about in gangs of 12 or 14, and often molest and maltreat any white whom they may find alone and unprotected." In the case in question the watchman had interrupted a group of blacks making a disturbance, whereupon David Anderson, "a negro fellow," becoming "surly and insolent," had attempted to hit the watchman, who promptly and, as the court reporter related with some relish, "very properly *maced* him over the forehead and soon rendered him submissive."[43]

If an African American walking down the street was enough to prompt whites to harass her or him, then the sight of a well-organized, proud and smartly dressed group of blacks striding down the middle of the main thoroughfares of town was an act of provocation almost too much to bear. All of the major African American parades were disrupted by jeers, catcalls, and stonethrowing from white bystanders. Watching the 1833 parade celebrating the end of slavery in New York, the English traveler James Boardman could scarcely credit the "insulting behaviour of many of the coachmen and carters [that] was unblushingly displayed in their driving their vehicles so as to interrupt the progress and order of the procession." In Philadelphia in 1842, a temperance parade held on August 1st, the anniversary of West Indian emancipation, was attacked by angry whites, and the ensuing riot lasted for several days. It was not just parades but any organized activity of well-dressed African Americans that became a target for local whites. Disturbances and scuffles inside and outside African American churches in Philadelphia and New York were a regular occurrence. Nor did places of amusement escape. In August 1822, nearly two score white "ruffians" bought tickets for New York's African Grove Theater and, once inside, did their best to trash the premises and beat up the cast and proprietor. It turned out that several of the white rioters were employed at the nearby Broadway Circus and, apparently, did not welcome the competition. In these years there were also a dozen or so full-scale race riots in northern cities, in which marauding mobs of whites destroyed black property and killed a few blacks unfortunate enough to get in the way. One of the largest riots, in New York in July 1834, began with a fracas over the double-booking of a church hall by blacks celebrating the anniversary of emancipation and the all-white New York Sacred Music Society. Over the next several nights whites' pent-up resentment at blacks was released convulsively, with thousands of New Yorkers roaming the streets. One theater manager diverted a mob by having an actor amuse them with a spirited version of "Zip Coon," an imaginative move on his part but also a telling illustration of the link between racist caricature and racial violence. These riots were driven by a passionate and explosive hatred of free blacks by working-class whites, many of them Irish, and the violence and destruction of property were particularly directed at any sign of African American progress. Institutions such as churches, halls, and schools and the houses of some of the more well-to-do blacks were the obvious focus of white rage.[44]

Blacks were not the only victims of violence in these years. On a Sunday in late November 1829, the lower part of Philadelphia, near Eighth and South streets, erupted into "a furious battle between an immense gang of blacks and a number of white men and boys." Several whites were seriously hurt by brickbats and stones hurled at them by angry blacks. The circumstances of the riot are not known, but as it occurred near the black meeting house and just "after the conclusion of divine service" it would seem likely that a group of whites went along to disrupt the black churchgoers and met stiffer resistance than they expected. The *Philadelphia Chronicle's* editor was in little doubt that, whatever might have sparked the incident, the blame should be attributed to the behavior of the city's blacks. After all, on "Sundays, especially, they seem to think themselves above all restraint, and their insolence is intolerable."[45]

But it was the threat of compatriots—whether kidnapped local blacks or escaped slaves—being sent to the South that was most likely to produce an aggressive and violent response from African Americans, and this type of action was required with depressing frequency. For example, in Boston in 1820, a well organized group of forty blacks "armed with bludgeons" tried to free a fugitive slave about to be returned to the South. In Philadelphia in April 1830, "colored persons to the number of sixty assembled and attempted a rescue" of an escaped slave in a similar plight. In New York in 1836 a "gang" of armed blacks attacked the crew of the Brazilian brig *Brilliante* at midnight, caught them by surprise, and succeeded in freeing two of the five slaves who were on board. When the mate, awakened by a noise, ran up on deck, "one of the gang cocked a pistol at him and threatened to blow his brains out in case he interfered." Behavior such as this was the realization of the worst nightmare of all those opposed to black freedom. Little wonder, then, that the *New York Journal of Commerce's* story was printed under the caption "*Gross Outrage.*"[46]

In many (in fact most) ways the story of what happened to the first generations of free African northerners is a dismal one. Increasingly they were forced into appalling housing and segregated from all but the poorest whites. They were shunned in public and cordoned off, whether they wished it or not, into separate churches, separate schools, and later separate street cars. They were condemned to scraping together a living in low-paying and menial occupations, cruelly caricatured in print, in paint, and on the stage, and denied the right to vote and even to walk down the street without harassment. Not only that, but they, their lives, and their culture were appropriated by whites and packaged for entertainment and profit into something that could fuel the fantasies and longings of their oppressors. Those relatively few African Americans who did manage to get ahead in this hostile environment—men such as Thomas Downing in New York and James Forten in Philadelphia—were very much the exception. During the antebellum years, for the first time, a substantial number of free African Americans ended up living in the cities. Their initial encounter with an urban environment, was, however, hardly a propitious one; for the majority of African northerners, life turned out to be a hard and unrelenting struggle.

But there was rather more to the story of African northerners than this. No longer slaves, blacks could participate in a whole range of activities previously denied them. They could, and large numbers did, attend those "separate churches" that John Fanning Watson complained of, start black newspapers, and agitate for African American rights. They could parade through the city, stroll along the battery or Broadway, or go out dancing, drinking and gambling, and they could do so whenever they wanted to, rather than in the few hours of leisure grudgingly granted them by their owners. They could even, as did one enterprising group of African New Yorkers, stage their own performance of Shakespeare's *Richard III*. To be sure, poverty imposed limits and the possibility of harassment by whites was ever-present, but whenever one probes beneath the surface in early nineteenth-century Boston, Philadelphia, and particularly New York, it is difficult not to be impressed by the vitality of urban black life. If African northerners had failed to gain full citizenship, their future, they must have felt, was more in their hands than ever it had been before. No matter what obstacles they might face, they were determined to show that they were active players in an increasingly important urban scene.

The history of the Boston July 14th celebration of the end of the slave trade provides an impressive example of this determination. The Bobalition broadsides pasted up all over town made it extremely unlikely that the parade would pass unnoticed, and, invariably, large numbers of white Bostonians turned out to view the spectacle. In 1821 the *Columbian Centinel* noted that the streets were nearly as thronged for this African American event as they had been for the July 4th festivities and for the recent procession of President Monroe, though, as the newspaper went on to report, "the cheers were not so loud, nor so unanimous." This was understatement with a vengeance. In fact, by the late 1810s and 1820s, increasingly hostile crowds were gathering to observe and participate in the verbal and physical harassment to which the black marchers were subjected. Black Bostonians were "assailed, insulted, and hooted at" as they proceeded along their route, and gangs of white boys threw stones and dirt at the marchers, particularly at the officers proudly striding out in front of the procession. Twenty-five years later a participant writing in the *Liberator* recalled graphically that the marches in the early 1820s "were followed by the rabble; hissed, hooted and groaned at every turn," to the extent that "one would have supposed that Bedlam had broken loose."[47]

The marchers tried to avoid trouble. In 1820, for example, when they heard that a particularly large crowd in an ugly mood had gathered in State Street, they "disappointed" them, as the *Boston Daily Advertiser* reported, and "very judiciously adopted a different and shorter route," so bypassing "much of the ridicule which they usually encounter." But the patience of Boston blacks was wearing thin, and on at least once occasion they decided to retaliate. Years later, Lydia Maria Child remembered that the "colored people became greatly incensed by this mockery of their festival," and that "a rumor reached us, on one of these anniversaries, that they were determined to resist the whites, and were going armed, with this intention." The upshot was a running brawl, with whites chasing blacks from the Common back to Belknap Street.[48]

In the end, however, what impresses most about this July 14th celebration is the way in which, each year for a quarter of a century, several hundred black Bostonians were prepared to dress up in their best clothes, assemble, and once more, quite literally, run the gauntlet of white Boston. In so doing, they were making a point—tenaciously, courageously, and with precious little support from the white authorities. Their liberty from slavery had been hard won and they were determined to commemorate both the abolition of the slave trade and their own freedom, even though an intolerant Boston would neither allow them to do so peaceably nor acknowledge their right to participate in the wider political discourse.

To a considerable extent, the struggle over what freedom meant centered on the bodies of African Americans, that is to say, on the appearance of individual blacks and on the ways in which they collectively presented themselves in public. What emerged in the early decades of the nineteenth century was a pattern of black initiative and white response, as many of the consequences of emancipation were worked out publicly on the streets of Boston, Philadelphia, New York, and other northern cities. African Americans were only a small minority of the population in these cities, but the very openness and exuberance of their public behavior attracted a disproportionate amount of attention from whites. In the short term African northerners were swamped by a wave of racist ridicule and violence, but now that they were free they could at least play an active role in determining their fate, and in that lay their hope for the future.

Swingin'
Like Crazy

With the first cut of the knife, the former slave Sandie sliced deeply into his ankle joint, severing the muscles. With the second, he drove the blade into the hip joint on the opposite side of his body. Then, as the incredulous group of whites witnessing these events in the central square of an antebellum Florida town gathered around him, he hacked off the fingers of his left hand with an ax. Finally, holding the bloodied knife aloft, Sandie shouted to his horrified audience that, should they continue to try to return him to bondage after he had successfully bought himself out of it, he had strength enough for one final thrust, after which they could sell his corpse for whatever it would fetch.

A decade or so before the Civil War, Sandie, a Maryland slave, had purchased his freedom for $3,000, moved with his wife to Florida, and gained employment on a railroad. But when, some time later, the documents attesting his freedom were incinerated in the fire that destroyed his house, a group of local whites determined to kidnap and sell him in the New Orleans slave market. Sandie had been able to repulse their first attempt, beating back no less thán six assailants. It was upon learning that a second, more determined effort would be made to subdue him that he had resolved upon his very public act of self-mutilation.

Yankee journalist Whitelaw Reid, who heard this story while traveling through the South at the conclusion of the war, was sufficiently intrigued by it to seek Sandie out. He eventually located the former slave at his Key West farm, where, as the journalist recounted, "there came hurrying up a stalwart negro, with the *physique* of a prize fighter; body round as a barrel, arms knotted with muscles that might have belonged to a race-horse's leg, chest broad and deep, with room inside for the play of an ox's lungs." Though seventy-two years of age, Sandie was the island's most successful farmer and reputedly its strongest man; but, as Reid could readily observe, the signs of his ordeal were plainly visible, in his badly mutilated hand and the "still fearfully distinct" scars on his ankle and hip.[1]

Here is dramatic testimony indeed of the way in which the human body may serve as a site for the inscription of historical processes. In freedom, as in slavery, the black body could become a surface on which the struggle between black and white was often cruelly etched, and on which the record of that struggle may be read.

The incident involving Sandie is informative on a number of levels, and bears interesting comparison with the deployment of the body by African Americans in the postslavery period.[2] Within a social context that denied blacks any kind of discursive access to the public world, we can sense Sandie's determination to control his own fate, to write his own script, as it were. We can also sense how circumscribed the realm was within which such an expression of autonomy could take place. Given Sandie's inability to document his freedom by producing the lost emancipation papers, he was compelled, by the limitations faced by a free black in a slave society, to inscribe that freedom on his body, and in the most dramatic of ways.

Sandie's desire to attain some kind of public recognition is conspicuous in his choice of the town square—the most public space available to him—as the stage for his performance. Marginalized by social custom and law, he forced himself to the literal and symbolic center of his immediate society, and compelled those who would customarily reduce him to a cipher in their own "text" to become the passive spectators to his reordering of events.

Sandie's dramatic gesture took place before slavery's abolition, but the same determination by blacks to act as instigators, and to use their bodies and public space to write themselves into the American story, would be reiterated in the postwar years. Like Sandie, other African Americans would resort to public spaces and there present their bodies with a degree of flamboyance and forcefulness that announced their determination to refute the bodily regime imposed upon them by whites, with all the notions of black identity and power relations which that regime implied. It can hardly have been accidental, for instance, that, on being informed that they were free, one group of Charleston slaves disported themselves on a major city thoroughfare "arrayed in silks and satins of all the colors of the rainbow."[3]

The hostility that such assertive acts often aroused in whites points to the ambiguity of the new social order. As blacks probed the boundaries of their freedom, behavior that infringed the rules of the old social system was resisted by whites, who were determined to maintain that system and the racial ideology and etiquette that buttressed it. As in the antebellum period, the outraged or irritable comments of whites alert us to such black infractions. Belle Kearney, the daughter of a former Mississippi slaveholder, complained that "since gaining their freedom, the negro women's natural love of dress has developed inordinately"; African American women, Kearney declared, "bought brilliant-hued stuffs and had them made with most bizarre effects."[4] Englishman A. G. Bradley, journeying through Virginia, noted archly that on Sundays the black factory hand, miner, or waiter might be found wearing "a covert coat and pot-hat, while his wife struts at his side attired in a caricature of the latest New York fashion."[5] Northern journalist Sidney Andrews, surveying the South at war's end, was told by a "ladylike-appearing woman" in Salisbury, North Carolina, that "the chief ambition of a [Negro] wench seems to be to wear a veil and carry a parasol." "The nasty niggers," the proprietress of a Charlotte hotel confirmed to Andrews, "must have a parasol when they ha'n't got no shoes."[6] Many southern whites had keener reasons for their resentment. Attending a church service in Savannah, Georgia, in 1866, Francis Butler Leigh, struck by the number of white females wearing mourning clothes, declared how "piteous" it was "to see so many mere girls' faces, shaded by deep crape veils."[7] In the immediate postwar context, the spectacle of young African-American women donning black veils—painful symbols, now, of white bereavement—aroused particular hostility.[8]

Underlying such language as "bizarre" and "caricature" we can sense not only obvious racial resentment, but the cultural difference separating black and white, an inability on the part of whites to recognize that an alternative set of cultural values was at work. On another level, an element of provocation and also of celebration was surely present in these public acts by blacks. Not only their intention to proclaim social parity but also their desire to share in the material attractions of the wider society are suggested by African Americans' decision to adopt such characteristically "white" apparel as veils and parasols and by the alleged pursuit of New York fashions.

Whites' *physical* response to the sartorial strategies of blacks suggests that they clearly recognized, in the black adornment of the body, a highly political subtext of struggle, a determination to renegotiate the social contract. The frequency with which whites resorted to violence signaled their determination to resist such pressure. "Even after the war things were pretty tough for us," Georgia ex-slave Lewis Favor told his W.P.A. interviewer. "White men cut the clothes from the backs of ex-slaves when they were well-dressed," and, should the former slaves not "beg hard enough, they might even be cut to death!"[9] Charlie Davenport, another W.P.A. interviewee, detailed the emphatic white reaction to a bold attempt by a group of Mississippi blacks to announce their presence as free people. One night, Davenport recalled, "a bunch o' uppity Niggers went to a 'tainment in Memorial Hall." They had "dressed detsef's fit to kill," but when they "walked down de aisle an' took seats in de very front," outraged whites "marched out de buildin' wid dey chins up an lef' dem Niggers a-settin' in a empty hall." Nor did the matter end there; that night the Klan "rid th'ough de lan'," and "grabbed ever' Nigger that walked down dat aisle, but I ain't hear'd yet what dey done wide 'em." "Dat same thing happened," Davenport averred, "ever time a Nigger tried to act lak he was white."[10] Here, in the usage of the body, the battle of Reconstruction that ultimately ended in the enforcement of Jim Crow is readily apparent.

In the immediate postwar years, not merely the clothing, but the demeanor and gestural language of some blacks became more provocative, or, at least, was seen to have become so by southern whites, who feared the effects of emancipation and the possible termination of laws encoding sub-servience and inferiority. Reflecting this heightened awareness on the part of whites, as well as certain shifts in black demeanor, some southern legis-latures declared the use of insulting gestures a criminal offense. At an indi-vidual level, whites protested that blacks no longer yielded the sidewalks to them or behaved in a suitably deferential manner. "The colored persons are awful sassy in Charleston," an Irish woman visitor to the city noted. "They take the inside of the walk of a white person, . . . and if you say a word they make faces at you." Some took their protests further. In Texas, a white man killed a former slave for failing to take off his hat.[11] In Mississippi, a mem-ber of the state legislature described to Whitelaw Reid how he had dealt with his servant, Sam, who had committed the same infraction. Sam had "had the impudence to stand up and say he was free," and would not re-move his hat "unless he pleased." "I jumped at him with my knife," the lawmaker declared, "but he run. Bimeby he came sneakin' back, and said he was sorry. 'Sam,' says I, 'you've got just the same rights as a white man now, but not a bit better. And if you come into my room without takin' off your hat I'll shoot you!' "[12]

Blacks transgressed territorial boundaries as well. Expressing the same determination that characterized Sandie's actions, newly freed African Americans moved collectively into formerly white-controlled space, pre-senting their bodies to whites in public and highly visible celebratory pa-rades. Spectacular black processions had occurred in the South even before the end of slavery. Timothy Flint, who visited New Orleans in the early 1820s, witnessed, on one of the African Americans' traditional holidays, a parade of hundreds of male and female slaves joyously following their "king" through the city's streets. "All the characters . . . ," Flint wrote, "have their own peculiar dress, and their own contortions. They dance, and their streamers fly, and the bells that they have hung about them tinkle."[13] Two decades later, Bishop Henry Benjamin Whipple, while touring in Georgia, encountered a public procession of local slaves, evidently a climax of their Christmas celebrations. "The negroes are out in great numbers," Whipple wrote, "arrayed in their best. . . . Already they have paraded, with a corps of staff officers with red sashes, mock epaulettes & goose quill feathers, and a band of music composed of 3 fiddles, 1 tenor & 1 bass drum, 2 triangles & 2 tamborines." The slaves were "marching up & down the streets in great style," followed by a second line of paraders, "some dancing, some

walking & some hopping, others singing, and all as lively as lively can be."
Those who refused to join the procession were subjected to mock trials and
floggings. "Here they come again," Whipple enthused, "with flags flying
and music enough to deafen one." [14] As William Piersen has recently shown,
such parades, which typically (and unlike white parades) were marked by
vividly colored and often mismatched clothing, improvisational music,
and joyous interaction between marchers and followers, were often associated with African American festivals, such as Jonkonnu, or, as in the case
of the procession witnessed by Bishop Whipple, with Euro-American holiday celebrations. [15] In the immediate aftermath of freedom, however, black
parades would become more formal, more pointedly political, and much
more numerous.

Emancipation and the protective presence of Union troops allowed far
greater scope for the staging of public parades, an opportunity which
southern blacks were quick to exploit. On March 30, 1865, for instance, approximately 4,000 African American men, women, and children marched
in procession through the main streets of Charleston, South Carolina, celebrating their freedom. As a *New York Times* correspondent described the
event, the parade included a company of African American militia, members of numerous black societies, volunteer fire companies, groups of
school children, and "colored citizens generally." American flags, visible
here and there among the marchers, reminded whites of blacks' "victory"
in the recent conflict and of their claim for social inclusion. A mule-drawn
cart containing two black women, seated on a block, with a man standing
over them ringing a bell and shouting "How much am I offered?" invoked
for onlookers the memory of a slave auction, and a cart bearing a coffin in-
scribed with the words "slavery is dead," followed by "a long train of female
mourners," somberly dressed, announced the marchers' central theme. To
the *Times* reporter it seemed that the mock funeral "would have been improved had young girls, attired in gay dresses, taken the place of the mourners, for we should naturally suppose that the colored people would not be
greatly afflicted with grief after having been assured of their freedom." As
for the white citizens of Charleston, who watched the great parade with its
many troubling signs move by, the reporter concluded that "the expression
on the countenances of many" suggested that "the thing was not altogether
agreeable." But, he added, "of course they wisely swallowed objections." [16]

Parades of this kind were richly symbolic: in events virtually unprecedented in the South, large numbers of black men and women, bearing banners and accompanied by bands, marched formally along main thoroughfares, their dress smart and neat, their bodies moving pridefully, straight and striding out, the whole performance encoding a stark visual repudiation of the effacement of human worth that slavery entailed. Reducing whites to onlookers, as had been the effect of Sandie's act, blacks, however briefly, took center stage, proclaiming their new-found status to whites and to each other, asserting their right to the streets.

Deeper meanings were stored in the Charleston parade's mock auction block and funeral carriage. Portrayal of the auction block surely recalled to blacks not only the most painful ritual of their lives, the trauma when family and community relationships were brutally sundered, but also the site at which the slaveholders' power over the black body was most humiliatingly displayed. Former slaves interviewed for the Federal Writers Project more than seventy years later spoke eloquently of the resentment and shame experienced by African Americans who had been bought and sold like so many cattle. "The first thing they had to do," former Tennessee bondsman William Coleman told his interviewer, "was wash and clean up real good and take a fat greasy meat skin and run over their hands, face and also their feet, or in other words, every place that showed about their body so that they would look real fat and shiny. Then they would trot them out before their would-be buyers and let them look over us real good, just like you would a bunch of fat cows that you were going to sell on the market and try to get all you could for them."[17] It was not uncommon, other ex-slaves testified, for blacks to be stripped "stark naked" before auction,[18] or to have their bodies rendered more salable in other demeaning ways. "I had long hair," Francis Black declared, recounting an attempt to sell her when she was a young girl, "and they cut it off like a boy."[19] Ex-slave autobiographer Solomon Northup recalled how the keeper of the New Orleans slave pen required his charges to "appear smart and lively" and to "open our mouths and show our teeth, precisely as a jockey examines a horse which he is about to barter for or purchase."[20]

It was surely their recognition that the ritual of the auction block was central to the dominant culture's dehumanizing mythologization of blacks and to the most traumatic moments of their own experience that prompted the Charleston marchers to make this image central to a symbolic commentary on slavery that was wending its way through former slave territory. Hitherto victims of a white process of signification, enveloped within a system over which they had little control, blacks who re-enacted the slave auction were taking power over signification. They were re-presenting in a different light that terrible moment at which they or their families or kin had been sold, so that it became theirs. During slavery times, the ritual of the slave auction had served the symbolic function of constantly reiterating the lesser humanity of blacks and hence permitting inhumanity to be directed at them: one would not callously sell, or inspect as one would a beast, a full, worthy human being. But when enacted by blacks, the moment of sale took on a whole different meaning. In effect, while ever slavery lasted, there had been an implicit denial by whites that the auction of human beings did in fact entail terrible trauma, a denial founded on the rationalization that blacks lacked a strong sense of family, kinship, emotional bonding, or other sense of constancy. The very fact that the Charleston blacks chose to hold this ritual up to the scrutiny of white southerners within a theatrical African American emancipation parade was undoubtedly a rebuttal of such assumptions. The fact that two women had been chosen to take the part of "merchandise" was a deliberately emotive gesture intended to emphasize the point with utmost rhetorical force. Furthermore, the denial inherent in whites' attitudes toward the auction was based on racial theories that polarized "white" and "black," tying skin color to the positive and negative connotations these terms had accumulated within Western culture. The difference in skin color between the seller and the saleable human property was the authorization for this transaction. But when, on the cart, a black man took the place of a white vendor, the contrast of skin coloration could no longer authorize the event. The assumed distance between master and slave and the denial of human interconnection were obliterated, and the absurdity, injustice, and outrage inherent in the act itself were presented in stark relief.

For their part, the women who followed the pall-covered coffin were engaged in something more subtle than the *New York Times* man had been able to discern. Pretending sorrow where they felt only joy, they offered a straight-faced, parodic representation of white grief at the passing of an institution that had seemed to whites both just and economically essential. Like the blacks re-presenting the slave auction, the women funeral marchers reproduced the forms of the dominant culture, but by merely inserting themselves into white roles they achieved an ironic reversal. In effect, they reflected back to whites their own attitudes and practices, and if those attitudes and practices now appeared questionable, it was clear who was to blame. Had the women funeral marchers dressed gaily, as the white reporter wanted, the blacks' presentation of the funeral would no longer have constituted a reversal, but merely a black celebration of slavery's demise. The impact of the moment would have been lessened, the point of the satire lost, the force of the irony dispelled.

Ralph Ellison has pointed out how the masks that whites imposed on blacks "veil the humanity of Negroes," in the process reducing them "to a sign,"[21] which, like most signs, can be readily manipulated to an ideologically serviceable end. Through the masks imposed during slavery—the docile, infantilized Sambo, for instance, or the faithful, contented servant—blacks were effectively silenced, unable to speak out and articulate their resentment or views without the threat of terrible punishment. The new freedom that the former Charleston slaves enjoyed brought empowerment, the capacity to refute the dominant culture's version of reality. In their parade, the blacks claimed the freedom to impose black meanings on white ritual, to make a subversive commentary on whites' practices, one which could not previously be said to the face of the master (or to whites generally). That which was previously confined to private space or articulated in carefully coded forms was expressed in a new cultural text. Here at last was an opportunity to break the imposed silence and broadcast "blackness" into the public realm; to force whites to register the African American perspective and to see through the two-dimensional masks that had been imposed upon blacks to a recognition of African Americans' humanity.

From Reconstruction through the early decades of the twentieth century, African American parades became an established feature of the southern urban landscape. Some were overtly political. On the occasion of state Republican party or state constitutional conventions, for instance, African American men and women in major cities organized street marches to demonstrate support for the party or policies of their choice.[22] Similarly, branches of the Loyal League, offshoots of a northern patriotic organization, their members wearing colorful sashes and badges and beating drums, paraded at election time in support of Republican candidates.[23] Black militia companies, organized in the immediate postwar period in part to protect African Americans from white harassment, not only practiced their drills in public streets but also regularly staged or participated in parades.[24] These volunteer militia units were common in the postbellum South, the *Atlanta Constitution* estimating, in August, 1878, that "there is not a city of any importance in the state where there are not one or more colored military companies."[25] Members of these units often wore striking uniforms— the Capital Guards, for example, formed in Atlanta in 1878, sported "neat fitting uniforms of dark blue with buff trimmings and white plumes in their hats"—and whenever they took to the streets they drew large crowds of African Americans.[26] In addition, the years following emancipation saw a burst of associational activity in the South, with thousands of black organizations—lodges, volunteer fire companies, pleasure clubs, mutual aid societies, and the like—being established. In New Orleans, for instance, some 226 African American societies were registered between 1866 and 1880.[27] Members of these associations, in full regalia, staged parades to mark such occasions as the anniversaries of their founding and also participated, as did units of the black militia, in larger processions celebrating major events in the black calendar, particularly Emancipation Day and the 4th of July.[28]

African American parades could prove particularly confronting to whites, not only because (as with Emancipation Day processions) the events they celebrated evoked painful memories, but also because they signified growing black unity and pride, traversed major thoroughfares, and often terminated at symbolically sensitive public sites. The parade by 2,000 of Richmond's blacks on April 3, 1866, to mark the anniversary of their city's capture by Union forces did all of these things. At the front of the procession was an "immense cavalcade of black horsemen," led, in the words of a white observer, by "a dusky son of Ham tooting on a worn-out bugle, and sounding original calls ever and anon." Next came a "Patriarch," wearing an apron of black and gold, a pair of trousers with a gold stripe down the sides, and a black-feathered hat. This man also carried a staff, on the top of which was a gourd (an emblematic African and African American utensil) covered with ribbons. A band followed the gourd-bearer, and behind it marched row upon row of members of Richmond's numerous African American societies, all in full regalia. Colorful banners identified the various groups of marchers as they passed. Bringing up the rear of the parade were "squads" of farm hands, walking, by the white onlooker's account, "without commander, uniform, or decorum." The procession terminated at Capitol Square, where the marchers, together with some 15,000 spectators, listened to speeches calling for equality among people of all races.[29]

In the immediate postwar context, groups of African Americans on horseback would not have provoked comment, but the spectacle of dozens, perhaps hundreds of black horsemen—the "immense cavalcade" referred to by the white onlooker—parading through the streets of this southern city must have been an unusual, even a unique sight, and surely an arresting one. The observer's description of the massed black riders suggests a sense of awe, an impression he hastens to counter with his derisory reference to the "dusky son of Ham" with his worn-out bugle. But black unity, pride, and assertiveness can be read not only in the vanguard of mounted horsemen and the impressive numbers of African Americans who took part in the procession but also in the smart dress, dignified bearing, and tight formation of the uniformed marchers (obliquely acknowledged in the observer's assertion that the field hands, trailing at the rear of the parade, possessed neither commanders, uniforms, nor decorum). Once again, African Americans had chosen the center of their city, an area of formerly white-controlled space, for spectacular public display. In assembling in their thousands before the Capitol, a site which formerly they had been forbidden to occupy,[30] they forced themselves on the attention of whites and confronted the most visible symbol of white political power.

This tendency to confront white power where formerly it had been most complacently displayed continued through the postbellum era. The extremely large and often boisterous Emancipation Day parades which became an annual event in Washington, D.C., wound their way through the center of the nation's capital, the imposing site not of municipal or state but of national political authority. Describing the 1868 celebration, a *Harper's New Monthly Magazine* correspondent wrote of "an endless black cloud stream[ing] through the town, here the throngs that compose it frolicking in exuberance and effervescence that know no bounds, and there marching serious and stately."[31] Also arresting, in its way, must have been an African American procession in Macon, Georgia, in April 1870, in which "a gang of perhaps two hundred negroes . . . paraded the streets," carrying pine knots and a number of signs, one of which read "Thank God, thank Lincoln, thank Grant for the 15th Amendment."[32] The route of a huge Washington parade of April 1870, organized to mark both Lincoln's emancipation of the District's slaves and the ratification of the fifteenth amendment, took it not only along the city's major thoroughfares but through the grounds of the White House, where, in the presence of a vast throng of African American spectators, the President acknowledged the contingents of marchers as they passed.[33] Emancipation Day parades in Greenville, South Carolina, in 1891,[34] and Rome, Georgia, in 1896, were others in which African Americans successfully asserted their right to occupy those cities' most prominent streets. In the case of the Rome parade, the several hundred blacks involved marched down Broad Street to the city's opera house, filled that building "to overflowing," and left the street outside "thronged with the overflow."[35]

Parades that intruded on formerly white-controlled social space or violated racial codes were likely to provoke an angry white response. A Fourth of July parade by Richmond blacks in 1866 produced complaints from the *Richmond Dispatch* that African Americans had virtually taken over that sacred day in the white calendar and that the city's main thoroughfares and the square in front of the Capitol Building had been "black with moving masses of darkeys."[36] A report from its Sumter correspondent, carried in the *Charleston Daily Courier* on July 9, 1866, registered strong objection to the behavior of a group of African Americans who, two Sundays previously, had attended a freedmen's religious meeting. "At the close of the service," the writer complained, "fifty or sixty negroes, with their guns and pistols, marched up Main Street," an act "justly considered . . . an open challenge and act of defiance to the authorities of the town." In July, 1868, the *Macon (Georgia) Telegraph* commented in outraged tones on a parade "through some of the principal streets" by a large number blacks, who had gathered to ratify the nomination of Ulysses S. Grant and Schuyler Colfax as the Republican presidential and vice presidential candidates. "A more humiliating scene was never witnessed," the *Telegraph* declared: "nearly three thousand ignorant field negroes, armed with clubs, marching through the streets, shouting and yelling the names of men whose principles they know nothing of, and could not understand if explained to them."[37] Transgression of racial boundaries provoked particular outrage. In August 1868, the *Atlanta Constitution* was almost beside itself as it described a Republican election parade which was made up of 672 blacks, two white members of the state legislature, and, in a "triumphal car" near the front of the march, "thirty-seven (supposed to be) white girls, representing the several States,

each dressed in white, and waving a miniature flag." Inclusion of the white
girls had excited "universal disgust," the *Constitution* assured its readers.
"What monsters of corruption and infamy," the newspaper protested, "must
be the parents who would thus prostitute the tenderest and fairest." The
writer went on to suggest that some of the "young nymphs" may have been
sexually promiscuous, or "etherialized by a liberal tincture of the *sanguine*
de Afrique."[38] The spectacle of black militia units, proud in their military
uniforms and bearing arms, regularly drilling on the city's streets or marching in major parades also proved disconcerting to whites. "How the rich
folks hated to see us," former Mississippi militiaman George Washington
Albright recalled, "armed and ready to defend ourselves and our elected
government!"[39] And the participation, from the late 1870s, of an African
American women's militia unit in Richmond's great Emancipation Day parade must sharply have challenged prevailing assumptions among blacks as
well as whites about the appropriate place of women in public space.[40]

On occasion, the composition of African American parades, the demeanor of the marchers, or the iconography on display pushed tensions
within the black community to the surface. By 1886, Frederick Douglass
was objecting to the garish exhibitionism and general unruliness that had
come to characterize Washington D. C.'s Emancipation Day parade, to
"the tinsel shows" and the "straggling processions, which empty the alleys
and dark places of our city into the broad daylight," forcing the public to
be confronted by "a vastly undue proportion of the most unfortunate,
unimproved, and unprogressive class of the colored people." Douglass's attack signaled a growing distaste among middle-class blacks for this annual
event, leading to their withdrawal from it; by the late 1880s, the national
capital's Emancipation Day parade, its exuberant character intact, had become a working-class celebration.[41] Conflicting African American agendas
were displayed, too, in the Emancipation Day parade in Charleston, South
Carolina, in 1878. Among those who participated were several black militia units, a number of bands, contingents of the Liberian Exodus Association and other African American societies, and volunteer fire companies,
one of whose wagons, adorned with American flags and flowers, featured a
young girl dressed as the Goddess of Liberty. In this instance, the numerous bands and organizations expressed the orientation toward both sepa-
ratism (as in the case of the Liberian Exodus Association) and inclusion
(the young girl surrounded by American flags and dressed as the Goddess

big bass drum strikes three extra loud booms and the band starts swing-ing *The Saints,* or *Didn't He Ramble,* or *Bourbon Street Parade,* and the wild, mad, frantic dancing starts, and the hundreds of all-colored umbrel-las are seen bouncing high above heads to the rhythm of the great crowd of second-liners." [59]

At least since the early years of the twentieth century, New Orleans blacks have been able, also, to find expressive space within the extravagant pageantry of Carnival parades, especially those associated with Mardi Gras, a traditional time for merriment and release before the abstention and re-ligious contemplation associated with the Lenten period in the Christian calendar. In the main, blacks who joined the Carnival celebrations chose to mask (that is to say, to dress up) not as whites, which they had the op-portunity to do, but as Native Americans or, in the case of members of the Zulu Social Aid and Pleasure club, as "primitive" Africans. The "Zulus," who, until the post-World War II period, paraded mainly in black neigh-borhoods, have directed their parody at the more lavish and dignified pro-cessions of the white Carnival societies or krewes, mocking their racial ex-clusiveness and aristocratic pretensions (membership being all-white and, to varying degrees, socially exclusive). While white krewe (carnival society) members, elaborately and elegantly attired, rode on richly decorated floats, carelessly tossing trinkets to the eager crowds who scrambled for these "riches," the Zulus, clad in grass skirts and set amidst jungle scenery, threw coconuts. While the whites peered down haughtily at the "common people" through dominoes and other styles of mask redolent of aristocratic revels, the Zulus toasted the crowds with beer. Against the imperious and splen-didly presented Rex, the King of Mardi Gras, and his beautiful Queen, were counterpoised the "wild" Zulu monarch and his consort (a transves-tite Queen for a number of years), with their tawdry costumes and tacky regal paraphernalia. Members of the Zulu Social Aid and Pleasure Club not on the royal float masqueraded in costumes that burlesqued famous lo-cal figures; on his release from jail in 1918, Louis Armstrong was delighted to see Papa Gar dressed as Captain Jackson, the meanest officer in the New Orleans police force, at whose hands Armstrong himself had suffered. [60]

The pointed exaggeration inherent in the Zulu king and his entou-rage's brandishing of spears, their blackening of faces, and donning of woolly black wigs and a second, darker skin of dyed black underwear clearly held up to ridicule the stereotypical conceptions of blackness as relating to the "savagery" and "primitivism" of "deepest, darkest Africa" (see Figure 20). Perhaps, too, there was here an affirmation of "blackness" as an alternative culture and tradition to "whiteness," a mockery of white traditions as repressive, stiflingly genteel and pretentious. The occasional practice, in more recent times, of the Zulus in handing out jars of hair straightener[61] would reinforce this message, signifying upon blacks who aspire to white standards rather than embracing their own physical nature and cultural traditions. On another level, the "blacking up" by the Zulus—the darkening of "insufficiently" dark faces, artificial enlargement of lips, and whitening of eyes—strongly recalls the rituals undertaken by the minstrel-show black (commonly a white in blackface), whose comically distorted appearance served the function of reassuring whites by affirming patronizing conceptions of blacks as harmless buffoons. One is particularly reminded of the experience of such a richly talented African American performer as Bert Williams, who was forced to darken his skin and highlight his lips and eyes

Figure 20: Pointed exaggeration was used to ridicule stereotyped conceptions of blackness. King Zulu and members of his court at Carnival in New Orleans, 1940. The Historic New Orleans Collection, accession no. 1980.54

before he could display his art. Once again we see that, when blacks take control of, rather than situating themselves within, these masking rituals, those rituals take on a very different and altogether more aggressive level of meaning. In the Zulus' mode of signifying, the masks or identities that whites impose upon blacks—that of the wild savage in this instance—are exposed as ludicrously distorted stereotypes that obscure the humanity of blacks. Whatever the specific associations the Zulus' appearance evoked among African American watchers, the general point of the satire is clear: their emphasis on masks, or imposed identities, effectively unmasks the labeling practices by which whites routinely demean black people.

The Zulus' parody cut deeper still. In the eyes of the boisterous crowds of blacks who greeted the arrival of the royal barge at the head of the New Basin canal with such wild enthusiasm and cheered their returning "African" monarch through the streets, King Zulu routinely outshone Rex, the designated ruler of the day's proceedings. The issue of the African American *Louisiana Weekly*, published on March 5, 1927, just after Mardi Gras, made this very point, featuring on its front page a large photograph of King "Arnold the Only," together with an article claiming that the Zulu potentate had "ruled supreme over New Orleans' Mardi Gras festivities, eclipsing the glory of His Majesty, Rex." What is important here is to realize just how monumentally tacky the Zulu King's performance typically was. In 1928, for example, His Majesty arrived in a barge (Rex, by contrast, disembarked from a stately yacht), decorated with "whatever scraps happened to be at hand." He was seated on a tattered chair under a canopy of sacking. He wore long black underwear, a grass skirt, and a fuzzy black wig. His crown was of tin and his scepter was a broomstick with a stuffed white rooster impaled on one end. Once ashore, His Highness mounted his mule-drawn chariot (really just a platform on wheels) accompanied by similarly dressed lesser dignitaries, who decorated the royal float with potted palms and some bunting and paper flowers hastily salvaged from the barge. As the king, leading a motley collection of floats and marchers (on the second float, an old woman fried fish and distributed it to favored members of the crowd), proceeded on his royal way, he saluted his subjects by quaffing beer from a bottle and exchanged lascivious banter with female admirers.[62] Through the effusiveness of their greeting, the Zulu king's rambunctious followers were claiming that even this grotesquely distorted caricature of a black man—the product, after all, of whites' own racist imaginings—was

superior to the most comely and dignified personage the main Carnival had
to offer. And in that claim, of course, lay a hilarious repudiation of whites'
idealized standards of beauty and worth (See Figure 21).

Toward the end of the nineteenth century, small groups of African
Americans adopting the appearance of Native American braves began to

Figure 21: The extravagantly tacky Zulu monarch acknowledges his subjects, Carnival, 1952. The Historic New Orleans Collection, accession no. 1979.333

appear at Carnival. They adorned themselves in war paint and feathers, carried various implements of battle, and ran through the crowds whooping and chanting. By the early decades of the twentieth century, a number of black "Indian" tribes, associated with specific neighborhoods in the African American sections of the city, had been formed, and on Mardi Gras these tribes, bearing names such as the Yellow Poker Hunters, the Wild Squatoulas, and the Black Mohawks, paraded through black neighborhoods, following no fixed route and stopping from time to time at local saloons. When tribes encountered one another, challenges were issued and, not infrequently, violence ensued. Over time, competition between the tribes centered increasingly on aesthetic display; sartorial brilliance and dancing skills were the major determinants of superiority. By 1925, according to one account, the Indians' costumes "were of deer skin packed with beads and hieroglyphic designs." On Mardi Gras in 1932, costumes were described by the New Orleans *Times-Picayune* as "magnificent, . . . with a huge feather headpiece and bead-strung leather garments." Though most members of the Indian tribes were poor, the *Times-Picayune* pointed out, their "suits and headpieces are not carelessly put together from odds and ends, but equal the beauty of the costumes of the great American Indian chiefs"[63] (see Figure 22). In more recent times, the regalia of the Indians have become magnificent assemblages of ostrich and peacock feathers, sequins, beads, rhinestones, and other reflective materials, meticulously hand-sewn into intricate patterns and dazzlingly colorful (see Figure 23).

It has been suggested that blacks originally adopted Indian headdress and face paint during Carnival because they were forbidden to wear masks. Whether or not this was so, the effectiveness of the black Indians' semiotic play depended to a significant extent on their *not* wearing masks. It is precisely the semiotic disjunction caused by the appearance of blacks in the role of Indians that prompts reflection on the nature of the relationship between the two groups. As George Lipsitz has observed, the image of the Indian already had powerful symbolic meaning for whites, calling attention to, among other things, "the initial genocide upon which American 'civilization' rests." When blacks presented themselves as, and symbolically allied themselves with, Indians, this unwelcome reminder of past wrongs committed against nonwhite groups and of the racial nature of the ideology underpinning those wrongs was doubly effective; blacks, too, were a historically marginalized group, whom whites had stigmatized as racially inferior and oppressed. As Lipsitz has pointed out, "the Indian tribes' disguise brings out into the open dimensions of repression that the dominant culture tried to render invisible." [64] In dressing not merely as Indians, but as warrior Indians, African Americans also registered their admiration for a people who had resolutely resisted whites' geographic expansion and cultural domination.

Through the medium of the parade, New Orleans blacks turned the streets of their city into performance space. Here, in the quilt-like dazzle of high-affect colors, in flexible bodily movements with their dramatic changes in dancing or marching steps, the totality of black style was displayed. Here again were the privileging of improvisation, the cultural imperatives of vibrancy, aliveness, and constant surprise. Here again was the cultural aesthetic that had informed not merely slave dance and textile design but African American quilting and musical styles as well.

Figure 22: A tribe of Indians in the Gypsy Tea Room, St. Joseph Night, March 19, 1940, New Orleans. By this time, dazzlingly colorful, intricately worked costumes were in vogue. Courtesy of the Louisiana Division, New Orleans Public Library

Figure 23: Aesthetic competition and display taken to fantastic lengths. This photograph, taken in 1980, is of Lionel "Bird" Oubichon, Wild Man of the White Eagles Mardi Gras Indian tribe. Courtesy of Christopher Porché West

The earlier postbellum African American parades had been joyous or defiant expressions of dignity and assertiveness. Groups of smartly uniformed blacks, their bodies upright and moving in close formation, marched proudly through formerly white-controlled public space, celebrating their newly gained freedom, marking important symbolic events in the black calendar, and calling for political empowerment. Through parody and ironic reversal they signified against whites, unmasking the masking practices that erased blacks' humanity. Elements of pride and parody are present in the New Orleans parades as well, in the splendid uniforms and dignified marching of African American societies and in the Zulus' parodic play, but the addition of interactive second-liners, as well as dramatic and exciting rhythmic changes, transformed those parades into ebullient celebrations of African American cultural difference.

Black cultural distinctiveness is manifested as uniformity is displaced by diversity, stately marching by strutting, prancing, and "shakin' it on down." It is signaled by the unexpected transformation of an orderly parade of serious marchers into what Danny Baker describes as a "large group of black folks dancing, . . . each dancing his or her thing,"[65] a spectacle that, especially when jubilant second-liners surround the band, evokes the "shouts" in slave cabins, the Sunday dancing of slaves at New Orleans's Congo Square, and the ring dances of Africa.[66] Black style is displayed, too, in the paraders' free-flowing body movement, in the revolving hips and angular motion of arms, in the spontaneous waving of hands, flags, and multi-colored umbrellas, in the parade marshal's exciting choreography, with its twists, fancy steps, and playful directional changes. It is present in the wonderful intricacy and brilliant color combinations of the Indians' costumes (each one necessarily different from those of all other members of the tribe), costumes that, like the dancers' varied steps, celebrate diversity and improvisation within the established parade form.[67]

The black parades of New Orleans put African American performance style on bold, public display. Folklorist Alan Lomax's cross-cultural study of such styles led him to conclude that "black African nonverbal performance traditions had survived virtually intact in African America." African performance style, Lomax found, was notable for its "velocity and changefulness . . . making the most use of marked shifts of level, direction, limb use, pacing, and energy in dance . . . along with the greatest facility in shifting style collectively in close coordination." Lomax saw these traditions exemplified in an impromptu performance he witnessed during an African American family party in the Mississippi Delta. As Ed Young and his brothers, Lonnie and G. D., began to play (Ed on the fife, Lonnie and G. D. on drums), dancing as they did so, a crowd of family members, relatives, and neighbors gathered around them, and "an electrifying rhythmic exchange" began, "a dancer breaking out and a musician responding, and then the reverse." There was "constant interplay within the whole group, with the musicians picking up hot rhythmic licks from the dancers nearby them so that everyone is dancing." Watching Ed Young's band move across the yard, Lomax was reminded of "the jazz parades of New Orleans, where the band is a pulsing artery in the belly of a huge dancing throng." [68]

In both this Delta fife-and-drum band and the New Orleans parades, the relationship between musicians and second-liners is interactive rather than linear. Second-liners not only respond to the musicians' rhythms, making those rhythms visible, as it were, but, through their dancing and their use of such percussive instruments as drums, tambourines and cowbells, they initiate rhythmic changes of their own. This creative fusion becomes more obvious when, as sometimes happens, the crowd moves among the musicians, splitting the band up. Musicians and dancers improvise, taking their cues from each other, effecting a complex, rhythmic interchange. [69] Music, costumes, dance and other body and body-connected movements—fancy steps, swaying trombones, pulsating umbrellas—become integral parts of an overall performance that communicates a sense of vitality, excitement, spontaneity, and joy.

This fluidity of black forms has been emphasized by Samuel Kinser in his study of black New Orleans parades. Kinser cites the "nonlinear, nondirected general quality of performance," contrasting it with the white Carnival krewes' linear thinking and style. Orderly white parades follow a predetermined route to a gala social event, the annual ball, at which style of dress is mandated and social etiquette strict. "In [white] letter-centered culture," Kinser writes, "you obey the letter of the prescribed program." The black Indians, by contrast, follow no fixed route, stop every so often for refreshment, and interact with second-liners in a way that makes rhythm, dance and probably even destination indeterminate. The Zulus' route was often advertised in advance, but their progress along it was haphazard; in 1928, Lyle Saxon, who followed the Zulus' parade, found the floats aban-

doned alongside an African American barrel house, from which there came
sounds of singing and dancing.[70]

In African Americans' orally centered culture, meaning itself is fluid,
rather than predetermined, "aris[ing] most often from face-to-face, inter-
personal exchanges," as in the call-and-response, interactive character of
the paraders' music and dance. Orally centered cultures, Kinser points out,
"prize performance above the exchange of views." They also, we can add,
prize performance over specified destination; where one is going is less important than how one gets there. Thus the stepper who is the best performer, who shows the greatest ingenuity, becomes the parade Marshal; the
Indian whose attire is most glorious, or whose dancing most skillfull, is
made chief.[71] Performance is sufficiently prized for African American society members, who are not generally well-off, to purchase expensive uniforms or special clothing, often featuring brilliantly colored garments:
"fancy expensive silk shirts," as Danny Barker described them, "new pants,
hats, ties, socks—everything new and costly."[72] It is sufficiently important
for the black Indians to spend a good part of the preceding year creating
their costumes, laying out large sums of money for materials, meticulously
hand-sewing thousands of beads, sequins, and rhinestones to form the dazzling and intricate patterns that distinguish their Mardi Gras attire. These
performances are intensely competitive, placing bands in aesthetic competition with bands, tribes with tribes, societies with societies, Grand Marshal against Grand Marshal—but they are primarily competitive as between
African Americans, not as between blacks and whites. In characteristic
fashion, New Orleans blacks use the medium of the parade to celebrate African American culture through competitive aesthetic display.

As an orally centered culture, African American culture is polyvalent,
finding expression through a process of *bricolage,* or "make-shift construction." "People who are part of orally centered cultures," Kinser writes,
"construct their lives and their cultural activity from interchangeable parts,
parts which one can make do in many different situations. Since resources
are so limited, everything must serve six purposes." Those who belong to
orally centered cultures display a "willingness to play with the elements of
meaning," the "fantasy" of such cultures being "infinite flexibility."[73] These
valuable insights recall for us the surprising, seemingly haphazard combinations of garments worn by some slaves; the "odd" combinations of colors, patterns, or materials that could exist within the one clothing ensemble;

the black dancer's simultaneous expression of several rhythms and surprising juxtaposition of dancing steps; the switching, in parades, from solemnity to hilarity, from stately, coordinated movement to fluid and individualistic dancing forms. In a classic expression of *bricolage,* the New Orleans Indians, in constructing their parades, draw on European carnival traditions, African cultural principles, and Native American costuming.[74] As Kinser points out, "their music sometimes approaches calypso rhythms, their beadwork imagery seems to be taken from movie Westerns, the call-and-response pattern of chanting is African."[75] To create their costumes, the Indians use a diverse profusion of materials "all organized," Michael P. Smith has written, "into a fantastic explosion of funk and flash."[76]

Since the early years of the twentieth century, black parades have functioned in New Orleans as the primary vehicle for the public display of African American culture. The cultural product exhibited in those parades is distinctive in some respects and expressed in a particularly exuberant and uninhibited form, but the principles underpinning it and the processes of its creation are familiar. Vibrant and provocative displays of color, pattern-breaking variations in movement, and a general privileging of improvisation and love of surprise not only exemplify the "velocity and change-fulness" of black artistic performance[77] but celebrate an aesthetic that, appearing intermittently in slave clothing and textile design and more conspicuously in black quilting, dress, music and dance, lies at the heart of African American style.

Strolling, Jooking, and Fixy Clothes

In his autobiography, *Born to Rebel,* Benjamin Mays relates an incident that occurred during his junior high school years, and that he would always count as the "bitterest and most embarrassing interracial experience" of his life. On a Saturday afternoon in 1911, he called to collect his mail from the local post office in Epworth, South Carolina. The post office was at the rear of a store, with entry to it through a swinging half-door or gate, and Mays took up his position near this gate, waiting to be served. Moments later Wallace Payne, a local white physician, intent on retrieving his own mail, moved past Mays, and as he did so he struck Mays "a mighty blow in the face." "Get out of my way, you black rascal," Payne told him, adding, by way of explanation, that Mays had been "trying to look too good anyway." That, Mays conceded, had been his "greatest sin": he had been "standing

153

erect; and I am sure that I had on clean clothes. . . . But a Negro was not supposed to look neat or intelligent, or to stand erect around Dr. Payne. Maybe he expected me to start to grin and cringe when I saw him or to jump when he spoke to me." Explaining why he did not strike back, Mays pointed out that "the store was filled with white men dressed in overalls, smoking and chewing tobacco, some drinking"; had he retaliated, "I would have been shot dead on the spot."[1]

Mays's story alerts us to the myriad ways in which Jim Crow impacted on the presentation of the African American body. Just as slaves, in the antebellum world, had been expected to look the part, shunning any sign of assertiveness and even demonstrating their contentment, so, under the racial system that had crystallized by the turn of the century, African Americans were required to dress, walk, comport themselves, and direct their gaze in a manner that registered uncomplaining subservience. Blacks understood, for example, that it could be dangerous to wear expensive clothes or, particularly in rural areas, to don Sunday attire during the week.[2] "White folks are terrible in this place," a former Works Progress Administration employee from Greene County, Georgia, explained to his interviewer. "If you go down town and stump your feet they put you in jail. . . . And don't go down town all dressed up. They liable to beat you cause they say they don't know you and they been knowing me all my life but if I go down town dressed up they won't know me."[3] White people "don't like nobody who don't wear overalls and don't work like digging ditches," a young black man told Hylan Lewis, who studied the African American community in Kent (actually York), South Carolina, in the 1940s.[4] "If a man dress decent, he's a smart nigger." The mere wearing of glasses could be sufficient to earn white disapproval.[5] Even in sizable urban centers, attempts to dress in a stylish manner were likely to cause offense. When the train carrying circus impresario John Ringling's private Pullman car stopped at Houston, Texas, Taylor Gordon, a Ringling employee on his first trip to the South, decided to explore the city. Gordon dressed in his "new Jack Johnson plaid suit, patent leather shoes, [and] hotcap," and began to stroll through the rail terminal, but almost immediately he was roughly seized by a large man with a star on his chest and a billy club in his hand. "You're a Yankee Nigger, ain't cha?" the man demanded. "No," Gordon replied, "I'm a Ringling's Niggah." "Well, by God! that saves yah," the man declared. "You sure look like a Yankee Nigger. They're too damn smart." The officer of the law then showed Gordon to a small shed adjacent to the building, advising him that that was where he belonged "in them clothes," and telling him that, if he wished to "see the sights," he should change into his porter's uniform. Gordon did as he was instructed, donning an outfit which, of course, signified an appropriate subservience.[6]

Around the time of World War I, African American soldiers, whose crisp uniforms and dignified bearing denoted pride and self-assurance, proved especially affronting to whites. In Vicksburg, Mississippi, in 1917, angry whites threatened to strip the uniforms of black officers from their backs. In Jackson, the state's capital, second-lieutenant George Washington Lee, who appeared on the street dressed in his officer's garb and moving with a precise military gait, was forced to flee for his life.[7] Those returning to the South after hostilities had ended became particular targets. At Blakely, Georgia, in April 1919, a soldier was fatally beaten for wearing his uniform for a longer period than his attackers thought appropriate.[8] "What did they do to the niggers after this first world war?" former tenant farmer Nate Shaw asked rhetorically. "Meet em at these stations where they was gettin off, comin back into the United States, and cut the buttons and armaments off of their clothes, make em get out of them clothes, make em pull them uniforms off and if they didn't have another suit of clothes—quite naturally, if they was colored men they was poor and they might not a had a thread of clothes in the world but them uniforms—make em walk in their underwear. I know it was done, I heard too much of it from the ones that come back to this country even."[9]

Deference, or the appearance of it at least, had to be communicated by appropriate body language: submissive gestures, modest deportment, and suitably downcast eyes. Sociologist Allison Davis and his coworkers, who studied race relations in and around Natchez, Mississippi, in the late 1930s, commented on the "respectful yielding . . . by Negroes in their contact with whites." Blacks waiting for a white person to answer a knock at the door would stand "respectfully," hat in hand; in rural areas, African Americans would tip their hats and greet "respectfully" any white person they encountered.[10] Blacks knew to step off the sidewalk so that whites might pass and to avoid eye contact with them; an injudicious glance could be highly dangerous if committed by young black men, but even very young females took care to avoid such infractions. As a child in Durham, North Carolina, Pauli Murray "learned to throw my eyes off focus whenever I passed a white person, so that I would not see the face or the expression." [11] "Most Negroes grinned, cringed, and kowtowed in the presence of white people," Benjamin Mays acknowledged in his account of life in Greenwood County, South Carolina, in the early part of the century. "Those who could not take such subservience left for the city as soon as they could—with or without their father's permission." [12] White people, a sharecropper from Boliver County, Mississippi, informed sociologist Charles S. Johnson, had to be treated "like they a silk handkerchief on a barb wire fence." [13]

The incident involving Benjamin Mays at the local post office also calls attention to the mechanism that ultimately fixed the racial system in place. Notwithstanding legal emancipation and the greater measure of political empowerment African Americans enjoyed during Radical Reconstruction, extra-legal violence, whether at the hands of individuals, mobs, or terrorist organizations such as the Ku Klux Klan, continued to be a commonplace of southern black life. The incidence of such violence did decrease once effective white rule had been restored in the 1870s, but it rose again from the late 1880s and continued high well into the following century. [14] Through all those years, African Americans whose dress or demeanor suggested that they might be getting "above themselves"—and this, precisely, had been the young Benjamin Mays's transgression—risked physical assault. Dr. Payne's brutal punch had sharply reminded Mays of that.

Fear of retributive violence, and especially of lynching, its most extreme form, became pervasive. John Dollard, investigating racial and social conditions in and around Indianola, Mississippi, in the mid-1930s, found that "the threat of lynching is likely to be in the mind of the Negro child from the earliest days." [15] By the age of ten, Mississippi-born Richard Wright recalled, "a dread of white people" had come "to live permanently in my . . . imagination," a feeling that "there existed men against whom I was powerless, men who could violate my life at will." [16] L. C. Dorsey, an African American woman born on a Mississippi Delta plantation in the early 1930s, related how, if someone in her community disappeared and was later found to have been lynched, folks were so fearful that "even at night with everybody at home in their own houses, nobody talked about this occurrence . . . out loud," that they went about with bowed heads, lest they be thought "uppity," that, if confronted by white women, men "removed their hats and stepped off to the side so as not to brush against them accidentally." [17] A "fine white woman," whom journalist Ray Stannard

Baker met in Atlanta in the early years of the century, graphically illustrated for him the fear that even accidental physical contact between the races could evoke. A few evenings previously, as she emerged suddenly from a doorway onto the sidewalk, a black youth accidentally brushed her shoulder. When the youth realized that he had touched a white woman, "such a look of abject terror and fear came into his face as I hope never again to see on a human countenance. He knew what it meant if I was frightened, called for help, and accused him of insulting or attacking me. He stood still a moment, then turned and ran down the street, dodging into the first alley he came to."[18] And if, as this story implies, "serious" breaches of the racial rules—in this case, physical contact between a black man and a white woman—could have literally fatal consequences, even minor infractions might provoke hideously disproportionate punishments. In one recorded incident in North Carolina, Matt Ingram, a black sharecropper, spent two and a half years in prison for assaulting a white woman, even though he had not been within seventy-five feet of her. Ingram had looked at the woman in what whites considered a threatening way.[19]

Black children were cautioned early against transgressing the South's invisible racial boundaries. As a child in Eatonville, Florida, Zora Neale Hurston enjoyed sitting on the gate post of her house and calling out to white travelers as they passed, but her family warned against this practice. Hurston's grandmother, a former slave, was particularly apprehensive. "Git down offa dat gate post!" the old woman would say. "Setting up dere looking dem white folks right in the de face! They's gowine to lynch you, yet. . . . Youse too brazen to live long."[20] In Stamps, Arkansas, in the early 1930s, Maya Angelou's grandmother instructed her to keep to "the paths in life that she and her generation and all the Negroes gone before had found, and found to be safe ones."[21] Charlie Holcomb, who grew up in Johnston County, North Carolina, in the 1930s, heard the same message from a grandparent, this time in parable form. One day, as he and his grandfather were fishing, the old man hooked a large catfish, but instead of landing it, he allowed the fish to swim around easily under the water, telling his grandson to watch it. The grandfather then pulled the fish onto the bank, where it thrashed around in a violent manner. He repeated the procedure, returning the fish to the water, where it became calm, and landing it again, only this time he allowed the fish to struggle violently until it died. "Son," the grandfather observed, "a catfish is a lot like a nigger. As long as he is in his mudhole he is all right, but when he gits out he is in for a passel o' trouble. You 'member dat, and you won't have no trouble wid folks when you grows up." [22] "Our mothers began telling us about being black from the day we were born," Mississippi native Charles Evers has written. "We got it hammered into us to watch our step, to stay in our place." [23]

Though the young Richard Wright was warned of the dangers he faced, he proved peculiarly inept at reading the elaborate codes that governed racial interaction—codes that Mississippian David L. Cohn has described as "written, unwritten, and unwritable"—and at fulfilling their subtly-nuanced requirements. For this very reason, Wright serves as a valuable register of Jim Crow's esoteric racial rules. After graduating from high school, Wright succeeded in obtaining a job in a clothing store, but he soon came to resent the contemptuous and callous manner in which its white proprietor and his son treated their black customers. "I watched the brutality with growing hate, yet trying to keep my feelings from registering in my face. When the boss looked at me, I would avoid his eyes." Despite his efforts at concealment, Wright's demeanor ultimately betrayed him. Demanding to know what was bothering him, the boss's son asked angrily why Wright did not "laugh and talk like the other niggers," and, when Wright could give no satisfactory answer, he was dismissed. "I don't like your looks, nigger," the son declared. "Now get!" [24]

Though Wright was able to obtain other jobs, he quickly lost them "because of my attitude, my speech, the look in my eyes." Seeking guidance from Griggs, a former classmate, he was advised to "learn how to live in the South," to behave in the presence of white people as if he knew they were white. But he could not follow this counsel: "it was simply utterly impossible for me to calculate, to scheme, to act, to plot all the time. I would remember to dissemble for short periods, then I would forget and act straight and human again, not with the desire to harm anybody, but merely forgetting the artificial status of race and class." "I knew what was wrong with me," Wright conceded, after recounting the circumstances of his dismissal from yet another job, "but I could not correct it. The words and actions of white people were baffling signs to me. . . . I had to keep remembering what others took for granted." Eventually, Wright did manage to effect at least a formal observance of social conventions, learning, as he said, "new modes of behavior, new rules in how to live the Jim Crow life." Deputed to obtain illegal liquor for the white prostitutes in a Jackson hotel, he became practiced at "walk[ing] past a white policeman with contraband upon my hip, sauntering, whistling like a nigger ought to whistle when he is innocent." His face, too, became a deceiving mask, concealing his feelings. Later, as an employee of a Memphis firm, Wright regularly spent his lunch hour with other African American employees in one of the rooms of the building, where they criticized white behavior and plotted revenge. But when they returned to work, nothing in their appearance hinted at the nature of their discussions. Asked by the foreman how he was getting along, Wright "answered with false heartiness, falling quickly into that nigger-being-a-good-natured-boy-in-the-presence-of-a-white-man pattern, a pattern into which I could now slide easily." [25]

Not surprisingly, in a world where even smart clothing could prove provocative and careless gestures dangerous, much black cultural display was pushed beyond the gaze of whites into the very spaces that Jim Crow's ordinances had created. Only in such locations could the deceptive masks that Wright describes safely be removed and creative energies given some play. Such a realization directs our search for expressions of African American style to black-controlled social space, to, to cite some of the more obvious examples, the streets in black neighborhoods of southern cities and towns, the jukes and dives and dancehalls where African Americans gathered to enjoy themselves, and the uncontested social terrain of the African American church.

In July 1881, a reporter from the *Atlanta Constitution,* curious as to the character of lower-class African American life, ventured into less salubrious sections of his city. Traversing Decatur, Ivy and Collins Streets, he surveyed such entertainment venues as the Beaver Slide and the Ant Hole before moving on to examine the condition of the communities of Ellis Row, Happy Hollow, Bone Alley, and Pigtail Alley. The newspaperman's verdict on the character of black Atlanta was a negative one. Not only were the people's residences in a deplorable condition, but "worthless negroes" congregated on street corners, and several commercial premises were little more than "nests where the worst forms of crime are born and bred." Concerned citizens, the writer concluded, "must hope that these dens, some of poverty and some of vice, . . . will be choked out of existence" as the expansion of the city brought more respectable people into the area.

But for all the *Constitution* man's evident distaste, there is enough ambiguity in his account to permit an alternative reading. His description of

Ivy Street, which he reached just at sundown, hints at the presence not merely of poverty and crime but also of a vibrant street life. Ivy Street was "packed with colored people of every size and class—big, little, old, young, black, yellow, mad, happy, sad, men, boys, women, girls, all together in such a squirm of confusion as to require an expert to make his way along the sidewalk in anything like a satisfactory manner."[26] There was no room here for the daily humiliations that Jim Crow exacted; no need to walk with head bowed, or eyes averted, or to step off sidewalks to allow whites to pass. Freed from hostile white oversight and in the company of their own people, African Americans on Ivy Street could dress, move about, and comport themselves pretty much as they pleased.

A correspondent for another city newspaper, the *Journal Magazine*, who explored black areas in Atlanta in 1912, was more prepared than was the *Constitution*'s reporter to acknowledge the positive aspects of black urban life. To him, Decatur Street east of Pryor appeared a "paradise for . . . negroes," a "kaleidoscope of light, noise and bustle from dawn to dawn." On Decatur, "the negro is found in his element of fried fish and gaudy raiment," and African Americans were able to "meet old friends, and talk and gossip to their hearts' content." On Saturday afternoons, "people flock up and down in shoals." It was hopeless to try to move quickly through this throng, this observer conceded, "nothing to do but fall in with the shiftless tread of the carefree colored folk who make up a vast part of the crowds."[27] Though obviously romanticized, this description of the black section of Decatur Street suggests a degree of expressive freedom uncommon in African Americans' contemporary world. Counter images of such spaces exist, of course; for example, black bluesman Perry Bradford commented that "it was a tame Saturday night in the notorious Decatur Street section if there were only six razor operations performed, or if only four persons were found in the morgue on Sunday morning,"[28] but what is important here is the recognition by both of these white journalists of the significance of African American street life.

Blacks' descriptions of Memphis's Beale Street bear the point out. W. C. Handy, who settled in Memphis in 1905, first heard stories of this famous thoroughfare as a boy in Florence, Alabama, and those stories enchanted him. Life on Beale, violin player Jim Turner told him, was "a song from dawn to dawn." Turner spoke of "darktown dandies and high-brown belles" and of "the glitter and finery of their latest fashions," alluring images that "planted in [Handy's] heart a seed of discontent, a yearning for

Beale Street and the gay universe that it typified."[29] To bluesman Muddy Waters, who traveled to Beale from Mississippi on Saturdays to earn money in the jukes, "Beale Street was the street. Black man's street." On Saturday nights, everyone was on the sidewalks, "somebody over here playing guitar, somebody singing gospel. . . . Walter Horton . . . , he's out there blowing the harp, and Honey Boy [David] Edwards, used to play guitar, and little midget, Buddy Doyle, he could sing good."[30] Much later, musician Rufus Thomas claimed to have said to a white man: "Hey man, if you were black for one Saturday night on Beale Street, never would you want to be white again."[31]

The same bifurcation of images that occurred in relation to Decatur is found in descriptions of Beale. Black musicians might eulogize Beale Street, but to Shields McIlwaine, a long-time white resident of Memphis, this concourse signified very differently. After midnight on a Saturday, McIlwaine warned, "nobody, white or black, who thinks much of his life should be around." During these hours, Beale "swarms with drunks, hop-heads, and hussies," and "blacks begin to slash each other with anything that will cut."[32] Like every other site where black people congregated, then, Beale Street carried many meanings, and the character of African American life there comes to us refracted through a variety of highly selective lenses.

What is clear, however, is that, for African Americans, streets such as Decatur and Beale served as performance sites, readily accessible urban stages for prideful or leisurely strolling and creative sartorial display. W. C. Handy has written of "powerfully built roustabouts saunter[ing] along [Beale Street's] pavement," of "fashionable browns in beautiful gowns," and of pimps in "boxback coats and undented stetsons," all of whom contributed to Beale's "color and spell."[33] The "Saturday night stroll" on Beale, African American George W. Lee declared, was "a thrilling adventure which the cooks in the kitchens and the men at the big plants on the Wolf River looked forward to all week." On that night, "golden browns, high yellows and fast blacks, some gorgeously dressed and others poorly clad, move together down the old thoroughfare. The working folks are on parade; going nowhere in particular, just out strolling just glad of a chance to dress up and expose themselves on the avenue after working hard all the week" (see Figure 24).[34]

The streets of black New Orleans offered similar prospects, a chance for the city's young black men, in particular (for the street, as Evelyn Brooks Higginbotham has pointed out, "signified *male* turf")[35], to exhibit their

Figure 24: Eudora Welty, The Saturday afternoon stroll, Grenada, Mississippi, 1935. Eudora Welty Collection, Mississippi Department of Archives and History

distinctive clothing and movement styles. By Jelly Roll Morton's account, many of these "tremendous sports" dressed spectacularly, but no matter how unpromising his circumstances, each sport strove to acquire "at least one Sunday suit, because, without that Sunday suit, you didn't have anything." To avoid being thought "way out of line," the sport had to make sure that his coat and pants did not match. Blue coats were favored, and trousers that were striped and worn tight. "They'd fit um like a sausage. I'm telling you it was very seldom you could button the top button of a person's trousers those days in New Orleans." Suspenders, while not functionally important, were essential, and needed to be "very loud." To ensure visibility, one strap was invariably left "hanging down." The swells made every effort to maintain their carefully constructed appearance: "If you wanted to talk to one of these guys, he would find the nearest post, stiffen his arm and hold himself as far away as possible from the post he's leaning on. That was to keep those fifteen, eighteen dollar trousers of his from losing their press." Morton himself habitually dressed in what jazzman Pops Foster described as a "very flashy" style, displaying "gold on his teeth and a diamond in one." "Those days, myself," Morton has acknowledged, "I thought I would die unless I had a hat with the emblem Stetson in it and some Edwin Clapp shoes." [36]

Their preferred style of walking contributed to the sports' visual impact. As a sport moved down the street, Morton has related, his shirt "busted open" to reveal a "red flannel undershirt," he displayed a "very mosey" style of walking called "shooting the agate." When one shot the agate, "your hands is at your sides with your index fingers stuck out and you kind of struts with it," a type of movement inconceivable, of course, in white-controlled public space.[37] This style of dress and movement was attractive to certain African American women: "if you could shoot a good agate and had a highclass red undershirt with the collar turned up," Morton explained, "I'm telling you you were liable to get next to that broad. She'd like that very much." [38] Here again, then, is the salience of performance; in the theater of the street, before an appreciative African American audience, these visually exciting and coolly moving actors placed an alternative aesthetic on ostentatious, competitive display.

Dressing well on the street was tremendously important to middle-class blacks as well, as the recollections of former residents of Atlanta's Auburn Avenue show. "You didn't find people coming to Auburn in their shirttails like they do now, and just kind of loosely dressed," long-time resident Dan Stephens declared when interviewed in the 1970s. "They had a lot of pride and [when] they'd come to Auburn Avenue, they would be dressed up." Kathleen Adams, who was born in 1890 in a house that fronted Auburn Avenue, remembered that on Sundays women churchgoers wore "their taffetas" and the grandmothers their "alpacas and even their brocades," and how the women's bellback skirts "gave you that flow, and as they walked down the street those skirts had a certain bounce to them." Men who escorted women to church wore "striped britches, two-button cutaway coats." Kathleen Adams's father, a lawyer, "walked down Auburn Avenue in his striped britches, his Prince Albert, his Stetson hat and his walking cane and, in winter, his tan gloves." The clothing of former slaves, now storekeepers on Auburn, was also formal, and their bearing grave. "They had a certain pride and dignity," Kathleen Adams remembered, "as they stood in their store doors or . . . walked the streets."[39] As Robin Kelley has perceptively commented, for African Americans, "seeing oneself and others 'dressed up' was enormously important in terms of constructing a collective identity based on something other than wage work." No less than the donning of flashy attire, the re-presenting of the black body through neat, elegant clothing constituted "a public challenge to the dominant stereotypes of the black body . . . reinforcing a sense of dignity that was perpetually being assaulted."[40] Seeing oneself and others moving about confidently, even proudly, on streets such as Auburn Avenue must have had a similar effect.

Like major streets, the jukes, clubs, and dancehalls in black neighborhoods were sites for pleasure and performance. "By the light of a few smoky oil lamps," the *Atlanta Constitution*'s reporter had written back in 1881, describing the premises on Decatur Street known as the Beaver Slide, "and to the soul-harrowing music of a string band, the colored beaux and dusky damsels . . . trip the light fantastic toe, not forgetting to refresh themselves at the saloon counter when each dance is ended."[41] What we glimpse here, through this witness's not wholly disapproving eyes, is a club, tonk, or juke joint, roughly appointed certainly, but a place where, in a familiar cultural ambiance and without serious hindrance, black people could dress up, socialize, listen to music, and dance. Through distinctive clothing and movement styles, but also through a range of gestural interactions that have largely gone unrecorded—facial expressions, eye-to-eye exchanges, rituals of touching (as in distinctive handshakes)—African American working people who congregated in such venues reconfirmed their identity as members of a cultural community (see Figure 25).[42]

In New Orleans, establishments such as the Big 25, Funky Butt Hall, Carrington's Saloon at 818 Rampart (described in one police report as "a Negro dive of the lowest type")[43], and Animule Hall afforded working-class blacks similar opportunities. By Danny Barker's account, the patrons of Animule Hall—stevedores, field hands, steel-driving men, washer-women, female factory hands—who came each Saturday evening, dressed smartly, the men in "box-back suits, high, broad-rimmed Stetson hats, yellow shoes (called yellow yams), and the women mostly [in] common gingham dresses, starched and ironed stiff." Well into the early hours of the

Figure 25: Marion Post Wolcott's photograph of a juke joint in Clarksdale, Mississippi, 1939. Courtesy of Mississippi Department of Archives and History

morning, Animule's patrons danced to the blues music of Long Head Bob's Social Orchestra, a music that, as Albert Murray points out, is a "good-time music" that "almost always induces dance movement that is the direct opposite of resignation, retreat, or defeat." In these ways, hardships could be forgotten and the blues driven away, if only for a time.[44]

For New Orleans's black middle class, more "worthwhile" premises were available, or so, at any rate, declared the *Louisiana Weekly* of January 16, 1926, in the first installment of a regular feature to be known as the "Folly Column." Readers of this African American publication were informed that the city's Parisian Roof Garden, the "most beautiful Roof Garden for Colored people in the United States" and a veritable "palace of pleasurable dances," was open "Monday, Wednesday, Friday and Sunday, . . . from 9 to 12," and that, for any "who ha[d] not stilled the irresistable [*sic*] desire to dance at such an hour as 12 a.m. . . . the Dreamland Cafe should fill the bill." "'Tis folly to listen long to the song of the Goddess Jazzmania," the writer added in mock apology, "but this is the Folly Column and the most righteous of us must admit that such folly is indeed enjoyable"—which is to say that, though elegantly clad and "respectable," the clientele of Dreamland Cafe danced to music that was hot. In its next edition, the *Weekly* announced that the Pelican, on Gravier and South Rampart, the city's "newest and largest dance hall," was about to open to the public. This venue would be "class A1, up to date in every way," with "a rest room for ladies, with a lady attendant," "choice lounges and dressing tables," a "free telephone," and a modern smoking room. In such settings, more well-to-do African Americans, their bodies clothed pridefully in fashionable evening wear, staged their own kind of glittering social parade.

Descriptions of clothing and dance styles feature in accounts of Beale Street's entertainment venues as well. Piano Red (John Williams) described the patrons of the Monarch, the "classiest" club in town, as "real dressed up, gambling men with diamond rings on and suits of clothes." As for the pimps, "you'd thought it was a preacher or lawyer, the way they dressed then. . . . They had tailor-made suits, nice gray and blue serge, and brown broadcloth, Manhattan shirts, and Stacy Adams shoes, and Knox hats and stetsons." Not infrequently, the pimps would exchange one clothing ensemble for another during the day. "Yes, Lord," Williams declared, "they were nice dressers. Wear two-and-a-half-dollar gold pieces in his cuff links, five dollar gold piece for a stickpin."[45] At Pee Wee's, which served as headquarters for W. C. Handy's bands and many other black musicians, one could see "glittering young devils in silk toppers and Prince Alberts."[46]

The dance scene on Beale was lively too. Early in the evening, long-time resident Nat D. Williams remembered, patrons of Beale Street's black working-class clubs would dance in the manner of whites, but later, when the "drink got to hitting just right, then people would do the type of dancing that suited them. You did what the spirit told you. If it said, 'Jump up and kick,' you jumped up and kicked. If it said, 'Turn around,' you'd turn around." African Americans could easily execute the "polite movements" characteristic of white dancing styles, Williams explained, but "when they got to the place where they felt they could release, just go on and enjoy themselves, they'd give a show." Better-educated blacks were not supposed to attend clubs of this type, but "sometimes if you took a notion to go native, . . . you'd be there jumping yourself and look over in the corner and there's another friend over there doing the same thing."[47] That sort of vigorous dancing could prove expensive. "At that time," Piano Red (John Williams) recalled, "women shoes costed one dollar and thirty-nine cents. And the next morning, they be in there 'catching the tiger' and doing the 'scratch' and be just as barefooted as a goose. Had nothing but the tops; done danced the soles plumb out."[48]

From W. C. Handy comes another striking, if more decorous, image of African American dance, this time at Memphis's Dixie Park. Here, the more than one thousand dancers resembled "a monstrous pin wheel, blazing with color and spinning magically," the whole scene becoming "an extravaganza, a pageant, a sea of gliding figures . . . ebony hands, brown hands, yellow hands, ivory hands, all moving in coordination with nimble dancing feet," and "gay smiling faces that had forgotten yesterday and never heard of tomorrow."[49] In such Memphis venues, and similar sites of night-time entertainment throughout the South, the African American body, so often the object of racist distortion, was proudly displayed and, in Paul Gilroy's words, "celebrated as an instrument of pleasure rather than an instrument of labor."[50]

Black clubs were not always as peaceful as these accounts suggest. New Orleans's Animule Hall received its name from the behavior of its patrons, who, as the night wore on and the cheap liquor took its toll, could become, in Danny Barker's words, "very antagonistic, belligerent, nasty, vulgar and provocative." As a result, challenges were issued and fights broke out. When violence erupted, Joe Baggers, the bouncer, allowed the contestants to settle the matter, using only their bare hands, while he kept the cheering crowds at bay by wielding an iron pipe. He would then eject the loser from the hall. In these fights, Danny Barker says, "men battled like bears and women like wildcats. . . . Most times the women fought until they were naked on the floor." In the early hours of the morning, at a signal from Joe Baggers, Long Head Bob's Social Orchestra would play the slow, slow drag and couples would begin dancing to the "sexy, body-twisting blues." But as dancers were discovered belly-rubbing with someone else's lover, the fighting would intensify. At a signal from Joe Baggers to the policeman on duty, Animule would be raided, and the rioters arrested and charged with disturbing the peace. Closing time at Animule was 3 a.m., but the evening's events never lasted that long.[51] Zora Neale Hurston also told of the violence that often seemed just below the surface at black entertainment sites. During a folklore-collecting expedition in 1927, Hurston and a woman called Big Sweet, who acted as her protector, attended a juke at a Florida lumber camp; when Big Sweet became involved in a fierce argument with two other women, knives were drawn and bloodshed was averted only by the intervention of a quarters boss, armed with two pistols.[52]

The contrast between New Orleans's Animule Hall on the one hand and its Parisian Roof Garden on the other signals once again the existence of class differences within the black community. Patrons of the Parisian Roof Garden and similar venues, who wore elegant clothing by night, were likely, by day, to have dressed in a "respectable," understated fashion, eschewing the more showy garments often favored by less well-off blacks. Hortense Powdermaker, who studied African American life in Indianola, Mississippi, in the late 1930s, noted that the "chief distinction" between the clothing of lower- and higher-class blacks was that "women of higher social status deliberately avoided bright colors" and were "offended if clerks in the stores assume that they want something 'loud.'" Not only were these better-off African Americans "pained by the Negro's reputation for wearing gaudy clothes," but "[a] few [were] sensitive about the insistence of some Negroes on having sound front teeth adorned with gold, when they cannot pay for dentistry needed on their back teeth." Disdaining such ostentatious display, middle-class blacks dressed with "quiet good taste."[53]

This understated style was certainly adopted by the African Americans depicted by the black photographer, Richard Samuel Roberts, in Columbia, South Carolina, in the 1920s. Roberts's studies plainly announce the desire of his subjects—dressmakers, morticians, nurses, barber-shop proprietors, physicians, pastors, teachers, college professors, grocers, cabinet makers, government officials, and members of their respective families—to present themselves as dignified, respectable and serious, certainly not flamboyant in any sense. Roberts's subjects are formally posed, often against a painted backdrop of plush drapery, flower-bedecked pillars and "a stylized cathedral window." They are conservatively dressed, usually in tailor-made gowns or suits, and their erect posture and firm gaze registers cool self-possession and pride in their hard-won social status.[54] The dress of these African Americans would easily have been distinguishable, by night as well as by day, from that of the working-class clientele of Animule Hall or of the glittering denizens of Beale Street's night spots.

Class differences were encoded in hairstyles as well, though here the picture is more blurred. Many of the women in Richard Samuel Roberts's studies have their hair styled in what, in the 1920s, was considered the modern way. By the time Roberts took his photographs, the use of new hair treatment techniques, notably those associated with the Madam C. J. Walker and Poro systems, was widespread in the South, and large beauty salons, operating in urban centers, were busily catering to a predominantly middle-class clientele. In the hairdressing department of Madame Eva B. White's Beauty Parlor and College in New Orleans, the *Louisiana Weekly* told its readers in February 1926, "twelve operators are constantly turning out practically twelve patrons at once." Specialties of Madame White's establishment included hair bobbing, curling, and marcelling, and trade was brisk: "Two thousand regular semi-monthly patrons are booked, besides the drop-ins." This "modernly equipped" salon—a large photograph on the *Weekly's* front page offered a view of its plush interior—was open from early in the morning and operated six days a week.[55]

Middle-class African American women, however, were not the only patrons of commercial hairdressing establishments. After observing that the beauty industry was thriving in Indianola, as in many other cities throughout the South, Hortense Powdermaker noted that even very poor women "go to a hair-dresser regularly, to have their hair greased and 'pressed.'" If money was short, a chicken might be offered as payment for these coiffures.[56] So popular among black women of all classes were commercial hair treatments that some Georgia towns, concerned that burgeoning employment levels in the cosmetics industry were depleting the supply of rural and domestic labor, imposed punitive taxes on hairdressing businesses, hoping thereby to ruin them.[57]

As a supplement to this commercial hair-styling activity, Southern black women from across a broad spectrum of income levels, and working from their homes, frequently dressed the hair of neighbors and friends. In his autobiography, *Colored People,* Henry Louis Gates, Jr., includes a wonderfully evocative account of his mother's hair-styling activities in the kitchen of the family home in Piedmont, West Virginia, a description that recalls the communal nature of slave hair-grooming practices.

> But the most important thing about our gas-equipped kitchen was that Mama used to do hair there. She had a "hot comb"—a fine-toothed iron instrument with a long wooden handle—and a pair of iron curlers that opened and closed like scissors: Mama would put them into the gas fire until they glowed. You could smell those prongs heating up.
>
> I liked what that smell meant for the shape of my day. There was an intimate warmth in the women's tones as they talked with my mama while she did their hair. I knew what the women had been through to get their hair ready to be "done," because I would watch Mama do it to herself. How that scorched kink could be transformed through grease and fire into a magnificent head of wavy hair was a miracle to me. Still is.[58]

Among many rural women, however, there was some sturdy class and generational resistance to anything that smacked of modern cosmetic methods. These women continued to wrap, braid, and cornrow their hair in the time-honored manner and also to dress young black girls' hair in the same way.[59] When Mamie Garvin Fields introduced new hair-styling techniques to the girls at the James Island school at which she taught, one mother, whose own hair was "wrapped the traditional way, with multicolor thread and a bandanna on top," berated her the following morning: "I ain' sen' my chile ya fo' to fix he-yah. I sen' em fo' *lun.* You let ee he-yuh stay like I hahv 'em!"[60] The former slave Jane Michens Toombs also appears to have regarded modern hair-processing techniques with uniform disdain. Recalling her early years in Georgia, she informed her W.P.A. interviewer that "ef a nigger wanted ter git de kinks out'n dey hair dey combed hit wid de cards. Now dey puts all kinds ov grease on hit, an' buy straightenin' combs. . . . Old fashion cards'll straighten hair jess as well as all dis high smellin' stuff dey sells now." [61] Ex-slave Mary Williams, of Arkansas, was equally dismissive. "I don't think nothin' of this here younger generation," she asserted. "They say to me, 'Why don't you have your hair straightened' but I say 'I've got along this far without painted jaws and straight hair! And I ain't goin' wear my dresses up to my knees or trail 'em in the mud, either.'" [62]

The usual interpretation placed on much of this hair-straightening activity (and black men, with their preference for close-clipped hair and their use of grease, stocking caps, pomades, and processes, are taken to have been similarly engaged) is that it was a dubiously successful attempt by African Americans to make their hair look more like that of whites. Subjected over a long period of years to derogatory references to, and distorted images of, their physical appearance, blacks, so the argument goes, had internalized whites' conceptions of beauty. By straightening their hair and lightening their skin, they hoped more nearly to approximate white standards. The wording of advertisements for hair treatments, and, more obviously, those for preparations promising a lighter complexion (not to mention the sheer volume of such advertisements in the African American press) certainly supports these assumptions. So, unforgettably, does the fantasy of revenge created by a young Maya Angelou, embarrassed before the other children in her church because of her appearance: "I was going to look like one of the sweet little white girls who were everybody's dream of what was right with the world. . . . Wouldn't they be surprised when one day I woke out of my black ugly dream, and my real hair, which was long and blond, would take the place of the kinky mass that Momma wouldn't let me straighten? My light-blue eyes were going to hypnotize them." [63]

Without denying the force of these imperatives, it is possible to see other meanings in the early twentieth-century vogue for hair straightening. Straightening of the hair, which is to say, removing the knots and some of the kinkiness from it, was nothing new in African American life. It had been an important part of African American, indeed African, cosmetic activity long before Madam C. J. Walker or any of her rivals in the cosmetics industry were born. Whether accomplished by traditional or modern methods, straightening was a practical necessity if some sort of styling were to be accomplished, a preliminary to styling, not its end point. Once that is recognized, advertisements for hair-straightening compounds appear in a somewhat different light. To Mamie Garvin Fields, the main significance of the improved, modern methods of hair straightening was that they broadened the opportunities for creative display; they "made it possible for black women to straighten their hair and then style it in whatever way they wanted to." [64] If those women then chose to borrow from prevailing white styles, that would hardly be a first in African American history, or necessarily an admission of perceived inferiority. Straightening the hair may be seen not as a sign of a defective black consciousness but as an integral part of a time-honored creative process. As Gates's discussion of his mother's hair-straightening and styling activities (and of his own deep admiration for Nat King Cole's "process") suggests, to dismiss such practices as "slavish copying" of whites omits virtually everything that is interesting about them. [65]

Although streets and entertainment venues in black neighborhoods allowed African Americans rich opportunities for self-expression, it was within the welcoming sanctuary of the black church, as well as during their Sunday journeys to and from it, that they discovered their most frequent opportunity for aesthetic display. In the world outside the church, the everyday clothing of many blacks was often rudimentary. Arthur F. Raper, who surveyed African American life in the Georgia Black Belt counties of Green and Macon in the early 1930s, reported that "most of the farm Negroes . . . literally live in overalls, in winter wearing one or more pairs of old pants under them, in summer wearing them 'agin de skin.'" Raper heard from black schoolteachers that some children were unable to attend school because their clothing was inadequate, and he himself saw children going barefoot in the middle of winter. It was only rarely that rural women or their daughters obtained a new dress, and when they did such garments were likely to be cut from cheap materials. The few items of clothing possessed by very young children were often made from feed- or salt-sacks. [66] Sacking was utilized by adults as well. Describing conditions in Mississippi in the 1930s, Ruth E. Bass stated that older African American women wore bandanna handkerchiefs made from "checked or flowered cotton, or a white flour sack," and, except on Sundays, "starched cotton aprons, many of them fashioned from well-washed and sometimes dried fertilizer sacks." Though canvas shoes were becoming more common among both the old and the young, it was not unusual for rural blacks to go barefoot for part of the year. [67] Loyle Hairston, born in Mississippi in 1926, remembers how poorly dressed the country children were who came to his mother's school classes, the boys in their "faded overalls, often patched at the knees and seat and denim jumpers and brogan shoes or rubber boots," the girls in "homemade gingham dresses and ragged ill-fitting coats." [68] Charles Evers, who was born in Decatur, Mississippi, in 1922, and his brother Medgar, went barefoot every spring and summer. Every two years their father would buy each child two pairs of shoes, one pair (always two sizes too big to allow for growth) for Sunday wear, and the other, "heavy, lace-up brogans," for winter. In summer, the boys removed their Sunday shoes immediately after church; in winter, they exchanged them for brogans as soon as they reached home. "If Daddy caught us playing in our Sunday shoes," Charles Evers has recalled, "he'd whip us good." The family practiced similar economies with clothing. "We'd have to go pull off our Sunday clothes, too. We had one pair of green tweed pants for Sunday, and we'd pull them off as soon as we came back from church or come from a funeral. We'd put on coveralls, Medgar and me; or an old pair of blue jeans. And blue jeans, even to this day, remind me of how poor we were. It's a personal thing now. I just can't put blue jeans on to save my life." [69]

As description after description makes clear, however, the freedom that blacks had won in slavery times to dress up for weekly religious observances continued into the postslavery period, and throughout the South, even during Jim Crow's most oppressive years, African Americans continued to exchange their tattered, faded, functional weekday apparel for showy Sunday attire. South African Maurice Evans, who studied race relations in the American South in the early twentieth century, thought the dress of African American urban congregations "more fashionable, with apparently more spent on gewgaws and frippery, than that of a middle-class English congregation probably ten times as wealthy." Young black male and female churchgoers were "often adorned in ultra fashionable attire" and were "obviously conscious of their finery." Evans surmised that "love of display enter[ed] largely into the attractiveness of church attendance." [70] In rural areas, the contrast between everyday and Sunday attire was even more striking. Lura Beam, who, as a superintendent of schools, traveled through the South in the second decade of the twentieth century, wrote that "[a] shack on the edge of nowhere would send to Sunday church two well-dressed children and a teenager with daisies on her hat." [71] Anthropologist Hortense Powdermaker, investigating conditions in the deep South in the late 1930s, was surprised by the standards of dress observed by members of a rural black Baptist church. "Men, women, and children are all in their best clothes," she wrote, and "on the hottest Sunday in August, the men wear their coats and the women their hats."[72] An African American rural storekeeper in Clairborne County, Mississippi, told Allison Davis that white people often complained that local blacks dressed better than they did. "And it's really the truth," the woman said. "You see these poor farm people and tenants goin' by here to church, and the men have on good well-cared-for suits, and nice ties and shirts and hats, and the women will have on good dresses they buy in Old City, and shoes, you know, and they'll have their hair all fixed and curled!" The storekeeper recalled for Davis an occasion on which, not wishing to embarrass local folk, a visiting churchwoman of some importance had worn everyday clothing to a local service, only to discover that the women of that small rural congregation dressed better than did those in Natchez.[73]

Sunday was "the best day of the week," plantation owner and writer Julia Peterkin decided after studying African American life in rural South Carolina in the early 1930s. On that day "Christians and sinners dress up in their best clothes, whether they expect to go to church or not." On Sunday mornings, women whose hair had been "wrapped all week in small tight rolls wound with ball thread" unwrapped it, combed it, rewrapped it, and covered it with a brightly colored bandanna. Those with short hair treated it with a relaxing compound and straightened it with an iron. As women donned their "finery," the men "walk around, looking and feeling important in their store-bought clothes and shoes." With hats "cocked jauntily on the side of their heads," they "visit . . . neighbors or gather in groups along the roads to talk." Young women appeared "very smart" in dresses and hats bought from local stores or obtained through mail-order catalogues, and while most men dressed conservatively, some left price tags on their suits to indicate that the suits were new and had been bought rather than made at home. Some of the young men were, however, "inclined to be gaudy" and wore "purple or green 'peg-top' trousers, with square-cut box coats of another color, along with bright tan shoes and fancy socks and loud ties."[74] "Colored people," white Mississippi resident Willa Johnson declared, "are very fond of fixy clothes and seldom do we find one who has not at least one dress-up outfit." Though blacks might "go about during the week in raggedness," Sunday was "a day of dress."

As in slavery times, the aggressive color combinations preferred by southern blacks attracted whites' attention. African Americans, Willa Johnson averred, showed a "decided taste for vivid colors," so that, "without hesitation, green, yellow and red are clashed together" and a "wild colored sash" was often added for effect. Black women, Johnson declared, would "spend [their] last dime for a color-crazy effect."[75] Lura Beam called the "color combinations" in African American clothing "exciting." "Negroes put red and pink and orange together before Matisse did," she observed. "Women who could wear only gray and blue in slavery came out in yellow, orange, cerise, green, scarlet, magenta and purple. Matrons in their best clothes displayed an opulent color sense, topped by hats that were extravaganzas. They had a characteristic style."[76] The preference for strong, vibrant colors was also noted by English artists Jan and Cora Gordon, who watched female students attending a religious service at Atlanta's Spelman College in 1927, even if its cultural significance eluded them. The Gordons decided that the young women "had not yet that touchy sense of white folks' ridicule which has made the northern Negro so self-conscious." The students "did not know that, because the traditional Mammy wore bright colours, therefore bright colours were taboo; so they wore what colours they liked and made a pretty bouquet as they filed into chapel on a morning."[77]

The African American church, to which countless well-dressed blacks throughout the rural and urban South made their way each Sunday, gave its members a sense of self-esteem customarily denied them. In black churches, "field hands were deacons, and maids were ushers, mothers of the church, or trustees," positions of respect and authority often signified by the wearing of special uniforms or accessories. The young women who showed members and visitors to their seats in a rural Baptist church that Powdermaker visited "[wore] around their heads stiff bands of white on which the word 'Usher' [was] embroidered," and white cotton gloves.[78] In the Rock Hill Baptist Church at Chapel Hill, North Carolina, which Agnes Brown attended in the late 1930s, the choir was attired in black robes, set off, in the case of women members, with large white collars; female ushers wore black dresses with white buttons, collars and cuffs, and male ushers dark suits, white shirts, black bow ties, and "at least one white glove." Senior ushers displayed distinctive metal badges, their junior colleagues small felt flags.[79] But the manner in which African American churchgoers constructed their appearance has a more general significance. By abandoning shabby work clothes, or such negative signifiers as mob caps and bib-aprons, for more dignified Sunday attire—clothes which, as Arthur Raper expressed it, were "not made to work in"[80]—black churchgoers were repudiating white society's evaluation of the black body as an instrument of menial labor. They were declaring, in effect, that there was more to life than work, and that a sense of dignity and self-worth could survive the depredations of an avowedly racist society. Work clothes—nondescript and uniform—tended to erase the black body; Sunday clothing enhanced and proclaimed it (see Figure 26).

In this private world of African Americans' own making, meanings were conveyed not merely through dress but through a range of culturally distinctive bodily movements that characterized religious celebrations. When R. Emmet Kennedy visited a number of black churches in the rural South in the early 1930s for the purpose of recording spirituals and other religious songs, the sense of cultural difference he experienced related, in significant degree, to the near-constant physical movement of the various congregations. Everywhere, singing was accompanied by "the rhythmic clapping of hands and patting of feet." Among members of the Sanctified Church, "dancing before the altar [was] an important feature of their ritual." After one of the churches Kennedy visited had filled, a "mournful humming" began, in response to which the congregation began "to sway like an undulating wave." Testimonies given by church members were "accentuated at times with hand clapping and boisterous stamping." As the congregation began to sing a holy song, adults and children stood up and began to dance. Before long they moved into the aisles and, as Kennedy related, "advance slowly towards the altar platform, where they continue to express themselves with joyful abandon," though "no two of them appear to be doing the same step." Deacons, their Bibles put aside, "join the celebration, doing fantastic steps and contortions on either side of the rostrum." An elder "walks back and forth, encouraging the harmonious tumult with loud hand clapping and vociferous singing."[81] During an evangelist's address to a revival meeting at a Chapel Hill church in 1938, Agnes Brown reported, the preacher vigorously acted out the biblical events with which he illustrated his sermon, such as the release of Paul from prison and the raising of Lazarus from the dead. As he moved energetically from side to side in the pulpit, the congregation "swayed with him."[82] During the prayers

Figure 26: Clothes "not made to work in." Eudora Welty's photograph of the preacher and church leaders, Holiness Church, Jackson, Mississippi, 1939. Eudora Welty Collection, Mississippi Department of Archives and History

and the sermon at a small Baptist church near Natchez, which Hortense Powdermaker attended, the congregation beat time with their feet, and during the otherwise unaccompanied singing, Powdermaker observed, "many wave their hands in rhythm, and clap out the beats." [83]

In offering a scriptural justification for his congregation's dancing, an elder from the church which R. Emmet Kennedy attended referred to the fifteenth chapter of the Book of Exodus, which told "how Aaron sister took a cymbal in her hand, an' all the women went after her with cymbals an' with dancin'." Holy dancing was altogether different from the kind of dancing indulged in by unbelievers at frolics and balls, the elder declared, and "the kind of gladness that makes these people want to dance in the house of Gawd, ain't the same kind of feelin' *a-tall* them pleasure-seekin' people has when you see 'um get up an' strut in the common dance-hall." [84] Zora Neale Hurston's explanation was cultural rather than theological. Referring to the Sanctified Church, which she contrasted with more high-brow black Protestant congregations that were prone to adopt white ways, Hurston noted that "the service is really drama with music," and that "since music without motion is unnatural among Negroes there is always something that approaches dancing—in fact *IS* dancing—in such a ceremony." "Negro songs," Hurston declared, "are one and all based on a dance-possible rhythm." [85]

Hurston's reference to the all-but-inevitable confluence of music and movement in black life points to a deeper cultural influence. West African religions knew nothing of the dualism in Western culture between mind and body, or, in religious parlance, between spirit and flesh. Whereas, as Sheila Walker has observed, in most Christian worship "the activity of the body is suspended," in West African cultures dancing was integral to religious celebrations. As J. H. Kwabena Nketia tells us, "in the [Akan] dancing ring, participants . . . mime and interpret the rhythms of drummers . . . and mime the dramatic actions of storytellers," "especially attractive rhythms" being "accompanied by shoulder and head movements, foot stamping and hand clapping, and vocal shouts from spectators, dancers, and singers." [86] "So essential are music and dance to West African religious expression," Albert Raboteau has written, "that it is no exaggeration to call them 'danced religions.'" Though the complex syncretic process that blended West African and European religious observances in the New World obviously produced many variants, rhythmic bodily movements, ranging from the ecstatic dancing impelled by the Spirit to gentle swaying and (as a replacement for the drums) the rhythmic patting of hands or feet, remained a distinctive element of African American religious services.[87]

Again, the general pattern of clothing and movement styles described above, a pattern which depicts religious practices in rural and poorer urban black churches, was modified by class differences within the African American community. Broadly speaking, the higher up the socio-economic scale black congregations were, the more likely were they to disdain "ostentation" in dress or manner of worship, the so-called "gaudy" clothing and ecstatic behavior of working-class congregations. At the very top of the social order, it was not uncommon for the black elite to seek and achieve membership in white churches, where the bold clothing ensembles and degree of enthusiastic participation common in many black Baptist, African Methodist Episcopal, or Sanctified Church congregations would have had no conceivable place.

In the culture-affirming, interactive space of most Southern black churches, however, and particularly within the numerically dominant working-class congregations, African Americans reaffirmed their sense of cultural identity. Smart clothes, distinctive uniforms, and often vividly colored official robes communicated a sense of dignity and pride, and the expressive movement of the saints' bodies—in off-beat clapping and swaying, in holy dancing, in the synchronic waving of outstretched hands, in the rhythmic patting of feet—gave collective expression to the passion and joy they felt. In a world largely of their own making, these African Americans framed an alternative reality.[88] Rejecting evaluations of themselves by white society, they made strong visual statements about their identity and worth, and, free of white oversight and control, displayed the cultural forms that allowed them to transcend, for a time, the harsh circumstances of their everyday lives.

The Long-Veiled Beauty of Our Own World

Precisely at 8:00 p.m. on the night of Saturday, August 17, 1912, Master William M. Porter flicked the switch that would open black Chicago's State Street Carnival. Instantly, a section of this major thoroughfare between 31st and 35th Streets, commonly known as "The Stroll," burst into a blaze of light as a canopy of thousands of electric globes illuminated the richly decorated black business establishments. As the onlookers' initial gasps of wonderment subsided, the Elks' Military band struck up and strode out, leading a Grand Parade through the heart of Black Chicago. Over the Carnival's next two weeks much the same mixture of modernity and tradition enthralled African Americans, entertaining adults and entrancing children. The Stroll was lined with merry-go-rounds and ferris wheels; the brand-new $20,000 calliope, or steam organ, constantly made

181

The
Long-
Veiled
Beauty of
Our Own
World

the rounds, competing with numerous bands for the crowd's attention; and every night parades organized by various black associations criss-crossed the South Side. Among the Carnival's other attractions were a Jungleland show, Zazell's Old Plantation with its 100 boys and girls, Chiquita, a twenty-two-inch-tall lady weighing in at twenty-four pounds, and Mazeppa, a horse that could play musical instruments and use the telephone. Promoters of this gala event, including Jesse Binga, the most prominent African American businessman in the city, the *Chicago Defender*, one of the nation's most important black newspapers, and other black business houses, aimed to make State Street "a veritable walk of light and beauty" so that "people sit up and take notice of us as a people." [1]

The State Street Carnival was a well-organized display of imagination and vision, a creative amalgam of Barnum, the Chicago World's Fair, the minstrel show, the county fair, and other commercialized entertainments of the nineteenth century. It was also an event that had distinct echoes of eighteenth- and early nineteenth-century northern black festivals. But what was especially novel about this African American spectacle was that it took place in the middle of America's fastest-growing city, a city whose State street and South Side were, by the second decade of the century, beginning to cement a reputation among African Americans as the new promised land.

The climax of the carnival came with the crowning of the Queen on the Wednesday evening of the second week. Voting for the "most beautiful woman in Chicago" (no mention of color was made) was open to anyone who clipped a coupon out of the *Defender* and mailed it in. Alternatively, votes could be registered by those who attended any of the shows during the Carnival's first week or made purchases from special booths on State Street. The winner, Miss Hattie Holliday, described by the *Defender* as "Chicago's Most Bewitching and Popular Young Woman," garnered 37,098 votes, and between them the three most popular young women accumulated 87,210 votes, figures all the more remarkable when it is considered that, according to the 1910 census, there were only 44,103 black residents in the city at that time. The contest's celebratory procession began at Jesse Binga's bank at 9 o'clock in the evening, with the Eighth Regiment band providing the music. Behind the band came the soon-to-be crowned queen and four little girls riding on an elephant (one of the *Defender*'s many headlines read "First Woman of the Race to Ride an Elephant Outside of Africa").

Somewhere in the vicinity of 10,000 people gathered at 36th and State to watch Miss Holiday, garbed in Royal Purple (see Figures 27 & 28), accept her prize of a one-hundred dollar bill from Jesse Binga and a crown and scepter from Col. Marshall. Reflecting on the fortnight's events, Jesse Binga declared the Carnival "the greatest race achievement in the history of Chicago."[2]

Of course, the organizers of the State Street Carnival had not invented the idea of either a beauty queen or a beauty contest. As Lois Banner has shown, in the decades after Barnum held the first modern beauty contest in 1854, numerous events of this type were held in association with festivals, expositions, carnivals, and dime museums or organized by newspapers. This was not even the first contest for African Americans. A brief notice in the *New York Times* in 1877 recorded the results of a colored baby show, at which prizes were awarded for "Best One-year Old," "Best Two-year Old" and more curiously, if not ominously, "Whitest Mother" and "Blackest Mother." In Philadelphia, in November 1900, white organizers welcomed African Americans and their money to the Grace Baptist Temple's fair but

THE CROWNING OF THE CARNIVAL QUEEN

A Flashlight Photograph of a Few of the Many Thousands That Viewed the Crowning of Miss Hattie Holliday, Wednesday Night.

Figure 27: *Chicago Defender*, August 31, 1912.

Figure 28: *Chicago Defender*, August 31, 1912.

excluded black children from the "baby show": the committee, swayed by the "blandishments" of white mothers, "sent word to the colored mothers that 'they needn't come 'round.'" At this point, the *Philadelphia Item* intervened and organized a separate contest for black children, with numerous prizes, including the "finest baby-carriage in Philadelphia," worth some $27. But the exclusion of blacks in the first place, and the way in which the *Item* promoted and wrote up the contest, with pieces on the front page talking of the "grand pickaninny contest," almost certainly offended Philadelphia's African Americans; only twenty-seven contestants entered, far fewer than the paper seemed to expect. Although in the South at this time there was never any question of whites and blacks entering the same competition, similar contests were held there. At the black celebration of the Fourth of July at Piedmont Park in Atlanta in 1892, for example, the "event of the day" was a baby show featuring about "six hundred lusty little ones." Local societies and church groups, in the South as well as the North, occasionally used beauty contests to raise funds. Thus, in 1909, the St. Paul's AME church in Rockingham County, North Carolina, held what Sharon Ann Holt has called "a species of beauty contest," at which the young woman who raised "the most cash in tribute to her beauty was declared the winner." Proceeds went to the building fund.[3] Notwithstanding these various activities, however, the State Street Carnival's spectacular selection of its queen prefigured an interest in African American beauty and in the display of female African American bodies that would fascinate blacks and many whites in the interwar years.

As we have already seen, even under slavery African Americans had devoted precious free time to the care of their hair and to their general appearance. In the South, these activities continued after freedom, especially on Sunday mornings in preparation for attendance at church, though mainly on a private and non-commercial basis. By the turn of the century, the swelling black populations of northern cities had created an urban African American consumer market of some significance, and commercial beauty products—at first hair oils and later creams for the face—quickly became a regular item in the expenditure of many blacks, even those who were hardly well-off. Black women were the major purchasers, but very soon black men too realized that the new hair preparations allowed them more creative scope in styling their hair. In 1911 the *Age* wryly drew attention to what it called the "latest fad," asking "Have you had your hair

185

*The
Long-
Veiled
Beauty of
Our Own
World*

straightened yet?" "Up and around 135th Street and Lenox Avenue," the story continued, "colored men can be seen in large numbers who are wont to take off their hats repeatedly . . . and stroke their glossy hair with their hand in an affectionate manner."[4] What the *Age* reporter had observed was rather more significant than a mere fad; almost certainly, it was an early ancestor of the conk, a style favored by many African American males in the 1930s and 1940s, most notably the young Malcolm X.

Initially, most of these products were manufactured by white establishments, but early this century a remarkable group of black entrepreneurs, including Anthony Overton, Annie Turnbo Malone and, most famously, Madame C. J. Walker, started their own businesses and managed to secure a share of the market. In part, this initiative seems to have been prompted by the patronizing, exploitative, and demeaning way some of the white companies treated black customers—in 1916 the *Defender* reprinted a circular letter, sent by the company promoting Palmolive Soap to white retailers, which concluded with the phrase "Yours for Nigger Business"— but, more interestingly, the cosmetics business appears to have been one of the few areas of commercial activity in which black consumers showed a preference for products manufactured and marketed by African Americans.[5]

As Kathy Peiss has shown, Anthony Overton aggressively pushed his products into mainstream routes of distribution. At an Exposition in Chicago in 1915, a correspondent of the *Defender* noted, by far the most popular stand was that of the Overton Hygienic Company, where "several pretty and charming girls tell you all about the High Brown powder." Indeed, the reporter "could hardly make his way to the exhibit, the crowd was so thick." In 1918, Overton became the first African American to have his product sold by Woolworths. Probably even more important were the networks set up by women entrepreneurs. Annie Malone's "Poro System" for styling the hair and Madame Walker's hair-care techniques were taught in beauty schools to thousands of young black women, and, since the costs involved in starting a business were modest, many graduates of these schools promptly set up shop, often beginning out of their kitchens and tending to the needs of friends and neighbors. A series of conventions, dating from the 1910s, allowed operators to meet and find out about new products and techniques and gave a rudimentary organization to this new commercial activity (see Figures 29 and 30). Though by the end of World War One signs of the burgeoning beauty industry were evident wherever there were

Figures 29 & 30: These photographs of the first convention of the traveling salesmen of the Overton Hygienic Manufacturing Company held in Chicago in 1916, and a gathering of Poro agents in Birmingham, Alabama, in 1912, highlight the different approaches these businesses took. Both Madame Poro and Madame Walker utilized a large number of African American women, whereas Overton relied on a few African American salesmen. *Half Century Magazine,* August 1916, 10. *The Light* 3 (February 19, 1927), 21. Chicago Historical Society

concentrations of African Americans in the South as well as in the North, this new field of black commercial endeavor was most evident in northern cities. In Chicago, for example, the 1920 Blue Book, a directory of black businesses in the city, listed no fewer than 211 barbers and 108 hairdressing shops, figures which did not include the numerous establishments run by women operating part-time out of their homes, always an important characteristic of the black cosmetics industry. Only groceries and delicatessens, with 119 establishments, registered anything like these figures.[6]

The rapidly expanding cosmetics industry made a considerable impact on African American life, and it and its products have remained a lasting and important aspect of twentieth-century black culture. Not only did hair treatments, for example, make hair more malleable, allowing scope for "fashion" and for changing the way most black women and many black men chose to look, but, for many African American women, the consequent and seemingly insatiable demand for cosmetic products of all sorts opened up the possibility that they could work for themselves, rather than as domestic servants for white employers. Furthermore, both the black and white manufacturers of these products were acutely aware of the power of advertising and of the importance of giving their product a prominent profile, and the space they bought was extremely important to the always-precarious finances of the black press. When, in 1925, Guy Johnson conducted a rudimentary content analysis of the advertisements in a selection of black newspapers, he found that almost 80 percent of those in the *Defender* and *Negro World* (the Garvey paper) were devoted to products listed in his category C, which included notices for good luck charms, clairvoyance, and firearms but was preponderantly made up of promotional material for beauty preparations. Johnson's study may not have been all that sophisticated, but a ten-minute perusal of any of the prominent black newspapers in the 1910s or 1920s will easily convince the reader of the importance of this sort of advertising.[7]

Cosmetic products, often abbreviated to the shorthand of hair straighteners and skin whiteners, were controversial at the time, and, if anything, have become more so since. In 1909, the *New York Times* weighed in with a ponderous piece attacking advertisements that implied that "negroes should be ashamed of their own features and should by all means mask them into some resemblance to the Caucasian race." "While the negro disesteems himself and seeks to be something else," the *Times* concluded rhetorically, "will he be respected as he is?" This was hardly the first occasion, and nor would it be the last, on which the *New York Times* managed to simplify and distort a complex aspect of black life and culture.[8]

On the one hand, it is undeniable that color discrimination had been and would continue to be an important and debilitating factor in African American life. For the most part, very dark-skinned African Americans, particularly women, were treated much worse than were their brown-skinned or very light counterparts, a phenomenon discernible in everything from blues lyrics and jokes through to the behavior of children in the schoolyard. Undoubtedly some blacks had internalized whites' conceptions of beauty and saw the new cosmetics as a means of improving their status, but it seems unlikely that this was generally the case; Madame Walker, for instance, emphatically denied that her products were designed to do anything of the sort. What is crucial here is context. As Kathy Peiss has shown, in the late nineteenth century cosmetics were associated with prostitutes—the painted woman as whore—but by 1920 they were accepted by respectable women as an essential part of everyday life. The boom in African American cosmetics occurred in the middle of, and was an important part of, this larger transformation. It was not so much that most African Americans who used cosmetic preparations wanted to look white; it was more often the case that they wanted the same freedom to construct their appearance that whites were allowed.[9]

The other point to bear in mind here is that most blacks who used these creams and hair preparations simply did not, as a result, look white. In much the same way as the young white college women in the 1920s, who unabashedly and obviously used rouge, powder and lipstick, African American women were drawing attention to their face and highlighting the artificiality of their appearance.[10] The look of a young African American woman, whose features were clearly made-up and whose hair had been straightened, bobbed, and dyed red, was not some pathetic and inept attempt to imitate white mores. What it did signify, however—and here there was a clear similarity between what young white and black women were doing, although who was imitating whom could be difficult to work out—was difference from the "natural" look of their mothers and grandmothers. Indeed, the so-called debate about the use of cosmetics is probably more profitably viewed less as a debate about the supposed desirability of "whiteness" than as a struggle between generations and genders.

Some contemporaries placed African American beauty culture in this broader comparative context. Writing in the *Messenger* in 1918, Louis W. George attacked those who would "cynically" characterize the new cosmetics as preparations used by African Americans who wanted to "make themselves look like white people." Such a notion was "erroneous and fallacious" and rested on the assumption that people should be "natural." George went on to point out that civilization was based on the artificial. Houses, clothes, science, and education were not natural; indeed, if you wanted "natural," the most obvious candidate was "ignorance." White women were hardly promoting the "natural" look, whatever that may have been; by George's calculations, white New Yorkers were spending a minimum of five million dollars a year on beauty preparations, and he could see no reason why colored women should behave any differently. Indeed, given the level of discrimination she faced, "the colored girl to-day would greatly limit her opportunities did she not make use of hair dressing, manicuring and facial massaging." For George, beauty culture was "proper, scientific and highly useful." [11]

To an even greater extent than was true of the white beauty industry, black cosmetics were associated with modernity and, most importantly, with progress. One writer in the *Messenger* pointed out that, although cosmetics were "new among the colored people," this was certainly not the case with other groups, and that African Americans' adoption of the new cosmetic practices demonstrated the distance that had been traveled from the "demoralizing effect" of slavery. Even critics less enamored than was this correspondent with the amount of energy being expended on cosmetic activities readily conceded the point. For example, in 1920 the *Chicago Whip* editorialized on the subject of "BEAUTY CULTURE VS. BRAIN CULTURE." Predictably, the newspaper was more concerned with promoting the latter, but what is most interesting about this piece is the way in which beauty culture was couched. The writer noted that beauty culture was "holding an all-important place in the life of colored Americans," who, he averred, "desire flowing and wavy hair, roseate cheeks and immaculate nails," in short, "to be beautiful." But he also acknowledged that the "most successful business institutions in the race are promoting *modern methods* of beautification and attractiveness." [12]

As members of one of the largest black business groups of the early twentieth century, African American cosmetics manufacturers were keen to present themselves as progressive promoters of the black community. The Walkers—both mother and daughter—were important supporters of numerous causes in Harlem and elsewhere, and the industry of which they were a part not only transformed the look of the new black woman but, for the hundreds employed in it, offered the chance of mobility. Not only did progressive reform-oriented women use cosmetic products, but quite a few had sold them at some time in their youth.[13]

If the daring and novelty of the new hairstyles and cosmetic techniques and the evident determination of the young women who consumed these products not to be limited to the ways of their parents and grandparents were clear enough in northern cities, these things were even more obvious in the South. As we have seen, some southern black women hated cosmetic products, but for many others, particularly the young, those products represented modernity, a term that meant, for them, change from the way things had always been. New ways of displaying their bodies hinted, above all, at the possibility of personal liberation, an improvement of their position as both women and African Americans in the South. Mamie Garvin Fields, living in Charleston around the time of World War One, who with her friend Mamie Rodolph made quite a bit of extra money through the Poro system, eventually set up an extra room in her house as a salon. For Fields, a woman like Madame Walker was an inspiring example: not only had she established her own business, but she had "a beautiful face, beautiful hair, dressed elegantly" and, when she lectured, "a go-ahead, up-to-date black woman was talking." Fields recalled that the first black woman to bring the croquignole curling iron to Charleston, Mrs. Ethel R. Brown, "made a sensation, because she not only had wonderful waves and curls all over her head, and a new style practically every time you saw her, but she had her hair dyed red." "We had never seen," Fields declared, "a black woman with red hair before." But Mamie Fields was most impressed by Mary Church Terrell, the great black educator and reformer, who came to Charleston to give an address on the "Modern Woman": "Oh my, when I saw her walk onto that podium in her pink evening dress and long white gloves, with her beautifully done hair, she *was* that Modern Woman."[14]

The demand for the new cosmetic products and the enthusiasm with which ordinary African Americans welcomed the opportunity to shape the way they looked and, for the first time on a mass scale, to participate in the consumption of fashion prompted public discussion of African American beauty and appearance. This discussion was conducted in an ebullient and

191

The
Long-
Veiled
Beauty of
Our Own
World

expansive manner that fitted in well with the mood of urban blacks in the 1920s. Notwithstanding blacks' disillusionment over their treatment during and after World War One and the vicious race riots of the summer of 1919, the immediate postwar years saw a new sense of optimism and self-assertion among African Americans in northern urban centers.[15] The political, literary and artistic manifestations of what later would be termed the "New Negro" are well-known, but this shift in consciousness also entailed a deliberate and prideful display of black bodies, particularly those of women, in a manner that transcended hoary white stereotypes. The clearest evidence of this concern with African American beauty comes in the form of two institutions that rose to prominence in the 1920s: the black beauty contest and the black fashion parade.

In October 1919, a writer in the National Association for the Advancement of Colored People's journal *Crisis* cast his eye back over a number of balls held during the previous summer, including one staged by the Pythians and Elks in Atlantic City, at which 15,000 African Americans had danced the night away on Young's Pier. The correspondent could only conclude that "there is nothing in white Europe or America that can measure up to the wonderful colorings of flesh, grace of movement and rhythm of music such as Black America can furnish." Those features of black cultural life—not merely music and dance, but the color and appearance of African Americans' bodies—were now being seen by many blacks as valued attributes and, as the 1920s proceeded, more and more whites would come to agree with this novel assessment. "We are," the writer of the *Crisis* story declared, "discovering at last the long-veiled beauty of our own world."[16]

A few months previously, in June 1919, the African American publication *Half-Century Magazine* had run a similarly assertive article entitled "Types of Racial Beauty," which was accompanied by a montage of photographs of black women. The author began by claiming that even "the beauty of Helen would be dimmed by the pulchritude displayed in any part of the world where Colored girls are to be found." As though the point had not already been made sufficiently clear, the writer went on to suggest that "our race has produced more varieties of beauty than any other race on earth." Colored men could choose from women ranging from "the bronze Venus with the mysterious black eyes and crispate hair, with cheeks of a dusky rose hue" to the "Indian peach variety with the baby grey eyes and brown curls." A year later, the magazine printed similar articles entitled "Crowned by the Gods" and "Beauty and Brains." The latter piece again emphasized "the variation in types of beauty" among African American women, while also making the point that these women were far from "brainless." Indeed, nearly all of the more than fifty African American women from across the country whose photographs illustrated the article were "active in the commercial, educational or industrial worlds." [17]

On the other side of the racial divide, Professor Frederick Starr, head of the department of Anthropology at the University of Chicago, created a stir in 1921 by claiming publicly that "there was no real beauty among white American girls." Not only did Starr suggest that "beauty in a blond race is next to impossible," but he also asserted that "only among Liberian and kindred races is real beauty to be found." The reasoning of this anthropology professor may have been at best curious, but he had provided an irresistible opening for local black newspapers. The *Whip* ran photographs of four African American women under the headline "Why We Agree With Prof. Starr, of Chicago U." The following month this publication put a photograph of a Mrs. Lorraine Jones, "One of Chicago's Beauties," on its front page, over the caption "Proof is here submitted to prove the Professor's statement." [18]

The *Whip's* polemics were part of a more general trend. From the end of World War One, and increasingly in the 1920s, African American publications prominently displayed pictures of black women. In 1924 the *Messenger* made this strategy explicit with an editorial entitled "Exalting Negro Womanhood." As the writer explained, although the photogravure sections of the Sunday papers contained page after page of pictures of white women, black women, unless they had done something "indecent and censurable," did not rate a mention. Beginning in January 1924, the *Messenger* would therefore display "in pictures as well as writing, Negro women who are unique, accomplished, beautiful, intelligent, industrious, talented, successful." [19] But this initiative was merely acknowledging an already wellestablished practice. Throughout the 1920s, not only the *Messenger* but such African American magazines as *Opportunity, Crisis,* and *Half-Century* illustrated their covers with images of young black women, and black newspapers ran similar pictures, often on the front page (see Figures 31 & 32).

Following the example of the *Defender* in its sponsoring the State Street Carnival in 1912, African American newspapers and magazines, partly no doubt with an eye to circulation figures, organized contests that emphasized the beauty of young black women. In 1921 *Half-Century Magazine,* probably the most up-market of the new black publications, ran a

Figure 31: In the 1920s, black magazines and newspapers deliberately set out to highlight African American women. In their pages, they printed photographs of the socially prominent but also of young, single women and older, married women who had sent in their pictures. *The Messenger* 6 (August 1924), 248

10 cents a copy

$1.00 a year

THE HALF-CENTURY MAGAZINE

JUNE, 1919

A Type of Racial Beauty

A Colored Monthly
For
The Business Man
And
The Home Maker

THE

B
E
A
U
T
Y

NUMBER

General Race News, Classy Fiction, Business, Fashion, Sports, Music, Fun

IN THIS ISSUE

Figure 32: In the immediate postwar years, African American publications emphasized what they termed "types of racial beauty." *Half-Century Magazine,* June, 1919

competition entitled "Who is the Prettiest Colored Girl in the United States?" Again, the focus was on the varieties of beauty: "Don't hesitate to send in your picture because you do not consider yourself unusually good looking," the organizers advised. "There are many types of Colored beauty. Not all of them appeal to every individual." Once again the message was one of racial uplift: "We merely want to show the unbelievers of our own and other races that there are as many beautiful Colored women as there are beautiful women in other races." One writer to *Half-Century* declared that he found the contest and the publication of numerous photographs of African American women "helpful" in rebutting whites' claims that "Colored" women were ugly.[20]

At times, the results of these promotional efforts are, to the modern reader at least, somewhat disconcerting. The juxtaposition in the *Messenger* of earnest articles on serious subjects and photographs of the three winners of the Bobbed Hair Contest held at the annual ball of the Brotherhood of Sleeping Car Porters is certainly eye-catching.[21] But the best examples of this sort of dissonance occurred in the *Crisis,* the journal of the NAACP, edited by W. E. B. Du Bois. Throughout the 1920s Du Bois printed literally hundreds of photographs of black babies: there were babies on the cover, pages with sixteen photographs of babies, half-page shots of babies, babies in cute outfits, and even naked babies artistically arrayed on rugs (see Figures 33 & 34). Indeed, it appears that baby contests were one of the principal fundraising activities of the NAACP. In 1924, for example, NAACP branches in fifteen states raised $9,409 from such events, and the National Office conducted a "National Baby Contest in which city is pitted against city." The following year, seventy-eight contests were held yielding some $20,000.[22] It seems that the NAACP created the style in which young black children were henceforth often snapped. Colin Powell's autobiography begins with a series of photographs from his Bronx youth, including one from 1937 when he was only a few months old, of the future four-star general naked on a leopard-skin rug.[23] The photograph could easily have appeared in *Crisis.*

It is difficult not to agree with the comment made by journalist Chandler Owen, early in 1924, that "the world [was] in a mad struggle for beauty." In the wake of the invention of the Miss America contest in 1921, numerous local contests of a similar nature were organized. Owen's warning that "the dominant group in a city or nation sets the standard" was probably little noted at the time, but within weeks of his observation a

The CRISIS

Vol. 31—No. 4   FEBRUARY, 1926   Whole No. 184

ONE DOLLAR AND A HALF A YEAR   FIFTEEN CENTS A COPY

Figure 33: In the 1920s the NAACP ran "beautiful baby" competitions, a continuation of a practice that had also been common in the last decades of the nineteenth century. These competitions were held all across America, and *Crisis* published many photographs of the entrants. *Crisis* 31 (February 1926), coverpage

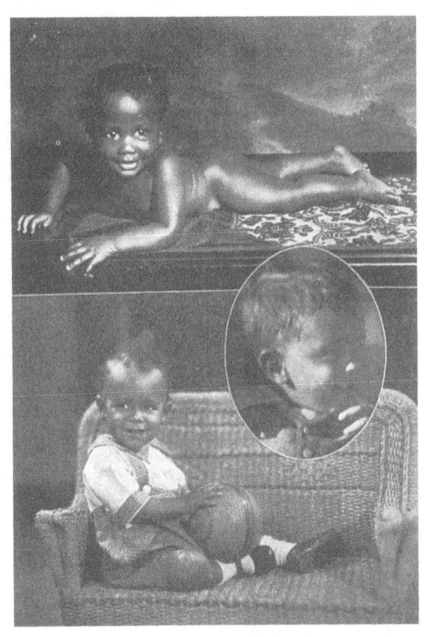

Figure 34: *Crisis* 30 (October 1926), 285

white-run beauty contest in Flushing, New York, was abandoned, apparently because "Dorothy Derrick, 17 years old, a negro girl was in third place and threatening to gain." According to the *New York Times,* Derrick, who had actually been running first but had then dropped away from the lead, was making a comeback when the officials intervened. The *Times* was unable to resist the snide comment that "She is said to be handsome in her way." "Don't you love that?" a writer in the *Crisis* responded. "Isn't it real Timesy? 'In her way!'" Perhaps the real difficulty for the organizers, the writer surmised, was that "colored girls are getting too attractive." The fashionable Green Twig Society, sponsors of the event, claimed that the cancellation had become necessary because the frontrunners were not members, and "therefore were not to be classed as society girls." That may well have been true, but the real import of the Society's action, the drawing of the color line, was not lost on anyone. Within a year, African Americans had organized their own national beauty contest.[24]

Nineteen twenty-five was the year in which Alain Locke published a collection of essays under the title of the *New Negro,* a volume which would become the key text of the Harlem Renaissance. It was also the year of the Golden Brown National Beauty Contest. That May a series of display advertisements in the major African American newspapers announced that Madame Mamie Hightower, a "beauty culturist of international repute," was to sponsor a nationwide search for Miss Golden Brown. According to the advertising copy, Hightower would "not be content until I find the most beautiful girl of our group in America" ("group," rather than "Negro" or "race," was her preferred term). Women interested in entering had to fill in a nomination blank (widely available in African American publications) and send in a photo. Voting depended on the purchase of the Golden Brown Beauty Preparation: 25-cent packets contained a coupon for 50 votes, 50-cent packets were good for 100 votes. These votes would determine the top five contestants, who would then be judged by the "foremost beauty authorities in the country." The winner would be announced at a special function to be held in Atlantic City.[25]

Mamie Hightower was actually the wife of the janitor of the white-owned cosmetics company that marketed Golden Brown beauty products to black women, but, as mythologized by the company's advertisements, she was transformed into another self-made African American entrepreneur in the Madame C. J. Walker mold.[26] A series of wordy advertisements in 1926 memorialized her success within a rags-to-riches formula: "From Obscurity to Fame and Fortune!" blared one caption, a claim that may already have been a cliché in America as a whole but, as applied to African Americans, was still unusual enough to retain a certain novelty. At a dance in Memphis, so the copy went, the young Mamie had been distressed by the way a young African-American woman named Selma, "whose unattractive complexion persistently marred an otherwise pleasing countenance," was ignored by all and sundry. She had reassured Selma that at the next function it would be a different story. Luckily, Mamie was "naturally inclined toward chemistry," a talent which, combined with her delving into the "mysteries contained in many books" and practical knowledge from "one or two of her druggist friends," allowed her to concoct a preparation that, by the time of the next dance, had transformed Selma's blemished and blotchy face into a "handsome golden brown complexion" that was "charm in itself." Soon after this, Mamie had married Zack Hightower and settled into domestic bliss, an idyll troubled only by the fact that she "heard some faraway voice calling." After "much thought" her husband "conceived the idea" that it was the "voice of Our Group calling her to her rightful position and place," whereupon she opened a beauty parlor on Memphis's Beale Street. From that time, news of the efficacy of her products spread quickly throughout black America. In outline, the story is much the same as the better-known one told of Madame Walker, although Walker's vision had come to her alone at the washtub and had not required a man to decipher it.[27]

Madame Hightower is now almost completely forgotten, but in the summer of 1925 news of the Golden Brown Beauty contest could hardly have been avoided by anyone reading the African American press. The contest was promoted as a part of racial uplift. "We must develop, in every member of our group," Madame Hightower was made to say, "that quality known as pride. It is not enough that some scientists are admitting that the glorious Cleopatra was of our race—let us prove once and for all that we have here in America some of the most beautiful women of the world." Editors accepted this aesthetic manifesto readily enough. In part, the Madame Hightower black beauty pageant was modeled on the Miss America contest, first held in Atlantic City in 1921; indeed, the decision to stage the final in Atlantic City highlighted the exclusion of blacks from that event. But the putative organizer was always careful to emphasize that her endeavors were not prompted merely by a desire to imitate white America and its standards. "We do not want to be white," she claimed, "but we do want that light, bright, velvety textured skin that is rightfully ours." Such statements do raise questions about how inclusive "Our Group" was likely to be in practice and what would have happened to a contestant with jet-black skin, but, in the context of contemporary and historical portrayals of African Americans, there is at least some plausibility to the claims of racial self-assertion.[28]

Local black newspapers, always keen to obtain attractive copy and to please advertisers (the beauty industry had become by this time a mainstay of the African American press), supported the contest. The *Pittsburgh Courier,* for example, placed photographs of two entrants on its front page under the headline "Pittsburgh and Chicago Vie in Big Beauty Contest." The caption noted that both women "possess smooth, creamy brown complexions, dark hair and large liquid brown eyes" (see Figure 35). Furthermore, the *Courier,* in conjunction with the Golden Brown Chemical Company, sponsored a ball at Liberty Gardens, at which aspiring local contestants could not only register for the contest but become eligible for gold prizes for prettiest girl, best Charleston dancer, and so forth.[29]

Figure 35: African American newspapers helped to promote the National Golden Brown Beauty Contest. These photographs ran on the front page of a Pittsburgh newspaper. *Pittsburgh Courier,* July 11, 1925

Approximately 1,400 young women entered the contest, and of these five won a trousseau and an all-expenses-paid trip to Atlantic City for the main ceremony, which was held on October 9. Thirty-nine state winners were awarded "genuine diamond rings." The national winner, receiving in excess of 300,000 votes, was Josephine Leggett, "star of the Shuffle Along Company on its triumphal tour," who was duly crowned Miss Golden Brown America and presented with a latest model Hudson Super-Six Coach Automobile. Madame Hightower, noting that the five finalists polled a million votes between them, declared that "emphatically our race is interested in beauty." Full-page advertisements proclaiming the victor's triumph were placed in the major black newspapers (see Figure 36). Fortuitously, it turned out that Leggett had herself used Golden Brown products "long before she was entered in this great contest." Madame High-

201

The
Long-
Veiled
Beauty of
Our Own
World

tower could only conclude that the event had been "one of the most stirring spectacles in the history of our race."[30]

There were other attempts to hold national beauty contests. For example, in 1928 the Nelson Manufacturing Company, makers of a hairdressing product, sponsored a competition in which African American women from thirty states participated by sending in their photographs. The winner—"The Nelson Girl"—and runners-up were awarded their "big cash" prizes at a function at the Alhambra Theatre in New York. But none of these events made anywhere near the impact of the Miss Golden Brown competition, and for the most part, after 1925, beauty and popularity contests continued only at the local level.[31] The *Pittsburgh Courier,* for example, ran competitions for the Pittsburgh area in which the winners received such prizes as a fur coat, a diamond ring, or a free trip to watch the Lincoln-Howard Classic football game in Philadelphia.[32] (See Figure 37.)

The original twist given to these competitions was the invention, in the summer of 1926, of the black bathing beauty contest. In March 1926, Harlem's Savoy Ballroom had opened for business. Occupying the second floor of a building that took up the entire block between 140th and 141st on Lenox Avenue, the Savoy rapidly became the area's most important social and cultural institution of the interwar years. Within six months, the management hit upon a novel idea that picked up on the vogue for displaying female flesh and quickly attracted the large crowds that the huge dancehall needed to survive. The Savoy announced that, on Tuesday August 17, it would hold a bathing beauty ball, the climax of which would be a bathing beauty contest. First prize would be an all-expenses-paid week in Atlantic City; second prize, a hundred-dollar bill. As it happened, the Savoy garnered considerable publicity from what turned out to be a controversial affair; it was discovered that one of the judges was the brother of the woman who came second, and the *Age* and the *Amsterdam News* became involved in a dispute with the *Interstate Tattler* over the ethics of the whole undertaking (see Figures 38 & 39).[33]

Since the beauty contest had been the "biggest sensation" of the Savoy's 1926 program, in February of the following year the management organized another one. This time the event would be a "Jungle Bathing Beauty Ball," a theme that necessitated the transformation of the dancehall into "a veritable jungle, to add warmth and local color to the affair." Over two hundred women entered a contest that promised "much for those who

Figure 36: The National Golden Brown Beauty Contest made extensive use of black newspapers, both by getting "news stories" about the event published in them and by placing advertisements in their pages. This advertisement announced the winner of the contest. *Amsterdam News,* October 7, 1925

203

*The
Long-
Veiled
Beauty of
Our Own
World*

have eyes for beauty and pulchritude." During the summer, the Savoy ran such contests each Saturday night. As the *Amsterdam News* gushed, "Saturday night is the big night of the week." The titillating prospect of forty or fifty of the "most beautiful girls in town parading before you" guaranteed that Saturday was "by far, the most popular night at the Savoy."[34]

Though the Savoy advertised its bathing suit contest as a "unique affair," other cities were running similar competitions at about the same time. In Chicago, a Miss Anna Hughley was crowned queen in a contest staged at Dreamland, one of the biggest clubs in the city (see Figure 40). For a while, Miss Hughley wrote a column entitled "Beauty Chats" in the black publication *Heebie Jeebies,* in which she confessed that to be "an acknowledged beauty in the city of Chicago with its multitude of beautiful girls gives the thrill that comes once in a lifetime."[35] These novel events spread to the South as well. In July 1928, the second Annual Bathing Beauty Contest was held at the Pelican Roof Garden in New Orleans. More than thirty young women from Mississippi, Illinois, and Louisiana paraded through the hall,

Figure 37: African American newspapers also ran their own contests. Those pictured above are contestants in the *Chicago Defender*'s Prettiest Girl contest. *Chicago Defender,* August 29, 1925

which was "landscaped into a big beach, the stage representing aristocratic Atlantic City, with sea, sand, beach parasols and lounging pillars." As with beauty contests generally, the bathing suit contest rapidly became a vehicle through which numerous local organizations could raise money. For example, Thomas L. Higgins, exalted ruler of the Brooklyn Lodge, came up

Figure 38: The Savoy, one of the most important institutions in interwar Harlem, invested heavily in bathing suit contests. *Amsterdam News,* July 27, 1927

205

The
Long-
Veiled
Beauty of
Our Own
World

with the idea of combining his organization's charity ball with a bathing beauty contest. He hoped that the presentation of a "bevy of beauties" clad only in swimsuits would aid the Lodge in its laudable aim of dispensing charity "among colored people in Brooklyn by colored people." [36]

If this splintering of national black beauty contests into numerous local events did not portend their demise—they would surface again later in the century—it did signal that their novelty was at an end. Increasingly, from the mid-1920s, black media attention became focused not on beauty contests but on African American fashion parades, a related institution that also relied on the display of black female bodies but that would prove to have more cultural force and staying power.

The Savoy Management Absolved

The Young Lady in the Center of This Picture Was Awarded First Honor in the Savoy Contest. Reading Towards the Left We See the Next Young Lady, Who Came Second. The Little Lady Next to Her With the Curls Came Third, but Many Feel, and so Does The Savoy, That She Should Be Recognized as Second. See Story in This Issue.

Figure 39: Almost inevitably in the multitude of competitions being run in the 1920s, there were occasions on which the objectivity of the judges was questioned. In this case, controversy arose because the woman who came second was related to one of the judges. *Amsterdam News,* September 8, 1926

Figure 40: Cover of *Heebie Jeebies* 2 (September 4, 1926). Courtesy of the Chicago Historical Society

According to William Leach, the new urban and secular culture of consumption, epitomized by the department store, that swept through America in the early decades of the twentieth century had an emancipating impact on the lives of women. It was the department store that brought fashion to ordinary Americans, and it was fashion that "intensified the excitement of commodities." In the nineteenth century there had been only a very limited market for such goods, but "fashion swelled to huge proportions by the 1920s." Starting in the early years of the twentieth century, department stores had run fashion shows, and these had immediately proved successful. By the late 1910s and 1920s, the stores were putting on style shows organized by more than one establishment, screening fashion movies, and staging huge fashion pageants replete with models, orchestras and special effects. As Leach has argued, the "engine of fashion existed now in thousands of cities at the heart of everyday life, churning up desire for commodities that carried with them the promise of personal transformation."[37]

Signs of fashion were everywhere in the cities—on billboards, in advertisements and news items in such publications as the *New York Times* or *Vanity Fair,* at the movies, on the streets, and in department stores—but for most African Americans this essentially white world must have seemed distant. Blacks were not excluded by law from department stores, but the number of court cases brought by angry African American customers complaining about the service they had received indicates that they were far from welcome there. Yet blacks did in fact partake of this new world of fashion, in much the same way that they participated in the related revolution in cosmetic use: through the mediation of a set of black institutions that paralleled white ones.

The black press informed its readers of fashion trends. Major black newspapers, such as the *Amsterdam News* and the *Chicago Defender,* ran Women's Page beauty columns that covered everything from tips on how to care for hair or fingernails to fashion advice. Most impressive was the fashion page in *Half Century Magazine.* From 1916, this publication printed Madam F. Madison's column, "What They Are Wearing," which predicted fashions for women in the coming season. On the same page, two or three models displayed relevant styles in clothing or hair. What was most striking about these women, clearly marking them off from the avalanche of blondes in other publications, was that they were distinctly and unmistakably black. As well, starting in January 1917, the magazine set up the Half-Century

Shopping Service. Readers who sent the necessary money could be supplied with everything from a natural hair switch that matched their own hair to "Hats for Early Spring" and "Pin Money Frocks," this method of purchase perhaps reflecting the difficulties blacks encountered when shopping in department stores.

But the clearest and most important example of the setting up of a black institution that paralleled those in white society was the creation, in the immediate postwar years, of the African American fashion show. Initially, these were small and often amateurish-sounding affairs. In Chicago, a Prof. Clark, who ran a dancing school, hired the Masonic Hall and ran a style show featuring "a large number of beautifully gowned women"; in Philadelphia, a Mrs. Idell Robinson displayed the work of her dressmaking students in a fashion show at the Waltz Dream Academy; in New York, a leading tailor R. R. Burt staged a "Midnight Fashion Show" at the Lafayette, one of Harlem's most famous theaters; and in Brooklyn, the Monday Circle held a "fashion promenade" in Arcadia Hall for the benefit of the Lincoln Settlement.[38]

As with the black beauty contest, which was becoming popular at the same time, the success of small, often local, events encouraged organization on a larger scale. In Chicago, an Annual Fashion Show for the benefit of the YWCA was inaugurated in 1923. A reporter for *Half Century*, present at the second of these functions, commented on the "brilliant array of beautiful women on the stage, displaying the newest in hats, gowns and furs to an audience arrayed in creations worthy of more than passing note," and surmised that the obvious success of that year's event meant that "its permanency is assured." In 1926, a Mrs. Bertha Lewis, who covered Chicago society events for the *Pittsburgh Courier*, gushed over the "galaxy of beautiful models display[ing] the newest styles to a packed house" in a show that surpassed "anything else in elegance and beauty." The mannequins included "recent brides, the most popular debutantes, girl scouts, stylish matrons and charming sub-debs," wearing attire ranging from negligees to formal evening wear. In New York, the longest-running and most important fashion event was the Utopia Fashion Show, organized for the benefit of the Utopia Neighborhood House on West 130th Street, but numerous other exhibitions were also staged. In 1925, for example, Mrs. H. Binga Dismond, New York society writer for the *Pittsburgh Courier*, reported rapturously on a fashion show at the Manhattan Casino that had attracted an

209

*The
Long-
Veiled
Beauty of
Our Own
World*

audience of two thousand, claiming that the Citizens' Christmas Cheer Committee, which organized the event, had "set a precedent in the history of fashion revues that will be difficult to surpass."[39]

The growing popularity of fashion shows provided African American newspapers with a further opportunity to display attractive young black women. During the spring or Easter season of 1926 the *Pittsburgh Courier* supplied its readers, in rapid succession, with photographs of dozens of models under headlines such as "Chicago Maids and Matrons Exhibit What is Proper in the Spring Mode," "Missouri Maids Exhibit The Latest in Feminine Foibles," "California Proves that Clothes Do Not Make The Woman, But Oh! How They Proclaim Her," "Pretty New Orleans Maids Know How to Wear 'Em," and "Leaders and Models in Louisville Style Revue."[40]

As these captions indicate, the fashion show quickly spread across America, even into the South. When plans for the first Crescent City Style Show, to be held in April 1926, were released, the organizers reassured New Orleans's African Americans that it would be "similar in all respects to those shows of the East and North." The event was eagerly anticipated, interest in it being stirred along by the *Louisiana Weekly,* the local black newspaper; in case anyone had managed to forget the function's voyeuristic basis, one of the *Weekly's* writers recorded that "the oculist is reporting a heavy increase of business, especially among the masculine contingent of the population, who are taking every precaution to be sure of missing nothing that is to be seen." The show, featuring over three hundred local African Americans and climaxing with a wedding scene, was a huge success, attracting, the *Louisiana Weekly* claimed, "the largest crowd in the history of the city." Two performances played to a jam-packed Pythian Temple Theater and, later in the week, a film of the entire proceedings played for four nights at the Lyric Theater. The following year the show was bigger and better, raising in excess of $1500 for charity. Again the wedding scene was "exquisite," but the new feature, "and one much appreciated," was "the display of lingerie and apparel suitable for Milady's boudoir." Footwear and hosiery were exhibited by a series of models walking behind a screen that descended to about knee level, an arrangement which meant, the *Weekly* was keen to note, that "shapely limbs were also displayed." Among the throng were the organizers of the Baton Rouge Style Show, seeking ideas for their own event, which was to be held a few weeks later.[41]

Fashion shows quickly became cultural extravaganzas, vehicles for the display of the talents of the local African American community. Roy Wilkins, stalwart of the NAACP for decades, remembered with particular affection one such event held in Kansas City in 1928. The Wheatley Provident fashion show, "the centerpiece of the spring social season," was organized under the watchful eye of "Mrs. Minnie Crosswaithe, a matron in her late sixties," and was designed to raise money for the hospital that catered to the African American inhabitants of the city. Months of work had gone into its preparation; indeed, one of the organizers had visited Chicago to study "the latest fashion pageants." The show, entitled "Artists and Models Revue Glorifying the Kansas City Girl," was held at the Convention Hall and over 6,000 blacks attended. It began with a Mrs. Roy Barker and her police dog, Pal, being driven around the ring in a "shiny La Salle sports Phaeton, followed by Mrs. Alberta Gilmore in one of Homer Roberts's flashing Hupmobiles." Then came the students of Lincoln High School in a "Bathing Beauty Revue" (beauty contests could easily be absorbed into fashion pageants). The actual parade was organized around a painter—played by Roy Wilkins, twenty-six years old and eligible bachelor-about-town—and his reveries of female beauty. Wilkins was positioned in the center, rakish beret on his head, palette on his arm, and brush clutched in his hand, and one by one his "dreams" of "Youth, Modesty, Innocence, Beauty, Charm, Passion, Vanity, a Blonde, a Brunette, an Opera Singer, and Pep, each played by a beautiful young woman" appeared before him. Wilkins remembered that the "applause was overwhelming," and "so were the models." Harlem's Cotton Club orchestra played at the party afterward "and Ethel Waters, then a slender young torch singer, fired up everyone." It was at this function that Wilkins was introduced to a Miss Badeau from St. Louis, who soon after married him.[42]

Fashion shows induced in Alice Dunbar-Nelson, widow of the famous African American poet and writer Paul Dunbar and a prominent member of the black elite (although, as her diary revealed, her finances were always precarious), both an appreciation of beauty on display and a sense of inadequacy, a combination of feelings that must have been quite common. In New York in November 1929 she recorded in her diary: "To the banquet hall . . . Such gowns! The fashions are definite. Stewart's [president of the National Federation of Colored Women] fashion show confirmed the awful news from Paris that had seeped through. Long-goshawful long skirts.

High-goshawful high waists! I felt like my own country cousin though I had on my tan lace. Oh, well!" Taylor Gordon responded in less ambivalent fashion, waxing lyrical about the fashion shows of the mid-to-late 1920s, in which "they have all of Harlem's beauties for manikens and they run in color from jet black to swansdown white, and the audience is the same. There is no way to write of the beautiful sight of this group on the dance floor after the show." Harlem—or whatever city was staging the event—was on display in these shows, and although reporters and photographers may not have been able to convey, to Gordon's satisfaction, the full texture of these glittering performances, they did supply black newspapers and magazines with reams of adulatory copy.[43]

By the mid-1930s the fashion show was flourishing on many levels. In New York, in April 1935, the 23rd Utopia Fashion Show took place at the Renaissance Casino. That same month, at the League Building in Flushing, the Corona Progressive Republican Club staged what was described as "one of the North Shore's leading social events" featuring "charming manikins" wearing the newest spring fashions (see Figure 41). In early June, the O. Clay Maxwell Club of the Mount Olivet Baptist Church on Lenox Avenue held its annual fashion show displaying spring and summer styles. Other affairs were more commercial. In April 1935, at a function at Club Danceland on West 125th Street, members of the University Fashion Club modeled dresses from the University Styles Shoppe on Seventh Avenue. In December, Ira, a "leading Harlem modiste," presented a musical fashion show at the Renaissance Casino. Reporting on this event under the headline "Ira's Fashion Show was a Parade of Gaudy 'Plumage,'" the *Amsterdam News* wrote of "beautiful mannequins, sleek and chic, strolling across the polished ballroom floor with all the grace and assurance of the peacock in its gorgeous plumage! Sweet music! Soft Lights!" The sixteen mannequins, selected from "the most popular debutantes of the season" and including a very young Lena Horne, wore "pajamas, negligees, nightgowns, sports wear, street wear, hats, cocktail gowns, and evening gowns." In early May of the following year, Blumstein's, a store on West 125th Street, exhibited on its premises garments fashioned from McCall's printed patterns and modeled by African American women.[44]

The reasons for the success of the fashion show are implicit in the innumerable press accounts of these events. If beauty contests were a novelty, emblematic of a new interest in the black body and of the modernist impulse, fashion parades and fashion became the means by which an African American middle class defined itself. Although a discernible black middle class had emerged in the nineteenth century, it had always seemed fragile. By the 1920s and 1930s, however, the sheer number of African Americans living in the cities—in 1930 there were well over 200,000 blacks in both Chicago and New York City—gave the middle class a chance to establish itself properly. What appears to have happened is that the black middle class rapidly assumed control of the burgeoning fashion show and used it to es-

-:- Manikins Pose for Photographer -:-

Amsterdam News Photos

PICTURED HERE are a few of the manikins who took part in the fashion promenade sponsored last Friday night by the Corona Progressive Republican Club at the League Building in Flushing. They are (left to right)—Betty Williams, in a clinging black evening gown of material with sweeping train, daringly low back trimmed with white mourf at the neck, designed by Rosemary Berry; Emmalena Jones of the teen-age unit wearing a silk taffeta evening dress of pastel blue, topped with a knee-length coat of self material; Adele Lindsey, in an English tailored sweetinburgh checkered tweed suit of putty tan and Marina green, side plaited skirt is buttoned onto a white tailored linen waist, topped by a double-breasted coat trimmed with cellophane buttons, a tan breton rolled brim straw sailor; Miss Sybil Prescod in a green, white and black printed cotton bathing suit lined with woolen jersey, designed by Rosemary Berry; Mrs. Reba Simmons in an afternoon costume of navy blue and checkered taffeta, featuring a cape and huge bow at the neckline, navy blue shoes, a side-turned straw hat and a matching quilted bag

Figure 41: The models at fashion shows were not professionals, but were usually drawn from a pool of respectable African American women. Married women as well as debutantes displayed clothes. As in the beauty contests, the emphasis in the fashion shows was on varieties of beauty. *Amsterdam News,* April 13, 1935

tablish itself as the authority on what respectable blacks should wear, and thus to differentiate itself from ordinary working-class African Americans. Fashion parades, sponsored by middle-class clubs and charities, organized by respectable society matrons, and using debutantes or society women as mannequins, set members of the middle class a standard to emulate and, with the newspaper and magazine coverage of these events and of fashion itself hinting at a glamorous, even opulent lifestyle, gave everyone else something to envy (see Figures 42 and 43).

The fashion parade must also have struck a particular chord with African Americans, echoing as it did a key black institution dating back to slavery times. In some senses, the black fashion parade constituted a more stagy and contrived variation of the Sunday promenade to and from church that, as we have seen earlier, was an important part of black life in both the North and the South. Both were spectacles in which participants expected and desired to be looked upon by their peers, as well as by those they considered to be their inferiors, and both were didactic rituals deliberately and clearly establishing social difference. It was this resonance with black history that allowed the African American fashion parade to combine ostentation and piety, consumption and religion (church groups and charities were the usual organizers and beneficiaries) in a way that sanctioned the cultural authority not only of the institution but of the black middle class itself.

In *Black Metropolis*, their classic study of Chicago, St. Clair Drake and Horace Cayton outlined the activities of the Amethyst Girls, "one of the small group of clubs that set

Successful Pilot of Harlem's Most Gorgeous Fashion Show Friday Night

Figure 42: The fashion shows were usually staged under the supervision of a respectable society matron. *Pittsburgh Courier,* October 31, 1925

the pattern in the middle-class social-club-world." In the 1930s, this exclusive group of eleven women, "in their late thirties and early forties, light-brown-skinned to 'very light,' stylish dressers, and cultivated in manner," organized two fashion shows a year, one for themselves and one for a Baptist church. The events were covered extensively in the African American press: in 1938 the *Defender* described an Amethyst Girl's function as "one of the most spectacular style shows ever staged and directed down church aisles." A member of the group commented: "We look forward to our fashion show every year. We always model our personal wardrobes at our own show. We make money on the fashion shows every year. Now we don't have to worry about selling tickets. They sell themselves without very much sales talk." According to Drake and Cayton, nearly a quarter of a century later, in 1961, prosperity had made possible "an extreme elaboration of the

Figure 43: Many of the fashion shows included a segment for children. This photograph, taken in Harlem in 1928, appears, however, to be of the participants in a show entirely devoted to displaying children's clothing. Photographs and Prints Division, Schomberg Center for Research in Black Culture, The New York Public Library, Astor, Lenox and Tilden Foundations

215

The
Long-
Veiled
Beauty of
Our Own
World

'cult of clothes,'" an elaboration that integrated "the world of 'Society' and the world of the Church in upper-class and middle-class circles." The fashion parade had become "a fixture of the Bronzeville sub-culture, and no one sees anything incongruous about the guild of a Catholic church sponsoring a 'Pert and Pretty Fashion Show,' or a Baptist church presenting 'Excelsiors in Fashion Review' at its thirty-third anniversary services." [45]

Perhaps the surest sign of the way in which the fashion show quickly established itself as an African American, middle-class institution was the way in which it was satirized and burlesqued in the famous Harlem Drag Balls of the 1920s and 1930s. As George Chauncey has shown in *Gay New York,* his brilliant exploration of gay life in the city, sometime in the early 1920s the Hamilton Lodge Ball, an annual event since 1869, was transformed into a drag affair that routinely attracted up to seven thousand participants, not a few of whom came from other cities on the eastern seaboard. Chauncey sensitively places the balls in the context of gay New York but does not develop as fully their position in African American culture. If Chauncey is correct in dating the transformation of the Hamilton Lodge Ball into what was commonly known as "the Faggots' Ball" in the early 1920s, then its rise coincided precisely with that of the African American fashion show. Indeed, as reporters and other observers noted, fashion was at the heart of these drag balls. Langston Hughes, present at at least one of them, commented: "For the men, there is a fashion parade. Prizes are given to the most gorgeously gowned of the whites and Negroes who, powdered, wigged, and rouged, mingle and compete for the awards." [46]

Patrons expended enormous amounts of energy on securing just the right outfit for these functions. Ethel Waters remembered the 1920s—"the great time of 'drags' in Harlem" when there "would be fashion parades for the male queers dressed in women's clothes"—because of the frequency with which her best gowns were borrowed for the evening (although she noted proudly that the borrowers won "many first prizes in my clothes"). On one occasion she lent her "black velvet dress, trimmed with ermine, to one of these he-she-and-what-is-it types. But he got to fighting with his 'husband' at the affair and was locked up in a cell." The dress was unwearable for months, reeking of carbolic acid, "the Chanel No. 5 of the cell blocks." According to Taylor Gordon, who was a judge at one of the drag balls at the Savoy, some of the dresses cost as much as $500. In 1936, the

Amsterdam News reported that Jean La Marr had won the first prize at the 69th Hamilton Lodge Ball with an "original creation" of a "white gown with pleat ruff of the same material—and backless, my deah" (see Figure 44). These drag balls, attended, in Taylor Gordon's words, by everyone "from bootblacks to New York's rarest bluebloods," and certainly including both white performers and spectators, involved the transgression of gender and racial lines, but the mostly black audience was also well aware of the way in which the middle-class pretensions of those involved in the black fashion shows were being lampooned.[47]

In his autobiography *Born to Be,* published in 1929 with a mostly white audience in mind, Taylor Gordon wrote that "the events I wished everyone could see in Harlem, are the Fashion Shows and the Drag Balls and a few Society Dances." As Gordon well understood, Harlem was on display at these affairs, but the display was designed, for the most part, not for whites slumming it uptown, but for African American inhabitants of the Negro Mecca. Here context is crucial. As is well known, for much of the 1920s Harlem was indeed in vogue among sophisticated whites. The musicals *Shuffle Along,* "a honey of a show," according to Langston Hughes, and *Blackbirds,* as well as the revues and performances at the Cotton Club, Connie's Inn, and other venues of their ilk, together gave nightclubbing white New Yorkers a taste of what seemed to them the exotic and erotic possibilities of black life. According to Jimmy Durante, one of the amateur guides to the hotspots of Harlem, "you go sort of primitive up there, with the band moaning blues like nobodies business, slim, barethighed brown skin gals tossing their torsos, and the Negro melody artists bearing down something terrible on the minor notes." As is also well known, many of these clubs excluded blacks—most infamously, W. C. Handy, father of the blues, was refused entry to the Cotton Club, even though he could hear his music being played inside—and employed only the lightest-colored African American young women in the chorus line.[48] These trends reached a climax in the revue "Brownskin Models," which toured northern cities in 1925. As the *Pittsburgh Courier* noted, this show contained "beauty, entrancing beauty of the brownskin type, with a smaller second chorus of creoles, to form a striking contrast." In the interwar years, the lithe, sinuous bodies of brown African American women were everywhere on stage, and black newspapers gave those bodies ample coverage, firing the imagination

Figure 44: The Hamilton Lodge Ball and other Drag Balls were generally reported in the African American press in a sympathetic fashion. This photograph is of Jean La Marr, a black who was the winner, and Connie Giako, a white who came second, at the 1936 Hamilton Lodge Ball. *Amsterdam News,* March 7, 1936

of white New Yorkers and inevitably of many African Americans as well (see Figures 45 and 46).[49]

Where black beauty contests, fashion shows, and even the drag balls differed from stage shows in the Cotton Club and similar venues was that they were primarily organized for a black audience, and, because of that, differences in skin pigment among black participants were of far less importance. Taylor Gordon claimed that the beautiful women who took part in the fashion shows ranged in color "from jet black to swansdown white" and, judging from the newspaper stories and the surviving photographs, his opinion is persuasive.[50] The ubiquitous rhetoric concerning the "varieties of beauty" that were on display at beauty contests and fashion parades also indicates that African American women with all shades of skin color participated in them.

"Glorifying The Brownskin Girl"

What was most important here was the public declaration that the black body was capable of being regarded as a thing of beauty. Against an unvarying background of demeaning visual portrayals of African American bodies in cartoons, magazine illustrations, advertisements, and film, black beauty contests and fashion shows were not merely vivid repudiations of black physical and aesthetic inferiority but salutary expressions of African American pride. That those who organized or took part in these displays may have been acceding, in part, to prevailing white standards of beauty was less significant than the fact that for the first time blacks were being presented, through the contests and fashion shows themselves and the widespread publicity given to these events by the African American press, in what was, by contemporary standards, an unambiguously positive way.

Figure 45: Stage shows put on for white audiences almost invariably allowed only very light-skinned African American women in the chorus line. This trend reached a climax in the 1925 production "Brownskin Models." *Pittsburgh Courier,* December 12, 1925

Figure 46: African American newpapers were very well aware that displays of female flesh sold papers. They were keen to publish pictures of beauty contests, fashion parades, and women from stage shows. *Amsterdam News,* June 13, 1936

CHAPTER

The Stroll

More than seven decades after the event, Naomi Washington, sister of Fats Waller, could still vividly remember an incident that occurred in Harlem in about 1910. The seven- or eight-year-old black girl had been hanging around a grocery store situated across the street from her home when a man—he was "dressed to kill—oh, a good-looking fellow," she recalled— entered the shop. "Hello, pimp," a young woman said to the man, a greeting that evoked from him nothing more than a good-natured laugh. That night, when Naomi Washington's father came home, she, too, welcomed him with the words "Hello, pimp." The father turned away, hung up his coat, and then beckoned his daughter over. "Who did you hear say that?" he inquired. "There was a man who came in the store," she explained, "and he was dressed, and that's what this woman said to him." "Now when I came in was I dressed like that?" the father asked. "Well, you dress like that on Sundays," she replied.

Naomi Washington accepted the distinction her father had sought to make even though she did not yet understand it. A respectable man who ran his own trucking business, Mr. Washington was a deacon (he would later become head deacon) of the Abyssinian Baptist Church. As he explained to his daughter: "I work every day to feed you, and I come home and bring my money to your mother. That man dresses up every day and takes his wife's money. He don't give her anything."[1] But to the as-yet-untutored eye of his daughter and, more importantly for the conduct of race relations, for the vast majority of casual white observers, the father's Sunday attire was all too easily equated with the clothing of a pimp. It was still the case that a well-dressed African American on the streets of a northern city, let alone one garbed with a dash of flamboyance, could raise the hackles of whites.

In a section of *Following the Color Line* tellingly captioned "Bumptiousness as a Cause of Hatred," the journalist Ray Stannard Baker recounted a conversation he had had with an acquaintance, as, in the early years of the twentieth century, they walked through the streets of Indianapolis. The two men came across "a young Negro," who was "immaculately dressed," whose "hat-band was blue and white," whose "shoes were patent leather with white tops," whose waistcoat was "flowered," and whose "tread as he walked was something to see." For Baker, the young black man was an example of the "airiness of the half-ignorant young Negro," who "mistakes liberty for licence." Baker's companion, "an educated Northern white man," was even less tolerant, commenting that "I never see that young fellow without wanting to step up and knock his head off." The "absolutely worthless" black man, who lived off "the wages of a hard-working coloured woman and spends all he can get on his clothes," almost automatically induced in Baker's friend the thought that "somehow I can't help believing that a good thrashing would improve that boy's character."[2] Over ensuing decades, not every white man who encountered a flashily dressed black male would be able to exercise a similar degree of restraint.

It was not only whites who were offended by displays of "extravagant" attire. No matter how ridiculous or unfair such attitudes may have been, the behavior of individual blacks was all too easily taken, by whites at least, to reflect on all African Americans. Partly for this reason, middle-class blacks and members of the elite were keen to distance themselves from the dress and demeanor of ordinary African Americans and, at the same time, to curb what they viewed as the sartorial and kinesic excesses of those they saw as their social inferiors. To this end, a number of etiquette books specifically targeted at a black audience were published in the late nineteenth and early twentieth centuries. Something of the exhortative quality of these manuals is suggested by the fact that, in the 1890s, a very young William Pickens, future stalwart of the NAACP, then attending a small school in Arkansas, received one of these volumes as a prize for being "never absent, never tardy."[3]

According to Edward S. Green's *National Capital Code of Etiquette*, a publication dedicated to the "Colored Race," the "two most essential points in a man's correct dress are at his feet and throat." Thus, Green's advice on neckties, for example, was detailed and specific: "be careful to avoid colors that do not blend with the remainder of your wearing apparel, and above all things shun the so-called 'loud' ties with colors that fairly shriek unto Heaven." Young black men should avoid "bright reds, yellows and light greens as you would the plague" and stick to "dark reds, dark greens, browns, black and white stripes or checks." The concern of these volumes was to teach young black men (women were barely mentioned) how to present themselves in public in such a way as to make them merge inconspicuously into the tableau of the street. This, as E. M. Woods in *The Negro in Etiquette* readily conceded, was a difficult task: "to say the moderately educated negro is totally ignorant of the fundamental principles of Chesterfieldian manners is putting it mildly," Woods wrote. "See him in peacock style, [when the fowl is proudest strutting with his wings in palmleaf shape,] swaggering down the broadway or popular highway of the place brushing against ladies and colliding with gentlemen." Particularly discomfiting to Woods was the way in which African Americans moved in public: "among the many bad habits of our race which we must get rid of before we can acquire an easy, graceful gait, is shambling or a shuffling, awkward walk—a kind of dragging the feet along, allowing the front part of the heels to strike first, and wabbling or moving staggeringly from side to side." "Do you not know," he continued rhetorically, "that some people

have a Sunday walk and a Monday walk?" The latter was "natural and
graceful," the former "unnatural and awkward."[4]

Implicit in such complaints was a recognition that the manner in which
blacks behaved on the street was readily apparent to whites, spectacularly
so in the cases of certain prominent African American thoroughfares. In
New York in the 1890s, Seventh Avenue between the twenties and the forties was known as the African Broadway. This area, a reporter for the *Trib-
une* noted in 1895, was always on "dress parade," although how "most of
the men support their wives and families is a mystery, for they seem to do
nothing but lounge about street corners." On Seventh Avenue one could
see a "daily promenade of gayly dressed girls and sprig young colored men.
Yellow is the prime tint of the young colored girls' clothes," while "the favorite dress of the young men 'in style' is a glossy silk hat, patent leathers,
a black suit with a sack coat of remarkable shortness, and a figured waistcoat." A few decades later, the action was much the same, although the setting had by now moved uptown to Harlem. Nora Mair, a migrant from
Jamaica, "loved it when my brother-in-law would take me strolling on Seventh Avenue." Like the other strollers, she was "dressed to the teeth."
"Everybody was out there," Nora Mair declared, and, she added emphatically, "we didn't walk, we strolled," a distinction that would not have been
lost on the despairing author of *The Negro in Etiquette* and other disapproving observers of the black scene in northern cities. In 1914, Adam Clayton Powell, Sr., complained archly of Harlem blacks that you "can see the
effect of the tango, the Chicago, the turkey trot, the Texas Tommy, and
ragtime music . . . in the movement of their bodies about the home and on
the street. Grace and modesty are becoming rare virtues."[5]

If African Americans were already, by the 1890s and early 1900s, noticeable enough in northern cities, their presence would become even more
obvious in the interwar years. Many Southern blacks had made their way
north before this, but with the opening up of employment opportunities
attendant on the outbreak of World War One and the continued deterio-
ration of race relations in the South, tens of thousands poured across the
Mason-Dixon Line. On Manhattan in 1890, for example, one in every seventy inhabitants was a black; by 1930, the figure was one in nine.[6] The
background of these migrants and the hopes and expectations for a new life
that they brought with them would substantially influence the contours of

African American culture in northern urban centers and the way that culture came to be expressed in the street.

Years after she had moved from Memphis to Chicago in 1918, Lil Hardin, a pianist and later Louis Armstrong's wife, could still recall the sense of wonder that she felt as she explored this northern city's streets: "I made it my business to go out for a daily stroll and look this 'heaven' over. Chicago meant just that to me—its beautiful brick and stone buildings, excitement, people moving swiftly, and things happening."[7] The awed walk through the city by the young African American fresh from the South rapidly became an archetype of black culture, an emblematic marker of the cultural migration from the South to the North, from the constraints of a traditional rural society to the apparent freedom of modernity and urbanity. (One thinks, for example, of Ralph Ellison's invisible man's journey uptown into Harlem.) But for all the undoubted magic of this exploratory journey, the experiencing and the telling of it were shaped by southern black culture, as migrants fulfilled expectations formed well before they arrived in northern metropolises.

For its numerous southern black readers, including those who, toying with the idea of migrating north, had sought out copies of this semi-clandestine paper, the *Chicago Defender* offered what can only have been a dazzling prospect for many of those confined by the strictures of Jim Crow in Mississippi or Alabama. In this famous African American publication were to be found articles on parades and events such as the State Street Carnival, and, most important, extensive entertainment pages extolling the wonders of the Stroll and the black bands that played until all hours at various clubs and night spots along the strip. Of course, as we have already seen, any southern town or city with any sort of African American population had its black street life, its own special thoroughfares affording sites for aesthetic display. New Orleans-born Jelly Roll Morton, self-confessed father of jazz, explained to Alan Lomax how, in the early years of the twentieth century, he took advantage of this situation to announce his arrival in the towns along the Gulf of Mexico. Morton would rent a room, "slick up, and walk down the street in my conservative stripe," a ploy made all the more conspicuous by his refusal even to nod to anyone else. A couple of hours later he would stroll by in a "nice tweed" and then, about "four in the afternoon, I'd come by the same way in an altogether different outfit and some babe would say,

"Lawd, mister, how many suits you got anyway?"
I'd tell her, "Several, darling, several."
"Well, do you change like that every day?"
"Listen, baby, I can change like this every day for a month
and never get my regular wardrobe half used up. I'm the suit
man from suit land."[8]

Exaggerated and self-serving though Morton's account doubtless is, it
nevertheless does suggest, once again, the importance of African American
street life—of a space in which blacks could watch and be watched—in
even the smallest southern town. Even so, many southern blacks, swayed
both by the travelers' tales of those who had been to the South Side or
Harlem and by the *Defender*'s urgings, must have anticipated that city life
in the North would be bigger, better, brighter and faster than anything
they had encountered. And those expectations were met frequently enough
for this image to persist in the South, in one form or another, well into the
second half of the century. The absence of Jim Crow laws, the relative freedom of the North, and the growing size and density of African American
urban populations gave fresh impetus and broader scope to a form of expressive behavior, the stroll, that rapidly developed into one of the defining
features of northern black city life.

In the 1910s and 1920s Chicago's "Stroll"—the section of State Street
between 26th and 39th—was the best known site for this behavior. (Later
in the 1930s, the focus would shift south to 47th and South Parkway,
the area adjacent to the Savoy Ballroom [see Figure 47].) An article in the
Chicago Defender in May 1914 recommended a walk along State Street,
"the most wonderful thoroughfare populated with Afro-Americans in the
United States." During the day, the reporter noted, the street corners were
so jammed with black men and women hanging around, gossiping or discussing politics (in this case the Mexican war), that he and anyone else trying to use the street had to make a wide detour just to get by. African American men, lounging comfortably against the patrol box at the corner of
29th, parted to allow a patrol man to "'pull the box,' but he saw no harm
in the idlers and laughingly moved away." In daylight hours, some of the
sights, particularly that of women, "with heads tied up with rags of various
gaudy hues" hanging out of the tenement windows, may have been somewhat tawdry, but at night the Stroll, ablaze with light, with its sidewalks

crowded, and with "music and laughter everywhere," transformed itself into something "sublime."[9]

It was precisely this aspect of Chicago's African American life that attracted the eye of Archibald J. Motley, Jr., perhaps the best known of the city's black artists. Eager to contest whites' stereotyped and often demeaning portrayals of blacks, Motley sought to communicate "the soul and the very heart of colored people" in a way that, he claimed, only an African American artist could do.[10] In a series of paintings completed in the 1930s and 1940s, Motley depicted, in vivid and striking colors, scenes from Bronzeville's streets and nightlife. Motley's *Black Belt* (1934), for example (see Figure 48), with its emphasis on the play of artificial lights on a tableau of brightly dressed characters, reprises the descriptions of the "sublimity" of the Stroll. If, for all the sincerity of his effort, Motley hardly managed to

Figure 47: Jay Jackson's "As Others See Us." *Chicago Defender*, March 3, 1934

break out of the straitjacket of whites' stereotypical depictions of blacks—
his paintings seem at times to be the visual equivalent of the work of some
of the writers of the Harlem Renaissance—his unabashed celebration of
the textures of African American life in Chicago does suggest something of
its exhilaration and vibrancy.

Hardly surprisingly, then, many of the stories and much of the gossip
and lore of the black city centered on the Stroll. Thus, black dance-band
leader William Everett Samuels remembered that many African Americans, employed as postal clerks, hotel porters, and the like during the day,
went home at quitting time, arose at 2.00 a.m., dressed up in their finest

Figure 48: Archibald Motley, *Black Belt* (1934). Motley wrote of this picture: "I have always possessed
a sincere love for the play of light in painting and especially the combination of early moonlight and
artificial light. This painting was born first of that desire and secondly to depict a street scene, wherein
I could produce a great variety of Negro characters." Oil on canvas, Hampton University Museum,
Hampton, Virginia

clothes, and hung out on the Stroll, before sobering up in a steam bath and going on to work. Even the relatively staid *Defender* occasionally carried stories of this kind. In January 1921, one of the *Defender*'s reporters, having heard that "a certain well known celebrity on the 'Stroll'" had had a big win "through an investment in 'bones,'" hustled across to the Colonial barber shop near State and 34th. There he beheld half a dozen attendants pampering the man's nails, buffing his shoes, and giving him the "'satin finish' with some of Madame Walker's best." His ablutions completed, the successful gambler spread enough money around to nonplus Buck, the shop's proprietor and a man not easily impressed.[11]

If the *Defender* retailed such stories only occasionally, they became one of the stocks-in-trade of a series of lively and entertaining black newspapers and magazines that came and went in the 1920s. For example, in 1925 *Heebie Jeebies* reported that "the boys on the 35th St. stroll have given little Smitty, the popular barber on the second chair of the Radio Shop, the name of 'Little Hog,' not on account of his eating so much, but because he has on his list a string of 'fat ladies.'"[12] As the *Whip*'s "Nosey's column," a melange of home-spun philosophy, humor, and thinly veiled gossip that even seven decades later is an entertaining and lively read, made clear much of the action centered on the Stroll. A tailor shop on the South Side had a special deal on cotton suits, Nosey revealed, and one of "our boys" had had one made, so that he could "strut his stuff down the Stroll in his new 'fit me quick.'" But the "rain gods" drenched the "State Street Sport," shrinking his suit alarmingly and making him look like Charles Ray, "the movie 'clodhopper.'" The purchaser stormed back to the "quack tailor," who greeted the irate black man by throwing up his hands in horror and exclaiming: "My, how thees boy has grown."[13] In a column entitled "Under the Lash of the Whip," another writer in the same newspaper posed the question: "Doesn't life mean more to the Negro than Clothes, Cabarets, Chicken and Church?" before drolly answering: "Ask the boys on the Stroll, they know."[14]

What was valued highly on the Stroll was not only the stylish way young black men-about-town presented their bodies but also their verbal agility and quickness of wit. If the humor, at times, went well beyond the bounds of good taste, that was too bad. In early April 1921, Alexander Johnson, a young African Texan, who had been accused of having sex with a white woman in the hotel in which he worked, was seized by some whites who branded three large K's on his forehead (see Figure 49). A few days later, on a Saturday night, Nosey, as was his custom, dropped into one of the "popular tonsorial parlors" on the Stroll and waited his turn for a shave. To Nosey's astonishment, as a black man sat down in the barber's chair, he sang out "put three K's on my head, old man." Nosey regained his "calm because the three K's wanted by this man was 'Kongolene Knocks Kinks,'" a method of styling his hair. Humor and public ridicule of this type helped to defuse the threat of extra-legal white violence; on the same page of the *Whip,* a brief editorial item suggested that the organizers of the Klan in Chicago arrange a march on State Street one night but warned that they should "ride horses that can run because they'll need them." [15] Protests of this type were also small signs of an increasingly aggressive demeanor, hints that African Americans in Chicago and other northern cities were not as interested in deferring to whites as they had in the South, an attitude that, to the chagrin of many members of the black middle class and some newspaper editors, was apparent also on city streets.

For this and other reasons, there was always an ambivalence in newspaper coverage of the Stroll, especially that of the *Defender,* ever eager to promote the uplift of the race. On the one hand, stories extolled the freedoms of the city (and the comparison with the horrors of the South, which were extensively catalogued in the *Defender's* pages, could never have been far from the reader's mind); on the other hand, Robert S. Abbott, editor of the *Defender,* clearly wishing that his compatriots would act in a more decorous fashion, continually hectored ordinary black Chicagoans about what he saw as their numerous failings. The pages of Abbott's and other African American papers and maga-

Figure 49: *Chicago Whip,* April 9, 1921. Alexander Johnson, a bell boy living in Texas, was accused of having sex with a white woman in the hotel in which he worked. The local Ku Klux Klan kidnapped, flogged, and branded him. Chicago Historical Society

zines were fairly peppered with complaints about the behavior on the Stroll and with imprecations to the authorities, in fact to any authority, to do something about it. In the 1920s and 1930s, the *Defender* ran a series of cartoons—"Folks We Can Get Along Without" and later, under the more assertive title, "Folks We Must Live Without"—hoping to shame African Americans into better behavior (see Figures 50 and 51). In the same vein, an irate letter-writer to *Half-Century Magazine* in 1919 demanded to know whether "our Colored Aldermen [are] doing their duty." The writer went on to object that "the corners of 31st and State, 35th and State and 47th and State are not properly kept clean of loafers who ungentlemanly turn to look at every decently dressed woman who passes those corners." [16]

Clearly, then, recent migrants from the South were the source of considerable tension, of irritable abrasiveness caused by rather different ideas about the way in which freedom from the oppressive southern racial system should be played out in the day-to-day life of northern cities. As early as August 1914, the *Defender* editorialized on "THE NIGGER," a term "rightfully" applied, this publication declared, to the "handkerchief heads that are coming to this city from many of the southwestern states." The author complained about the new migrants' unwillingness to be served by black rather than white assistants in stores, about the loudness of their talk and behavior, about a degree of shabbiness in their clothing that made it "sickening to wait on them," and about a general disreputableness made all the more obvious by the fact that on Sundays "these same people look like fashion plates." [17] Over the ensuing decades, writers in black publications kept up a constant litany of complaint against the offensive habits of many of their compatriots. In August 1920, an editorial in *Half-Century Magazine* asked: "is it true that the selfishness of the white man is the only cause of race prejudice?" and then listed, in a column and a half, reasons why African Americans were partly responsible for the current state of relations between the races. Blacks' practice of sprawling over the seats of street cars, or getting on in filthy, foul-smelling work clothes; of holding conversations across streets; of hanging out of the windows of tenements in summer or sitting around the front stoop "half naked"; of giggling and talking at the movies; of getting on street cars "early in the morning wearing absurdly elaborate, much-soiled silk and satin waists or dresses or bright colors more appropriate for evening wear than daylight"—these and other social infractions were deplored. What was even more worrying to the editorialist

Folks We Can Get Along Without

This disgraceful scene takes place any warm afternoon or evening at the entrance of some of our supposed to be first-class apartment buildings on the boulevards and up-to-date residence streets. Uncouth youth with college boy suits, sweatshirts or sweaters on loiter all over the steps and on the balustrades. They make it impossible for one to enter and when women attempt to call on friends in the building they have to run the gantlet of would-be heroes whose only weapons are insults. As a result many so-called kitchenet apartments are nothing more than breeding places for crime and the entire Race suffers from the outrage. It is an eyesore and needs not only the attention of the renters, but that of the owners who can call the police if the situation is out of their control.

Figure 50: *Chicago Defender,* May 9, 1931

was the belligerent attitude that many African Americans displayed as they went around town, the way in which southern blacks, in particular, were no longer prepared to allow whites to get away with perceived slights: "many go about defiantly with a chip on the shoulder, ready to quarrel with the first white person who looks at them," the writer noted, a rather pointed observation coming as it did only a year after the Chicago Race Riot of July 1919.[18]

Much the same sort of complaint could be found in any of the northern cities. A columnist in New York's *Amsterdam News,* for example, assailed young blacks who protested that they had "no chance," demanding that they "deport [themselves] with greater decorum and decency on street cars" and stop behaving "like so many jungle apes." For this type of young black, the writer lamented, the "street car is his stage and he is the star performer." The author had seen young African American men whistling at both black and white girls, playing guitars and banjos, using profanity and obscenity, and entering "the car in full monkey regalia and strut as though they were the princes of the jungle." "What we need among us," he hyperbolically concluded, "is about five million funerals."[19]

Partly, of course, these complaints reveal the frustrations of a black middle class forced by a residential segregation more severe than anything found in the South to live in a South Side teeming with working-class African Americans, a middle class lacking the power to force the city to curb behavior that inconvenienced and irritated them. In *Harlem: Negro Metropolis,* Claude McKay wrote scathingly of the "strenuous and pathetic" attempts of such better-off Harlem blacks "to create an oasis of respectability within the boundaries of Aframerica." Despite the presence of quite a number of doctors, dentists, lawyers, businessmen, teachers, nurses, social workers, and the like within it, this group was not yet large enough to establish an exclusive res-

Folks We Can Get Along Without

Numbered among the people we can get along without and who are fast becoming a menace to the community are those men who congregate on the sidewalks of principal streets, thus forcing women pedestrians to walk on the grass in order to pass them. They fail to realize that sidewalks are not the places to discuss the outcome of horse races and other topics of the day, and thus not only show lack of good breeding but an attitude of disrespect for the women of their Race.

Figure 51: *Chicago Defender,* October 15, 1932

idential area. "Wherever they move," McKay noted unsympathetically,   233
"the common people follow and threaten to submerge them." [20]

The

Stroll

What complaints about urban black behavior also reveal with particular clarity is the way in which the most important public space in the black
section of the city had come to be the preserve of African American males.
An item in the *Defender* in 1917 deplored the presence of "loafers and idlers
who infest 35th and State street," who made "insulting remarks about
women" and "flirt and 'make eyes' at passers-by." These men, some young,
some old, hung around on the corner for hours, "giving women what they
term the 'once over.'" Furthermore, they "watch women aboard street cars,
and even tip their hats to those they do not know." [21]

To be sure, one could always see women on State Street, but very early
in the piece the Stroll became a byword for an aggressive display of mas-
culinity. Always self-conscious about the way they looked and moved and
ever aware of the scrutiny and approbation of their peers, male denizens of
the Stroll engaged in a type of behavior that frequently amounted to what
nowadays would be labeled sexual harassment and, even when it did not,
was sufficiently raucous and unruly to be an affront to many middle-class
African Americans. In his novel, *The Walls of Jericho* (1928), Rudolph
Fisher captured some of the badinage of the black thoroughfares:

> "My Gawd—did you see that hat?"
> "Hot you, baby——!"
> "—co'se it's a home-made dress—can't you see that crooked
> hem?"
> "What is these young folks comin' to—dat gal's dress ain'
> nothin' but a sash!"
> "Now you know a man that black ain' got no business in no
> white linen suit." [22]

In 1921, the *Defender* published an account of events in the Vendome Theater, a venue for silent films, in which the writer captured well both the
style of these young men and the hostility it could engender among those
forced to witness their performances. The theater's program was evidently
being ruined by a bunch of "vain dandies," young men "who come in and
peacock up and down the aisles, cigars in their mouths and hats on their
heads," not "all of whom come from State street." If the point had not

already been made, the author went on to complain about "'Strollers' who strut up the aisles, mannikin-like, with their hats on."[23]

Every northern city had its equivalent of the Stroll. In Pittsburgh, it was Frankstown Avenue, labeled "Chocolate Boulevarde" by the *Pittsburgh Courier*'s columnist Ole Palmetto. In Kansas City in the 1920s, it was Eighteenth Street, where on Sundays in early spring, the "Faithful Christians and their hangers-on—the Sunday Morning Strutters—would look out at the golden sunlight, test a stray sweet breeze, and head for the churches," or so wrote an almost rhapsodic Roy Wilkins. Later, after dinner, the street would fill "with the rich and poor, the low-down and dignified, crooks and choir singers, riders, strollers, and [those who were] 'just standing.'" On Eighteenth Street "you could see a black man in a pearl-gray hat and a spotless gray suit, somber as any undertaker, except for one touch—a vivid, pink and blue moiré scarf" or a passing parade of "slick hair, flashing teeth, ladies' legs clad in silk—some good, some maybe not so good."[24]

Yet for all the vitality and vibrancy of these and many other locations there was, both in reality and in African Americans' imagination, only one serious rival to Chicago's Stroll, and that, of course, was to be found in Harlem, which by the 1920s had become the Negro Mecca. According to Edgar M. Grey, writing in the *Amsterdam News* in 1927, Harlem managed "to effect in clothing perfect chromatic harmony with its complexion." If one stood "on any of the corners any day, but especially on Sunday, when the town is out on dress parade, one would see that here were a people who, whatever their shortcomings, are masters in the art of gay dress." Not only were Broadway's newest fashions seen immediately in Harlem, but the "slender bodies of these black, brown and yellow people seem to have been made especially for the cut and trim of Anglo-Saxon garments."[25]

A *New York Times* reporter made similar points in a story emphasizing the "enviable physique" of blacks "with slim waists and straight broad shoulders," who were out "strutting the streets of the 'Black Belt.'" Some dressed conservatively and lived frugally, but many "like to dress up and appear the glass of fashion and the mold of form." The crucial difference that easily separated African Americans from whites who held similar laboring jobs was that blacks "run more to exaggerated styles and bright hues." When Harlem churches "disgorge their large congregations, men and women appear in the latest and newest creations of the tailor's and dressmaker's art."[26] Four years later, in 1931, an article in the same paper suggested that, rather than being followers of fashion, young African Americans were its cutting edge. According to the *Times* reporter, the streets—in particular Seventh and Lenox, the "two favorite avenues of Harlem where folks go a-strollin'"—were at their most thronged around 8 o'clock in the evening, but even as late as 3 and 4 o'clock in the morning, there were still plenty of "nocturnal strollers of both sexes" idling in front of store windows, "saunter[ing] up and down in lazy rhythm." At most times of the day, African Americans dressed soberly in black could be found easily enough, but, like us, the *Times* reporter was drawn to those denizens of the avenues who were "celebrated for their sartorial splendors":

> Both men and women display the latest creations of the art of the tailor and the dressmaker. There is a type of youthful Negro who affects garments of a daring cut and pattern, with exaggerated built-up shoulders and with wasp-like waists. These garments are frequently of delicate pastel shades. One gets the impression their wearer is all shoulders and is gorgeously upholstered from head to foot. It is said of Harlem that its fashion plates are several jumps ahead of the rest of the world.[27]

In the 1920s and 1930s, artists and writers, both black and white, tried with varying degrees of success to capture the spirit of African American streetlife. Palmer Hayden's *Midsummer Night in Harlem* (1936) (see Figure 52), a canvas jammed with black humanity, suggests the attractive spaciousness of the front stoop and avenue on an oppressive Harlem night, particularly when compared with the cramped and expensive apartments most African Americans were compelled to rent. But the most successful renditions of black urban life came from the jazz musicians and from those writers prepared to use the blues idiom, for, as Langston Hughes wryly noted, "the life of . . . Lenox Avenue" cannot be "expressed" in a "Shakespearean sonnet." Hughes' blues-infused poetry and Jean Toomer's novel *Cane* best exemplify this point. As Farah Jasmine Griffin has noted in relation to *Cane,* the "slow, sonorous, and cyclical" language—"the language of the spirituals"—of the first section, set in the rural South, transforms, in the first piece of the second section, set in Washington's "Seventh Street," into "an eighteen-line, one-paragraph-long prose poem framed on either side by verse." Griffin likens this "immediate change in rhythm, pace, and content" to the urban blues.[28] That the texture of the lives of

ordinary African Americans in northern cities found their most understanding and sympathetic expressions in the blues-infused works of some
black painters, writers, and musicians is hardly surprising, for it was the
blues idiom itself that animated the colors and rhythms of Lenox or the
South Side's Stroll.

Nowhere was this idiom more clearly displayed than in the numerous
parades that criss-crossed northern cities, almost invariably to the disapproval of the African American press. In 1920 the *Defender* complained
that, from early spring until fall, "every Sunday there is a parade of some

Figure 52: Palmer C. Hayden, *Midsummer Night in Harlem* (1936). This sympathetic image provides a
marked contrast with the way such behavior was viewed by the *Chicago Defender* in Figure 50. Museum
of African-American Art, Los Angeles

sort or other in the streets of Chicago," disturbing the quiet and peace of the day. The paper puritanically protested that for blacks "to tramp the streets, all dolled up in flashy regalia, behind a noisy band" was anything but "exhilarating." What is more, the participants "overtax themselves and are utterly unfit for their duties on Monday morning." The *Whip*, too, decried "parades, loud colored regalia, black horses and pompous 'street-marshalls,'" and would much have preferred all the energy expended in them to have been put into "labor organizations and behind Negro business." [29] Yet for all the invective against these events (much of it clearly directed at Marcus Garvey and his Universal Negro Improvement Association, whose street theater was so exciting northern blacks in the post-war years), it remains apparent that those who participated viewed the parades in a more positive light. James Weldon Johnson commented, in understated fashion, that "it is not a universal custom of Harlem to stand idly and watch a parade go by; a good part of the crowd always marches along, keeping step to the music," an interactive process that added much to the "movement, colour and gaiety" of street life. Some parades did receive the approbation of the newspapers, a notable example being the funeral procession through Harlem for Florence Mills, the famous singer, who died young in 1927, a parade which, according to the *Amsterdam News*, attracted 200,000 spectators. It was the more "irresponsible bodies," who used processions "to spread their particular propaganda," that drew the ire of much of the African American press.[30]

The issue of how blacks should present themselves in public space was obviously problematic. At one end of what is probably best viewed as a fluid continuum (although depending on the occasion the same people could be at different points along it) were middle- and upper-class blacks, who were often accused of adopting wholesale white manners and ways. For the benefit of this group and those who aspired to join it, the *Defender*, in the 1930s, carried a column entitled "Men's Corner" that dispensed fashion advice and commented on the ensembles of various men about town. "Men's Corner" also ran an annual pictorial feature on black Chicago's ten "Best Dressed Men," the majority of whom were professionals of one sort or another (although a postal employee and a valet were included in 1935), whose garb was again virtually indistinguishable from that of well-dressed whites.

For members of the respectable black upper and middle classes, church-going and attendance at weddings became occasions for the public display of a tasteful elegance, a refined appearance that did in fact closely resemble that of the white elite. Isabel Washington Powell, former wife of Adam Clayton Powell, Jr., recalled that after church on Sundays Powell "would walk down Seventh Avenue wearing tails and an ascot. He was immaculate. He was fantastic." Her own preparations were equally elaborate. She had the advantage of "my own milliner who did my hats" and "a lady that made my dresses." "My whole deal was getting ready for church on Sunday and strutting down the aisle of Abyssinian Baptist Church, oh sure."[31] And when, in November 1923, Miss Mae Robinson, granddaughter of the late Madame Walker, married Dr. Gordon Jackson at Saint Phillip's Episcopal Church in New York, the event was characterized, according to the *Crisis*, by "beauty, elegance and rare taste." The bride's dress was a "gown of chiffon beaded with pearls over bride's satin"; the bridesmaids "wore cream colored Chantilly lace over silver cloth"; and the bride's mother wore "a marvelous gown of gold metallic cloth which had been designed and made in Paris." Male guests wore formal suits and wing collars and, but for the color of their skin, were virtually indistinguishable from the guests at a white society wedding (see Figure 53). The Robinson/Jackson event was hardly typical—over nine thousand invitations were sent out—but, generally, middle- and upper-class African American weddings were ritualized and prescriptive (virtually every fashion parade had a section devoted to weddings) and differed little from their equivalent in the white community.[32]

Easter Sunday was another important sartorial occasion for the elite. On that day in 1935, the *Defender* sent out its photographer to catch "men, women and children, dressed in formal day wear and spring finery" (see Figure 54). Elton Fax, a black writer who first arrived in Harlem on an Easter Sunday, was impressed by what he saw: "that was something," he told an interviewer years later; there were African Americans "who were quite seriously elegant, in top hat, tails, cutaway coats, spats, cane." Indeed, he bitingly added, they wore "anything that mimicked white upper-class living, mimicry of that which was opulent, that which was approved, that which white folks aspired to be."[33]

But if Booker T. Washington, besuited and resplendent in the rectitude of his Victorian garb, and the nattily dressed and urbane W. E. B. Du Bois were at one end of the sartorial spectrum, the other end was occupied by a more colorful urban *demi-monde* that broke the rules, or set new ones, with a rainbow-like abandon. Chester Himes would later people his detective stories with characters drawn from his experience as a young black tearaway in 1920s Cleveland. Working as a bellhop, he was involved in prostitution and bootlegging, often making fifty dollars a night, which he promptly used to shoot dice. Whenever Himes had a win, "next day I'd go downtown and buy clothes. I was ridiculously vain." For the most part he bought expensive garments and accessories, "stylish but not outlandish" items, as he described them, his most "daring" purchase being "a pair of square-toed yellow pigskin bluchers by Florsheim."[34] For the theater-going classes at least, this urban milieu of pimps, prostitutes, gamblers, hustlers, numbers runners, bootleggers, and drug dealers was instantly recognizable in the

Figure 53: The marriage of Miss Mae Robinson and Dr. Gordon Jackson. *Crisis* 27 (January 1924), 129

character of Sportin' Life in *Porgy and Bess,* the "sexualized, hip and flashy descendant of minstrelsy's 'Zip Coon,'" as Ann Douglas has pointed out, who tried to entice Bess to leave on the boat for New York:

> An' through Harlem we'll go struttin' . . .
> Come along wid me, dat's de place . . .
> Dat's where we belong! [35]

From today's perspective, the most famous denizen of this world was the zoot-suited Detroit Red, or, as he later renamed himself, Malcolm X.

In the 1920s and 1930s, the arbiters of fashion, as well as its *avant garde,* were, as indeed they are now, African American musicians. Inhabitants of the night hours who often played in clubs run by gangsters and bootleggers, jazz musicians were associated with an element of risk, with the illicit (a few of the early players, most notably Jelly Roll Morton, were little short of being pimps, living off the earnings of a string of "sporting women"). Jazz musicians' performances and lifestyles were highly visible and influential aspects of city life, albeit hardly reputable ones. In February 1922, the *Defender* reported that there was to be a "determined drive against jazz music and dancing in the public schools of the city," and that one of the key measures in the attack on the "preponderance of jazz" in the system was to be "action against extremes in dress." [36] There was something exaggerated about the way jazz men presented themselves in public, an almost in-

Figure 54: *Chicago Defender,* April 27, 1935

evitable accompaniment to performing for an audience under the glare of the spotlight. Because they were very conscious of their appearance and frequently highly articulate about it, there is more than enough material surviving from interviews, autobiographies, and the like to approach the subject, for once, without having to struggle through the usual miasma of white ridicule and black middle-class disapproval. Looking sharp was an inescapable part of being a jazz musician; it was also an aspect that many reveled in.

Earl Hines, typically resplendent in his tuxedo, Chesterfield overcoat, bowler hat, walking stick, and carefully coiffed hairstyle, was renowned as the most elegant of the Chicago jazzmen in the 1920s. His reputation was hard won: as he wryly noted, he "practically lived at the barbershop, getting manicures and massages, as well as getting my hair fixed."[37] Hines had learned his trade in Pittsburgh, where, unsupported by a union, musicians dressed up and waited around on Wylie Avenue for the bookers to hire them. As William Howland Kenney has perceptively noted, "already, jazz musicians understood clothing as a form of show business advertising," a judgment with which Willie the Lion Smith, the famed Harlem Stride piano player, agreed: "the guys that dressed to kill always got good jobs."[38]

Dressing up was something Smith knew a good deal about. According to his good friend and fellow piano player, James P. Johnson, Smith was not only "one of the sharpest ticklers I ever met" but also "a fine dresser, very careful about the cut of his clothes."[39] Around the time of World War One, Smith, Johnson, and some of the other piano players fused their carefully crafted appearance with the way they moved their bodies to create a performance style that was the epitome of twentieth-century African American expressive culture. Many were very good dancers, an attribute that showed through in their "attitude and stance." Johnson recalled that "when Willie Smith walked into a place, his every move was a picture." "Every move we made was studied, practiced, and developed," he continued, "just like it was a complicated piano piece." The way such musicians approached the piano, took off their overcoats and hats, laid their cane on the music rack, and sat at the piano to show off the pleats in their jacket, as well as the distinctive manner in which they played the instrument, were integral parts of their performance. In their accounts of this style, both Johnson and Smith stressed that the aim was to "attract the young gals," but projecting sexual allure was only a part of what was going on. The almost arrogant, disdainful manner they assumed was not only intimidating for the other piano players in this highly competitive world but something that the knowing and demanding audiences in Harlem clubs understood and expected. As Johnson said, "you had to have an attitude, a style of behaving that was your personal, professional trade-mark."[40]

Jelly Roll Morton was among the more notable performers, a man whose "attitude" was admired by Johnson, Smith, and many others. He would come in to a club smiling "so everyone would get a glance at his diamond-studded tooth."[41] Then, according to Johnson, Morton

> would take his overcoat off. It had a special lining that would catch everybody's eye. So he would turn it inside out and, instead of folding it, he would lay it lengthwise along the top of the upright piano. He would do this very slowly, very carefully and very solemnly as if the coat was worth a fortune and had to be handled very tenderly.

Morton would then shake out his silk handkerchief, ostentatiously dust the piano stool with it, sit down, and hit his signature chord, the one that announced the presence of Jelly Roll Morton. He always began with a "spirited rag" in order "to astound the audience" with his undoubted skills.[42]

In his autobiography, *Music on My Mind,* Willie the Lion Smith gave the "correct lowdown on how we all dressed in the olden times." The three main tailoring establishments favored by the musicians were Bromberger's, Clemens and Ostreicher, and Wilkowitz. Smith's overcoat, "the first garment the customers would see you in—in the cold season," was a blue melton, with a full, boxlike back and plaid lining. It had cost him around 150 dollars and, most important, given the often precarious finances of these men, could, if new, be pawned for 100 dollars. Smith always wore a derby, in part at least because it was a hat favored by the English. When the derby was removed, it revealed hair styled by Hart, the barber up on 153rd Street, who had invented Kink-No-More—"Conk" for short—a preparation that, according to James Johnson, was "used by all musicians." Customarily, entertainers needed "at least twenty-five suits," Smith stated, because "you couldn't wear the same suits too often." Smith favored a "conservative blue or brown melton made out of the same material from which my overcoat had been cut," with square shoulders, a padded lining, and a full or box-back cut. The jacket was single-breasted "so I could show off my gold watch fob and chain." The trousers were "tight with long, peg-topped fourteen inch cuffs." The shoes were handmade from French, Shriner & Urner, the store that James P. Johnson also patronized. If one worked with one's jacket off, "it was a policy to have a real fancy silk shirt"— Smith preferred a "soft-blue" or a "candy-colored pink"—that cost anything from ten to twenty-five dollars. Expensive accessories were important components of the desired look: "if we had diamonds," Smith boasted, "we flashed them"—in tie pins, rings, or in one memorable case, set in the tooth of a bulldog that the player tethered to the leg of the piano. Clothing was expensive, even extravagant, but it was also carefully chosen with the necessary poise and elegance of the musician in mind. Smith remembered that "many of us carried a cane to balance our stride."[43]

Clearly, the music business was pervaded by a deeply entrenched ethic of conspicuous consumption. Not everyone participated—Smith used to call Fats Waller "Filthy" because of his disreputable and somewhat soiled appearance[44]—but it was, nevertheless, one of the distinctive characteristics of the life. In musicians' speech, clothing and accessories were abbreviated to brand names, and, whatever the *cognoscenti*'s requirements, there were only certain firms that they would patronize. Johnson frankly admitted that much of the inspiration for their look came from "the styles of the rich whites," but he also added that we "copied them and made improvements."[45] We would suggest that the phrase "made improvements" can bear some weight here. The constructed appearance of these musicians was, in time-honored African American fashion, an act of *bricolage*, a creative combination of clothes (many with small adjustments here and there), textures, and colors that frequently belied the origins of its constituent elements. Much the same can be said of the musicians' individual performance styles. Johnson learned how to move on stage, how to win over an audience, indeed, how to play the piano, from closely observing his peers and sampling whatever was original: "if they had anything I didn't have," he admitted, "I listened and stole it."[46]

Hardly surprisingly, stories about the appearance of its major figures entered jazz music's lore. Al Rose used to patronize Mike the Tailor in Philadelphia. One day in the late 1930s, Mike let Rose know that he had a remnant of imported English cloth—"a polychromatic, green-striped worsted, truly beautiful"—sufficiently large for him to make from it a three-piece suit, whereupon Rose ordered the suit to be made. When the splendid garment was ready, the tailor made recommendations about the color of the shirt and the accessories that Rose should wear, and Rose took his advice. But on visiting a club that night Rose was confronted by Jelly Roll Morton wearing an identical outfit. Clearly there had been more than just a "remnant" of the cloth. Morton came to Rose's table, and when Rose's companion introduced the two men they burst out laughing at one another. As Morton left to join his party he leaned over and quietly whispered in Rose's ear, "next time you see Mike the Tailor, you tell him I'm gonna kick his ass." [47]

It was not only the piano players who developed their own style. Some of the bands, notably Ellington's, wore especially snappy uniforms, and all of them acknowledged the importance of dressing sharply. According to Earl Hines, "the bands tried to outdress one another, but, with Jimmie Lunceford's and Duke Ellington's, we were considered the best-dressed band on the road. It meant an awful lot, because appearance was almost half the battle." [48] As we have seen, clothing and the look of the band were important in the South, but perhaps never to the same extent, or in quite the same fashion, as they were to African Americans based in the northeastern cities, something that often became apparent as bands swung through the rest of the country on tours. Ellington and his orchestra made a lasting impression on a young Ralph Ellison in Oklahoma City: they "came with their uniforms, their sophistication, their skills"; they "were news from the great wide world, an example and a goal." [49] But not everyone in the South appreciated this "news" as much as Ellison did. The *Chicago Defender* reported in 1922 that members of a black band had been beaten up outside a Miami hotel. According to the paper, their white assailants had warned them: "We'll teach you niggers to come here dressed in your white flannels and tweed coats, playing for our dances and looking at our pretty white women. Now, go back up North and tell all your nigger friends." [50]

But the views of unreconstructed and vicious whites were hardly likely to diminish, indeed would probably only increase, the cachet that peers accorded to musicians who, masters of the idiom, were able to set the new fashion standards. Though Miles Davis began getting "into clothes" as an eleven- or twelve-year-old in the late 1930s, his real education took place at the hands of Dexter Gordon in the early postwar years. The "super hip and dapper" Gordon was little impressed by Davis's wardrobe. "I know you think they hip, Miles, but they ain't. I can't be seen with nobody wearing no square shit like you be wearing. And you playing in Bird's band? The hippest band in the world? Man, you oughta know better." After Davis had bought a gray, big-shouldered suit, Dexter Gordon was reassured: "now you looking like something, now you hip. You can hang with us."[51]

Yet for all the elan of the jazz musicians' measured and cool display, there was always something fragile or brittle about it. Bouts of unemployment, well-publicized struggles with alcohol or drugs, sickness, and innumerable other possible disasters—all these threatened what was far from a stable way of making a living. Willie the Lion Smith's careful eye to the value of clothing at the pawnbrokers was an attitude born of the hard experience of many of his peers. Much the same characteristics marked the major northern black communities, of which the jazz musicians were such a vital part. Though many of the migrants did do better than they would have done in the South, the 1920s were hardly good years economically for northern blacks, and the 1930s, of course, were much worse. For many, life was an incessant and interminable struggle to make ends meet.

Outside the world of musicians, black style, as we have outlined it here, was hardly going to aid African Americans in overcoming the economic inequities they encountered in the northern cities; indeed, as many white and black commentators were keen to point out, the importance attributed to clothing, appearance, and the right "look," probably contributed to the impoverishment of some black families. But these men and women were well aware that there was more to life than rational economic calculation, and they saw no reason why they should merely exist. The majority of African Americans in the urban northern were employed as laborers, factory workers, domestic servants, and the like, jobs that were often backbreaking, badly paid and menial, and that usually placed black people under the supervision of whites. On Sundays and in their other leisure hours away from work, however, urban blacks regained control of their bodies and of their souls. Shucking off their work clothes—the overalls and maids' uniforms that more often than not were a mark of the degradation frequently associated with their employment—ordinary African Americans dressed up like "fashion plates" and congregated in convivial black spaces. Such activity, which, as Robin Kelley has astutely observed, tended to be "alternative rather than oppositional,"[52] was one of the liberating features decisively influencing the distinctive African American culture that was emerging in the northern cities in the first half of the twentieth century.

On Sundays and at night during the rest of the week, in Philadelphia, Pittsburgh, Detroit, and most obviously in Harlem and the South Side of Chicago, factory workers, doormen, maids, porters, writers, and even the self-employed, whose numbers included Naomi Washington's father, could forget the vagaries and troubles of their humdrum, workaday existence, put on their best clothes, and venture out into the city. For those who could afford it, there was dancing at the Savoy or at a rent party, the chance to see a show at the Apollo, or to watch a film, but for those who could not, there was still the local stroll and, on Sundays, the excursion to church. "The masses of Harlem," the songwriter and author James Weldon Johnson observed, "get a good deal of pleasure out of things far too simple for most other folks." Partly, of course, resort to the stroll was the product of a cruel necessity born of poverty, but there was more to it than this. For Johnson, the phenomenon he referred to was best exemplified by the way Harlemites went strolling on summer evenings and on Sundays. As he carefully pointed out, the word "strolling" did "not mean merely walking along Lenox or upper Seventh Avenue"; it meant "that those streets are places for socializing."

> One puts on one's best clothes and fares forth to pass the time pleasantly with the friends and acquaintances and, most important of all, the strangers he is sure of meeting. One saunters along, he hails this one, exchanges a word or two with that one, stops for a short chat with the other one. He comes up to a laughing, chattering group, in which he may have only one friend or acquaintance, but that gives him the privilege of joining in. He does join in and takes part in the joking, the small talk and gossip, and makes new acquaintances. . . . He finally moves on a few steps farther and joins another group and is introduced to two or three pretty girls who have just come to Harlem, perhaps only for a visit . . . . The hours of a summer evening run by rapidly. This is not simply going out for a walk; it is more like going out for adventure.[53]

To be sure, there is an air of wistful romanticism to this passage. Johnson ignores the class and color differences that were increasingly apparent, barely alludes, and then only inadvertently, to the masculine ethos that ruled in black public spaces. Yet Johnson also manages, as well as does any other writer, to capture something of the pleasures of African American street life in the first four decades of the twentieth-century North. The young Naomi Washington may not have been able to distinguish her fa- ther's garb from that of a pimp, but for Washington himself, and for thousands like him in Harlem and elsewhere in the North, dressing up on Sunday and strolling down Seventh Avenue to church was—and this too was some sort of comment on northern black life—about as sweet as it got.

EPILOGUE

Suit Men from Suit Land

Standing on the platform of a New York subway station, Ralph Ellison's invisible man watched the approach of three young African American men. They were "tall and slender," and walked "stiffly with swinging shoulders in their well-pressed, too-hot-for-summer suits, their collars high and tight about their necks, their identical hats of black cheap felt set upon the crown of their heads with a severe formality above their hard conked hair." The youths moved "slowly, their shoulders swaying, their legs swinging from their hips in trousers that ballooned upward from cuffs fitting snug about their ankles; their coats long and hip-tight with shoulders far too broad to be those of natural western men." The angular, almost cubist, appearance of these zoot suiters prompted Ellison's protagonist to recall the words of one of his teachers: "You're like one of these African sculptures, distorted

248

in the interest of a design." But, the invisible man quickly wondered, "what design and whose?" [1]

That was a question that intrigued a good many people in the decade before the publication of *Invisible Man* in 1952. The zoot suit had erupted into American consciousness in the summer of 1943. In a series of explosive riots in Los Angeles and northern cities such as Detroit and Harlem, mobs of armed servicemen, with at the very least the acquiescence of the police, beat up and stripped young African Americans and Mexican Americans caught on the streets wearing the daring and provocative garb of the zoot suit. It was not so much that these riots disrupted the smooth running of the home front that disturbed the white authorities, although that was cause for concern, but the way in which, at a time of crisis for the American republic, indeed for most of the world, a significant number of young men from the non-white underclasses thumbed their noses at their country's patriotic demands. Instead of fighting for America and democracy, the youths chose to hang around on city streets, flaunting their indifference to the war effort by wearing clothing that outrageously broke the newly introduced rationing regulations (see Figure 55). If only for its own peace of mind, white America needed to know the origins of this offensively flamboyant type of clothing.

The *New York Times,* authoritative as ever, provided the answer. In a story printed on June 11, 1943, as running brawls between armed servicemen and zoot suiters were occurring on Los Angeles streets, the *Times* was able to determine that the "first zoot suit on record" had been ordered and made in February 1940. Clyde Duncan, a young busboy from Gainesville, Georgia, had so amazed his local tailor by requesting a suit with a 37-inch-long coat, and trousers 26 inches at the knees and 14 inches at the ankle, that, after the tailor had had a Chicago company make the suit up, he had photographed the satisfied customer in his new garb and sent the picture in to *Men's Apparel Reporter.* The *Reporter* duly printed the photograph, and an accompanying story, in its February 1941 issue (see Figure 56). According to the *Times,* initially the trade had been "amused" by the zoot suit, but amusement had soon been transformed into astonishment "when the 'killer diller' caught on in Mississippi, New Orleans and Alabama and leap-frogged to Harlem." The paper went on to suggest that the inspiration for the zoot suit was the "authentic Civil War garb worn by Clark Gable as Rhett Butler in 'Gone With the Wind.'" As the reporter pointed out, the film had opened in Georgia in December 1939, a couple of months before busboy Clyde Duncan placed his order.[2]

Among the nation's black newspapers, there were some skeptical reactions to this story. The *Pittsburgh Courier,* suspicious of the motives of the "staid *New York Times,*" pointed out that, "in getting to the basic sociological and psychological causes for the 'Zoot Suit Riots' being raged on

"—*I cause I've deferred man. Someone has got to look fo' fine women.*"

Figure 55: *Amsterdam News,* February 14, 1942

the West Coast," the paper had gone "way down in its files and came up with the Georgia boy," who, the august *Times* "would have you gather," had "started it all."³ A week later, Horace Cayton, writing in the *Pittsburgh Courier,* also referred to the zoot suit's "alleged origin" with the order placed by the "Negro boy in Georgia" before going on to add that, whatever its source, "the motion picture's estimable star, that paragon of Negro culture, Rochester, made [the zoot suit] synonymous with Negroes."⁴

There was, however, an alternative genealogy for the zoot suit, one that had been revealed in the *Amsterdam News,* an African American newspaper, a fortnight before the publication of the *Times's* story. If the *New York Times* was propagating a myth of "fashion from below," the basis of the *News's* story was a more old-fashioned trickle-down theory of elite influence. According to Julius J. Adams, the first zoot suiter was the Duke of Windsor. "He probably would deny it," Adams conceded, "but the facts speak for themselves, and those of us who used to look to him for a cue to the advance mode, recall vividly that it is so." In the 1930s, on "Seventh Avenue in New York, and on 47th Street in Chicago, the boys were wearing wide-brimmed hats, peg-top trousers and long coats," and "fancy shirts, hand-colored socks, and odd slacks and jackets were the rage." The inspiration for this extravagant sartorial display had been none other than the

former Edward VIII, "he being the exponent of such attire." When, at a recent official function, the Duke and some newspaper reporters had laughed at the colorful garb of some zoot-suited Bahamian farm workers, the irony had slipped by everyone there: "what the reporters seem to have forgotten and probably didn't know and what the Duke of Windsor would like to forget is, that he, as Prince of Wales, wore the first, and is truly the father of the present-day Zoot Suit." But, as Adams added mischievously, "he was young and fly, too, in those days."⁵

Clearly, the black press did not view the origins of the zoot suit with quite the same gravity as did the *Times.* In an article for the Associated Negro Press, Frank Marshall Davis at first wheeled in the usual suspects. Some said the

Figure 56: According to the *New York Times,* at least, this was the first zoot suit. *New York Times,* June 11, 1943. NYT Permissions

zoot suit began with Clyde Duncan, "dusky Gainesville, Ga., bus boy"; others pointed to Clark Gable in *Gone with the Wind;* another group believed that "the Filipino colony in Los Angeles originated the style and then discarded it, only to have it later picked up by Mexicans and Negroes." But Davis had another nominee: "George Washington, the pappy of this country." At age fifteen, Davis was able to reveal, the young Washington had instructed his tailor to create a frock coat "very long waisted and in length to come down below the knee." Davis went on to observe that "in those days the men wore broad brimmed hats, two large fobs from the vest, which itself descended halfway between the hips and the knees, with breeches sitting upon the waist." By way of conclusion, the author stated that, as there were "several possible explanations for the style," it was up to the reader "to choose the one that zoots you."[6]

Leaving aside the story of George Washington, there is an immensely appealing ring to all these myths about the origin of the zoot suit. Indeed, there is something very modern about the suit itself; in many ways its appearance signals the beginning of our own time, an appropriate point at which to end this book. There is deep irony in the notion that the zoot suit, the subversive and un-American garb of young blacks and Chicanos, was possibly inspired by Rhett Butler's clothing in one of the icons of twentieth-century popular culture, *Gone with the Wind,* a film that perpetuates demeaning racial stereotypes and does its best to etch in stone the corrosive idea that the ending of slavery and the period of Reconstruction constituted the Tragic Era in the history of the South. Moreover, the complex interplay between genres of popular culture—from Rhett Butler to the streets and then back to the big screen in the figures of Rochester and, later, Cab Calloway in *Stormy Weather* (see Figure 57)—is similarly suggestive of a distinctly modern sensibility. Stories of Filipino and English influence, too, and indeed the fact that it was not just blacks but Chicanos and whites as well who wore the suits, point forward to the increasingly global nature of the creative influences that would shape African American culture and, of course, the impact that that culture would have.

There is also, in all likelihood, an element of "truth" to all these stories. With the benefit of hindsight, it is possible to see the zoot suit emerging at least as far back as the early 1930s; indeed, several of the descriptions quoted in the previous chapter obviously point this way. It is also correct to say that English fashion and tailoring—and the Duke of Windsor was important here—were highly valued among African Americans in that decade. There was, however, a distinct shift somewhere around 1939 or 1940, a transformation from precursors to the full-blown zoot suit. Clyde Duncan comes into the picture here because, by the accident of his Gainesville tailor's initiative, he entered the published record and could later be excavated by the print-conscious *New York Times*. In all probability, Duncan was but one of a number of individuals who were early wearers of this type of clothing.

Taken together, these stories of the zoot suit, and, indeed, the rather different motives of those blacks and whites who attempted to discover its origins, reveal something about race relations during World War Two. They are also suggestive of some of the changing elements of African American life, harbingers of the future. But, as is usually the case with black culture, the search for a genealogy for any particular cultural practice is less important and interesting than is the discovery of the uses ordinary African Americans were able to make of that practice, wherever its origins may have been.

In this latter context, the zoot suit appears as one element, albeit an important one, in a style being developed by young black men against the backdrop of World War Two. When Ellison's invisible man assumed the role of Rinehart, the author's protean ghetto character, he quickly realized that it "was as though by dressing and walking in a certain way I had enlisted in a fraternity in which I was recognized at a glance — not by features, but by clothes, by uniform, by gait."[7] The zoot suit, then, was but one part of a total "look" that included not merely clothing and accessories but also hair style and the way the body itself was carried (see Figure 58). After a very young Malcolm X had finished his makeover in a Boston department store, emerging from the process resplendent in a wild sky-blue zoot suit, baggy pants tapering to the ankles,

Figure 57: Cab Calloway in the famous zoot suit he wore in *Stormy Weather*. *Baltimore Afro-American,* March 20, 1943

The orchestra that played for the Elks' victory ball was stopped many times while a request was made for the boys in the audience to remove their hats. To the "jitterbug" like the one shown at right, such a request is the same as asking a well-dressed woman to remove her make-up because the hat forms a part of the "zoot suit." However, the boys paid no heed and members of the lodge and ladies' auxiliary took it upon themselves to remove the hats as shown in photo above. Results—The hats were off and on all evening.

Figure 58: *Baltimore Afro-American,* October 12, 1943

hat, gold watch chain and monogrammed belt, his first action was to take "three of those twenty-five cent sepia-toned, while-you-wait pictures of myself, posed the way 'hipsters' wearing their zoots would 'cool it'—hat dangled, knees drawn together, feet wide apart, both index fingers jabbed toward the floor." As Malcolm X and his compatriots well knew, the "long coat and swinging chain and the Punjab pants were much more dramatic if you stood that way." [8]

The term "zoot" meant something done or worn in an exaggerated style, and exaggeration was indeed the key to understanding the zoot suiters themselves. In the period before April 1942, when the cloth conservation order made the zoot suit illegal, tailors had classified it as an "extreme." The *New York Times* quoted the opinion of a Mr. Carlyle that the "'V-knot' tie, the zoot chain, the shirt collar, the tight 'stuff cuff,' the wide, flat hat and the Dutch-type shoes of the zoot suiter" displayed his "tendency toward exaggeration in all things." [9] The result was an appearance impossible not to notice: the chances of a zoot suiter remaining invisible on anything but a metaphorical level were negligible. This was hardly a new phenomenon. As we have seen throughout this book, where they had space to do so, African American men and women, particularly the young, had often fashioned for themselves a distinctive and visually arresting appearance. What was new was the context. For northern whites, the way in which African American zoot suiters were displaying their bodies in wartime America was no longer something to be dismissed with a joke, a raised eyebrow, a shake of the head, or an expression of annoyance; it was something they cared deeply about. In the summer of 1943, wearing a zoot suit was an illegal and, more importantly, a dramatically unpatriotic act.

Among the African American population, the main zoot suit wearers were the young and the musicians. North and South, this style was associated in particular with the jitterbug and the lindy hop. One Louisiana black remembered that zoot suiters "were guys who could really dance. Most guys who went to dances had them on." These were young men who liked "swing music, very fast music," music which displayed their clothes to best effect on the dance floor.[10] In the North, it was the crowds that flocked to the Roseland Ballroom in Boston, the Savoy in Harlem, and their equivalents in other cities, who donned the sartorially extravagant clothes. It was in such spaces, too, that the language of jive became embedded in the culture. Nowadays this youth and dance culture is best known through Malcolm X's description of it in his autobiography, but, as Robin Kelley has demonstrated, Malcolm X's later conversion to the Black Muslim religion fundamentally flawed his perspective on the events of these years. "The story is tragically dehistoricized," Kelley has written, "torn from the sociopolitical context that rendered the zoot suit, the conk, the lindy hop, and the language of the 'hep cat' signifiers of a culture of opposition among black, mostly male, youth."[11]

As befitting their status within this culture, black jazz musicians took the lead in wearing the zoot suit. Dizzy Gillespie remembered wearing "drape suits like everyone else," with "long coats, almost down to your knees and full trousers." "It was beautiful," he continued, and "I became pretty dandified, I guess."[12] But the most famous zoot suit was one of those worn by Cab Calloway, the leader of the band in which Gillespie played. The suit in question, which Calloway claimed to have had made up just before the rationing orders were introduced, cost what was then a phenomenal $185 (see Figure 57). It was the garb he wore to such effect in *Stormy Weather*, and in which, following instructions from the studio, he refused to allow members of the black press to photograph him.[13]

The specific meaning of the zoot suit derived from its context, from who was wearing it and where it was displayed. Very quickly the suit came to signify, as Stuart Cosgrove has aptly put it, a "refusal"; it was a "subcultural gesture that refused to concede to the manners of subservience." [14] In part, this gesture was directed at whites—if anything, the aggressiveness of some blacks on the northern streets in the 1920s and 1930s, a matter discussed in the previous chapter, increased in the early 1940s—and while the vast majority of black males of fighting age did end up in the armed services, a significant and obvious minority, regarding the war as something solely for the benefit of white America, did their best to avoid the draft and ignore the whole war effort. [15] Associated as it was with leisure and with a dance and music culture that displayed a studied indifference to a work ethic that, for many Americans, seemed even more important as the nation fought for its very survival, the zoot suit was correctly seen by many whites as an insult to their country.

But the gesture was also directed at other blacks, notably the respectable middle class, who, since their reaction to the suit was mixed with embarrassment for the "race," disdained the extravagance and lack of patriotism of the zoot suiters even more than did many whites. Some black commentators, by setting this garb in historical perspective, did advocate tolerance. Frank Marshall Davis began a column that ran in the African American press by claiming that "I can't run a temperature over the way in which today's hepcats strut in their zoot suits." After all, Davis pointed out, he and many of the blacks who now condemned the current fashion had probably provoked much the same outrage when they were young: Davis would not have been surprised if "some of the sundown brothers who blast loudest against zoot suiters weren't talked about in the same way by their elders of the 1920–24 era." [16] But others were unable to prevent their temperatures from rising. Ed Peterson of Chicago, writing to the editor of the *Amsterdam News,* began, quite reasonably, by claiming that the "suit itself is probably a reaction to the conventional-dressed and is a desire of the younger generation to show that they do not care what the older people wear," and that zoot suits "embody the new freedom thought and besides furnish the tailors with work and novelty in cloth cutting." But there was a distinct limit to the writer's sympathy: zoot suits were "extremely ugly it seems to many and do not have at all the grace and appeal that women can put in their newly designed clothes." The fact that blacks had gone for this item of clothing "in a big way . . . merely proves that [the Negro] is a willing fall guy for anything different." [17]

This indifference to respectable opinion, whether black or white, was probably even more obvious among the few African Americans in the smaller towns and communities of the South who dared to wear zoot suits. Among the categories of inhabitants Hylan Lewis used in his investigation of African American life in "Kent" (in reality, York), a community in South Carolina, was one that he admitted was rare, that of the "slick cat." The slick cat was usually the product of "contact with the urban prototype of the 'hep cat'" on the one hand, and "dissatisfaction with local status coupled with a certain disdain for local people and ways" on the other. Lewis manifested little sympathy for this group: in "dress and manner," the slick cat was "blatantly deviate"; he was also "prone to brag of his cleverness and superiority." The investigator's prototype was Lonnie, "a very dark fellow in his mid-twenties." "He wears his hair long and 'conked,' and walks with a self-confident swagger. He is unusually neat and colorfully dressed with a heavy 'zoot' accent—pastel shades and pegged trousers. He is an excellent and exhibitionistic dancer." Lewis went on to characterize Lonnie as a "lone wolf," who displayed considerable confidence in himself but "shows great disdain and distrust of local Negroes." Lonnie had not made "peace" with the local situation; indeed, "a significant quota of hatred and bitterness" was clearly evident in his words and demeanor. "I don't fool myself about the place of the colored man in the South," this young man told Lewis. "I'm educated, I'm the best dancer in town, but I know they'll treat me like everybody else." [18] And that, clearly, was not particularly well.

The small-town South was hardly the only site where the zoot suit fashion became a way of asserting individuality by bucking authority. The enmity between armed servicemen and zoot suiters, the basis of the "riots," has often been commented upon, but those soldiers were white. By late 1942 and early 1943, however, enough African American conscripts were embracing the zoot look by "adjusting" their uniforms for the practice to become a topic of discussion in the African American press. At Fort Huachua in Arizona, the *Baltimore Afro-American* asserted, the behavior of black troops had been impeccable, the sole exception being the violation of army regulations concerning their uniforms, a development which had given the Military Police a considerable headache. According to this newspaper, soldiers "not long removed from civilian life . . . have had their uniforms tailor-made in 'drapes' and long coats resembling the 'zoot suit'" (see Figure 59). A story published a few months after this, in May 1943, suggested that the army had finally managed to have its way, and that the "zoot suit boys" at Fort Huachua were now "a thing of the past."[19]

PEE WEE'S OFF-JIVE—By Ol Harrington

"Major, look down there—I knew we were going to have trouble the day they sent that tailor to this outfit."

Figure 59: *Baltimore Afro-American*, October 5, 1942

At the most basic level, the zoot suit was about youth (see Figure 60): the suit's emergence, and the associated riots, marked the beginnings of the modern invention of "juvenile delinquency" and of teen culture, both of which would flourish in the 1950s.[20] Even very young black teenagers desired, if not to wear a zoot suit, at least to incorporate some aspect of the zoot look in their appearance. Faith Ringgold's mother did not want Faith's younger brother, Andrew, "to look like those boys who wore zoot suits."

"Well, I agrees with the good Reverend when he says he's got to win over the young folks, but I thinks that's goin' a little too far!"

Figure 60: *Baltimore Afro-American,* November 7, 1942

"Musicians wore them," Ringgold remembered, "and so did boys who hung out on street corners." But of course that which repelled and alarmed the mother attracted this African American youth, who had to negotiate life with his peers on the streets of Harlem. After he left the house every day, "Andrew sewed his pants with big stitches at the ankles to make them appear pegged"; before he returned, he would take the stitches out and restore his pants to their original condition.[21] As some contemporary commentators recognized, the youthful exuberance associated with the zoot suit bared not merely racial but generational differences. J. A. Rogers, columnist for the *Pittsburgh Courier,* reported that, in the early summer of 1943, "zooters and jitterbugs" had "stormed" the Paramount Theater, queueing all over the sidewalk, in order to "hear their idol, Harry James." The audience "simply went wild" over James, but all Rogers could get out of his playing "was a piercing noise, annoying at best." The columnist was dimly aware, however, that the whole event represented something new and that the zoot suits worn by the audience on this occasion signaled the "revolt of callow youth against convention and authority." It was a development that Rogers did not welcome: even at best, he wrote, the zoot revolt was "shallow-brained," and "typical of the mentality of the wearers." It "gets the Negro group," he concluded, "nowhere."[22]

What is particularly interesting here is that Harry James, a virtuoso trumpeter who was in vogue in the late 1930s and early 1940s, was white. From colonial times, there had been whites in New York who were fascinated by black life and had mixed freely with blacks, but during World War Two this interest reached new heights. The elements of zoot culture—the dancing, the music, the language, and the clothing—appealed to the young among this group, who, even after the April 1942 regulations had made the suits illegal, continued to buy them from bootleg tailors. The desire to obtain a zoot suit was only one of the reasons why young whites continued to trek uptown into Harlem. They came, also, to dance, to be part of the scene. Thirty percent of the Savoy's patrons were whites, and the vast majority of those were Americans rather than foreign tourists; as one of the members of a band that played regularly at the famous dance hall remembered, the venue was "strictly interracial." This new youth culture—vibrant, autonomous, and not segregated—was of concern to the authorities; indeed, the failure to keep the races apart was the major reason why the New York police closed the Savoy down for three months in 1943.[23]

In a column in the *Pittsburgh Courier,* Horace Cayton observed percipiently that the zoot suit appealed mainly to "frustrated youth, often members of minority groups who can find no other means of self-expression." Cayton pointed out that blacks wore and probably invented this type of clothing, but that zoot suits were also worn by Mexicans in Los Angeles, and that there had even been reports in the papers that zoots were being worn in Paris "as a means of defying the Nazi conquerors." The zoot suit, this journalist concluded, "set the individual off as a person at variance with the dominant group in society." What particularly interested Cayton, though, was the way in which the suit cut across racial lines: zoot-suited African Americans, zoot-suited Mexicans, and "zoot-suited second generation foreign-born whites" all were criticized heavily by the established leaders of their communities, and perhaps, partly for this reason, an "affinity" had developed between the zoot suiters. "Negro and white zoot suiters mix, especially in Harlem, and in Los Angeles Negro and Mexican zoot suiters are closer together than they are to members of their own racial group." Cayton was not without sympathy for these young men, the "dispossessed of this generation," firmly locating their sub-cultural origins in their treatment by the dominant society, but he did warn readers of his column that the youths' distinctive style of dress had become a "badge of identification which symbolizes a mentality," the mentality of a "frustrated, thwarted, 'Bigger Thomas.'"[24]

As it turned out, Cayton overstated his case; few, if any, of the zoot suiters developed into anything approaching Richard Wright's terrifying literary creation. The alienation of these young blacks, which Cayton so correctly described, resulted in a resistance that was cultural rather than physical. That the zoot suiters were engaged in style warfare is now generally recognized by scholars, but what is less often realized is that their behavior was part of an African American tradition. In Ralph Ellison's novel *Invisible Man,* the protagonist's job was to get the zoot suiters back into the "groove of history." From the perspective of the invisible man, working at the time as an agent of the Brotherhood, this may well have been the case, but from our perspective, they are central figures in a long and important cultural lineage, and already firmly in the groove of history. What we have sought to show in this book is that the ways in which black men and women have presented their bodies have been shaped, in important respects, by a distinctive and identifiable African American aesthetic. The zoot suiters may have been more conspicuous in this regard, and may have garnered more attention than most, but, at the point where this study concludes in the early 1940s, they were still merely the last in a very long line.

In late 1939 and early 1940 in New York, Jelly Roll Morton attended his last recording sessions, cutting over twenty tracks for General Records. A few months later he drove across country to Los Angeles, where he would remain until he died on July 10, 1941. By the time these events occurred Morton was in his fifties, in ill-health, broke, and all but forgotten. It is difficult to believe, however, that he did not express a view about the young zoot-suited black men he must have seen in the streets of New York and Los Angeles. After all, Morton was nothing if not opinionated, and it is likely that the zoot suiters reminded him of the time when he was a young tearaway musician, cutting up in the towns along the Gulf, an era in which he, too, was the epitome of black style. Perhaps Morton, with his finely developed sense of history and of his role in it, laid claim to having been the father of the zoot suit, as well as of jazz. And if he did, there would have been some substance to that claim, for, far from being divorced from the African American past, the zoot suit was linked to it by a succession of clothing and movement styles, styles through which, to the extent that their circumstances permitted, black men and women had defiantly announced their presence, giving subtle or even, on occasion, aggressive expression to the aesthetic imperatives that marked them off from the norms of the wider society. Though the black youths on the New York subway platform who walked toward Ellison's invisible man, and their real-life compatriots on the streets of American cities, probably had little knowledge of the traditions involved, they were the rightful heirs of Jelly Roll Morton and a whole host of other African American figures, for surely, if they were nothing else, these young black men were, to borrow one of Morton's prideful self-descriptions, "suit men from suit land."

NOTES

INTRODUCTION

[1] Quoted in Arnold Rampersad, *The Life of Langston Hughes: I, Too, Sing America* (New York, 1986), 73–74.

[2] Frances Ann Kemble, *Journal of a Residence on a Georgian Plantation in 1838–1839,* ed. John A. Scott (New York, 1975), 93–94; Frederick Law Olmsted, *The Cotton Kingdom: A Traveller's Observations on Cotton and Slavery in the American Slave States,* ed. Arthur M. Schlesinger (New York, 1953), 28.

[3] Ralph Ellison, *The Collected Essays of Ralph Ellison,* ed. John F. Callahan (New York, 1995), 54.

[4] Our study of African American expressive culture has not included black spoken expression. This was a deliberate decision made in order to render our subject more manageable.

[5] Willie Morris, *North toward Home* (Boston, 1967), 81–90.

CHAPTER 1

[1] Quoted in John C. Inscoe, *Mountain Masters, Slavery, and the Sectional Crisis in Western North Carolina* (Knoxville, Tenn., 1989), 99–100.

[2] Philip D. Curtin, *The Atlantic Slave Trade: A Census* (Madison, Wis., 1969), 88.

[3] *The Life of Olaudah Equiano, or Gustavus Vassa, the African, Written by Himself,* in Arna Bontemps, ed., *Great Slave Narratives* (Boston, 1969), 1–192. This autobiography was originally published in 1789.

[4] *South Carolina Gazette,* June 5, 1736; *South Carolina Gazette,* June 5, 1756; *South Carolina Gazette,* January 31, 1736. Other historians have touched on the importance of slave clothing, but mostly in the nineteenth century. See, for example, John W. Blassingame, *The Slave Community: Plantation Life in the Ante-Bellum South* (New York, 1972), 192; John B. Boles, *Black Southerners, 1619–1869* (Lexington, Ky., 1983), 86–87; Robert William Fogel and Stanley L. Engerman, *Time on the Cross: The Economics of American Negro Slavery* (Boston, 1974), 116–18; Elizabeth Fox-Genovese, *Within the Plantation Household: Black and White Women of the Old South* (Chapel Hill, N.C., 1988), 120–28, 178–83; Eugene D. Genovese, *Roll, Jordan, Roll: The World the Slaves Made* (New York, 1974), 550–61; Charles Joyner, *Down by the Riverside: A South Carolina Slave Community* (Urbana, Ill., 1984), 106–17.

[5] The research for this book would have taken years longer if not for the publication of Lathan A. Windley, compiler, *Runaway Slave Advertisements: A Documentary History from the 1730s to 1790,* 4 vols. (Westport, Conn., 1983). Here we will cite the newspapers and then, in parentheses, the references to the Windley volumes. In this case the reference is: *Virginia Gazette* (Hunter), November 14, 1751 (Windley, *Runaway Slave Advertisements,* vol. 1, 24).

[6] *Virginia Gazette* (Parks), November 11 to November 18, 1737 (Windley, *Runaway Slave Advertisements,* vol. 1, 3–4).

[7] *South Carolina Gazette and Country Journal,* November 12, 1771 (Windley, *Runaway Slave Advertisements,* vol. 3, 339).

[8] The Works Progress Administration interviews with ex-slaves were conducted in the 1930s and published in several series in the 1970s. The full citation is George P. Rawick, ed., *The American Slave: A Composite Autobiography,* Series 1 & 2, vols. 1–19 (Westport, Conn., 1972); Supplement Series 1, vols. 1–12 (Westport, 1977); Supplement Series 2, vols. 1–10 (Westport, 1979). If the reference is to the Supplements it is stated in the note. In this case the reference is: Rawick, *The American Slave,* Supplement Series 1, vol. 9, Mississippi Narratives, 1415, 1417.

[9] *Virginia Gazette* (Purdie & Dixon), December 24, 1772 (Windley, *Runaway Slave Advertisements,* vol. 1, 126).

[10] John Thornton, *Africa and Africans in the Making of the Atlantic World, 1400–1680* (New York, 1992), 230–34.

[11] Richard L. Bushman, *The Refinement of America: Persons, Houses, Cities* (New York, 1992), 70–74; Jonathan Prude, "To Look upon the 'Lower Sort': Runaway Ads and the Appearance of Unfree Laborers in America, 1750–1800," *Journal of American History* 78 (June 1991), 129–30.

[12] Quoted in Peter H. Wood, *Black Majority: Negroes in Colonial South Carolina from 1670 through the Stono Rebellion* (New York, 1975), 232.

[13] *South Carolina Gazette,* August 28, 1736.

[14] *South Carolina Gazette,* June 8, 1765; *South Carolina Gazette,* July 20, 1765.

[15] *South Carolina Gazette,* December 1, 1766.

[16] *South Carolina Gazette,* June 22, 1734.

[17] *Virginia Gazette* (Purdie & Dixon), October 20, 1768 (Windley, *Runaway Slave Advertisements,* vol. 1, 65).

[18] *Virginia Gazette* (Purdie & Dixon), January 15, 1767 (Windley, *Runaway Slave Advertisements,* vol. 1, 48).

[19] *Virginia Gazette* (Rind), February 27, 1771 (Windley, *Runaway Slave Advertisements,* vol. 1, 312).

[20] *Virginia Gazette* (Rind), February 27, 1772 (Windley, *Runaway Slave Advertisements,* vol. 1, 317).

[21] *Annapolis Maryland Gazette,* June 15, 1775 (Windley, *Runaway Slave Advertisements,* vol. 2, 111–12).

[22] *Virginia Gazette* (Purdie & Dixon), June 30, 1774 (Windley, *Runaway Slave Advertisements,* vol. 1, 149–50).

[23] *Virginia Gazette* (Pinkney), June 15, 1775 (Windley, *Runaway Slave Advertisements,* vol. 1, 331–32).

[24] *Annapolis Maryland Gazette,* August 16, 1777 (Windley, *Runaway Slave Advertisements,* vol. 2, 170–71).

[25] *Charleston South-Carolina Gazette* (Timothy), April 11, 1771 (Windley, *Runaway Slave Advertisements,* vol. 3, 299).

[26] *Charleston South-Carolina Gazette and Country Journal,* November 5, 1771 (Windley, *Runaway Slave Advertisements,* vol. 3, 668–69).

[27] *Maryland Journal and Baltimore Advertiser,* May 25, 1787 (Windley, *Runaway Slave Advertisements,* vol. 2, 361).

[28] *Virginia Gazette and Weekly Advertiser* (Nicholson), September 4, 1788 (Windley, *Runaway Slave Advertisements,* vol. 1, 242).

[29] *Virginia Gazette* (Rind), September 22, 1768 (Windley, *Runaway Slave Advertisements,* vol. 1, 289–90).

[30] *Maryland Journal and Baltimore Advertiser,* December 17, 1783 (Windley, *Runaway Slave Advertisements,* vol. 2, 276).

[31] Quoted in Wood, *Black Majority,* 232.

[32] *Annapolis Maryland Gazette,* January 9, 1783 (Windley, *Runaway Slave Advertisements,* vol. 2, 133).

[33] *South Carolina Gazette* (Timothy), December 8 to December 15, 1766 (Windley, *Runaway Slave Advertisements,* vol. 3, 260–61).

[34] *Savannah Georgia Gazette,* August 1, 1765 (Windley, *Runaway Slave Advertisements,* vol. 4, 15). Obviously, the vast bulk of slave crime would not have been reported, but, in colonial Virginia at least, clothing and fabric were among the most common items stolen in those cases that were settled by a court. See Philip J. Schwarz, *Twice Condemned: Slaves and the Criminal Laws of Virginia, 1705–1865* (Baton Rouge, La., 1988), 126–27.

[35] Wood, *Black Majority,* 232.

[36] Quoted in Joyce E. Chaplin, "Slavery and the Principle of Humanity: A Modern Idea in the Early Lower South," *Journal of Social History* 24 (Winter 1990), 309.

[37] On the task system, see Philip D. Morgan, "Task and Gang Systems: The Organization of Labor on New World Plantations," in Stephen Innes, ed., *Work and Labor in Early America* (Chapel Hill, N.C., 1988), 189–220.

[38] *Annapolis Maryland Gazette,* July 15, 1784 (Windley, *Runaway Slave Advertisements,* vol. 2, 144–45).

[39] *Virginia Gazette* (Rind), May 9, 1771 (Windley, *Runaway Slave Advertisements,* vol. 1, 311).

[40] *Maryland Journal and Baltimore Advertiser,* September 3, 1782 (Windley, *Runaway Slave Advertisements,* vol. 2, 271).

[41] For an account of this market in used clothing in New York City, see Shane White, *Somewhat More Independent: The End of Slavery in New York City, 1770–1810* (Athens, Ga., 1991), 195–96. A similar situation appears to have occurred in England; see Beverly Lemire, "The Theft of Clothes and Popular Consumerism in Early Modern England," *Journal of Social History* 24 (Winter 1990), 255–76.

[42] *South Carolina Gazette* (Powell and Co.), May 10, 1773 (Windley, *Runaway Slave Advertisements*, vol. 3, 323–24).

[43] *South Carolina Gazette*, August 27, 1772.

[44] *Charleston South Carolina Gazette and Country Journal*, August 24, 1773 (Windley, *Runaway Slave Advertisements*, vol. 3, 689).

[45] *South Carolina Gazette*, November 5, 1744.

[46] *South Carolina Gazette*, August 27, 1772.

[47] *South Carolina Gazette*, September 24, 1772. On Charleston blacks, see Philip D. Morgan, "Black Life in Eighteenth-Century Charleston," *Perspectives in American History*, New Series, 1 (1984), 187–232.

[48] *South Carolina Gazette*, September 17, 1772.

[49] *Daily Advertiser* (New York), July 30, 1794.

[50] Prude, "To Look upon the 'Lower Sort'," 156. See also White, *Somewhat More Independent*, 198–99.

[51] *South Carolina Gazette* (Powell & Co.), May 10, 1773 (Windley, *Runaway Slave Advertisements*, vol. 3, 323–24).

[52] *Charleston Royal Gazette*, June 6 to June 9, 1781 (Windley, *Runaway Slave Advertisements*, vol. 3, 581).

[53] *Annapolis Maryland Gazette*, June 9, 1780 (Windley, *Runaway Slave Advertisements*, vol. 2, 125).

[54] *Maryland Journal and Baltimore Advertiser*, September 25, 1781 (Windley, *Runaway Slave Advertisements*, vol. 2, 253); *Virginia Gazette or American Advertiser* (Hayes), January 25, 1783 (Windley, *Runaway Slave Advertisements*, vol. 1, 346).

[55] *Charleston South Carolina Gazette and Country Journal*, December 24, 1771 (Windley, *Runaway Slave Advertisements*, vol. 3, 670–71). For a discussion of the African propensity to combine European garments in apparently haphazard fashion, see William D. Piersen, *Black Yankees: The Development of an Afro-American Subculture in Eighteenth-Century New England* (Amherst, Mass., 1988), 11.

[56] Shane White, "'It Was a Proud Day': African Americans, Festivals, and Parades in the North, 1741–1834," *Journal of American History* 81 (June 1994), 13–51.

[57] Quoted in Joyce E. Chaplin, *An Anxious Pursuit: Agricultural Innovation and Modernity in the Lower South, 1730–1815* (Chapel Hill, 1993), 211.

[58] *South Carolina Gazette* (Timothy), August 18–August 25, 1758 (Windley, *Runaway Slave Advertisements*, vol. 3, 163).

[59] *Charleston South Carolina and General Gazette*, January 21, 1779 (Windley, *Runaway Slave Advertisements*, vol. 3, 548–49).

[60] *South Carolina Gazette* (Timothy), December 19–December 26, 1741 (Windley, *Runaway Slave Advertisements*, vol. 3, 49); *South Carolina Gazette* (Timothy), July 27–August 3, 1747 (Windley, *Runaway Slave Advertisements*, vol. 3, 78).

[61] See T. H. Breen, "'Baubles of Britain': The American and Consumer Revolutions of the Eighteenth Century," *Past & Present* 119 (May 1988), 73–104; T. H. Breen, "Narrative of Commercial Life: Consumption, Ideology, and Community on the Eve of the American Revolution," *William and Mary Quarterly* 50 (July 1993), 471–501.

[62] Quoted in Chaplin, *An Anxious Pursuit*, 213. On the extent of reliance on Britain and its discouragement of plantation self-sufficiency in the colonial years, see Carole Shammas, "Black Women's Work and the Evolution of Plantation Society in Virginia," *Labor History* 26 (Winter 1985), 5–28, especially 24; Carole Shammas, *The Pre-Industrial Consumer in England and America* (Oxford, 1990), especially 65, 69.

[63] Chaplin, *An Anxious Pursuit*, 208–20.

[64] In West African societies the weaving of cloth had been the work of men, but in nineteenth-century America slave women performed this task, probably because their owners followed traditional European labor practice. See Maude Southwell Wahlman, *Signs and Symbols: African Images in African-American Quilts* (New York, 1993), 21, 25.

[65] Fox-Genovese, *Within the Plantation Household*, 181.

[66] Rawick, *The American Slave*, Supplement Series 1, vol. 9, Mississippi Narratives, 1640.

[67] Rawick, *The American Slave*, vol. 3, South Carolina Narratives, 159.

[68] Rawick, *The American Slave*, vol. 14, North Carolina Narratives, 286. On some large plantations textiles were produced in special buildings. See John Michael Vlach, *Back of the Big House: The Architecture of Plantation Slavery* (Chapel Hill, N.C., 1993), 84, 100–101.

[69] Rawick, *The American Slave*, vol. 14, North Carolina Narratives, 286.

[70] Rawick, *The American Slave*, vol. 8, Arkansas Narratives, 243–44.

[71] Rawick, *The American Slave*, vol. 14, North Carolina Narratives, 286.

[72] Rawick, *The American Slave*, vol. 3, South Carolina Narratives, 240.

[73] Rawick, *The American Slave*, Supplement Series 1, vol. 1, Alabama Narratives, 48; Rawick, *The American Slave*, vol. 5, Texas Narratives, 6.

[74] Rawick, *The American Slave*, Supplement Series 1, vol. 9, Mississippi Narratives, 1641–42.

[75] Rawick, *The American Slave*, vol. 12, Georgia Narratives, 324–25.

[76] Rawick, *The American Slave*, vol. 10, Arkansas Narratives, 315–16 (emphasis added).

[77] Rawick, *The American Slave*, vol. 7, Oklahoma and Mississippi Narratives, 44–45.

[78] Elizabeth Hyde Botume, *First Days amongst the Contrabands* (Boston, 1893), 236–37.

[79] The vivid colors and multiple design patterns of West African textiles signify social status and wealth; only the wealthy can afford such elaborate cloth. The bold and contrasting colors in such garments allow them to be "read" at a distance, insuring that the wearer will be treated in an appropriate manner. See Wahlman, *Signs and Symbols*, 35, 48, 110.

[80] Frederick Law Olmsted, *The Cotton Kingdom: A Traveller's Observations on Cotton and Slavery in the American Slave States*, ed. Arthur M. Schlesinger (New York, 1953), 467.

[81] C. Vann Woodward, ed., *Mary Chesnut's Civil War* (New Haven, Conn., 1981), 214.

[82] Botume, *First Days amongst the Contrabands*, 237.

[83] Robert Farris Thompson, *Flash of the Spirit: African Art and Afro-American Art and Philosophy* (New York, 1984), 209–10.

[84] Thompson, *Flash of the Spirit*, 208.

[85] Rawick, *The American Slave*, vol. 3, South Carolina Narratives, 82.

[86] Thompson, *Flash of the Spirit*, 209, 217.

[87] Quoted in Elsa Barkley Brown, "African-American Women's Quilting: A Framework for Conceptualizing and Teaching African-American Women's History," in Miche-

line R. Malson, Elisabeth Mudimbe-Boyi, Jean F. O'Barr, and Mary Wyer, eds., *Black Women in America: Social Science Perspectives* (Chicago, 1990), 11. See also Wahlman, *Signs and Symbols*, 12, 16, 17, 35.

[88] Brown, "African-American Women's Quilting," 9–18. On quilts, see also John Michael Vlach, *By the Work of Their Hands: Studies in Afro-American Folklife* (Charlottesville, Virginia, 1991), 36–40.

[89] Rawick, *The American Slave*, vol. 18, Unwritten History of Slavery, 229.

[90] Rawick, *The American Slave*, vol. 7, Oklahoma and Mississippi Narratives, 170.

[91] Rawick, *The American Slave*, vol. 18, Unwritten History of Slavery, 313–24.

[92] *Maryland Journal and Baltimore Advertiser*, June 27, 1780, Supplement (Windley, *Runaway Slave Advertisements*, vol. 2, 240–41).

[93] Rawick, *The American Slave*, vol. 4, Texas Narratives, 22.

[94] Chaplin, *An Anxious Pursuit*, 219.

[95] Rhys Isaac, *The Transformation of Virginia, 1740–1790* (Chapel Hill, 1982), 305–8.

[96] Rawick, *The American Slave*, vol. 5, Texas Narratives, 68.

[97] Rawick, *The American Slave*, vol. 5, Texas Narratives, 221.

[98] Olmsted, *The Cotton Kingdom*, 161.

[99] Rawick, *The American Slave*, vol. 4, Texas Narratives, 132.

[100] Booker T. Washington, *Up from Slavery* (1901; New York, 1967), 20–21.

[101] Quoted in Norrece T. Jones, Jr., *Born a Child of Freedom, Yet a Slave: Mechanisms of Control and Strategies of Resistance in Antebellum South Carolina* (Hanover, N.H., 1990), 98.

[102] Olmsted, *The Cotton Kingdom*, 164.

[103] Rawick, *The American Slave*, vol. 13, Georgia Narratives, 40–41.

[104] Frances Ann Kemble, *Journal of a Residence on a Georgian Plantation in 1838–1839*, ed. John A. Scott (New York, 1975), 93–94.

[105] "The Rice Lands of the South," *Harper's New Monthly Magazine* 19 (November 1859), 734.

[106] Quoted in letter from E. D. Worthington to David Ross McCord in Louisa McCord Smythe, *For Olde Lange Syne* (Charleston, 1900), introduction (unpaginated).

[107] Arthur James Lyon Fremantle, *Three Months in the Southern States: April–June 1863* (Lincoln, Neb., 1991), 75.

[108] Olmsted, *The Cotton Kingdom*, 37.

[109] Woodward, *Mary Chesnut's Civil War*, 316.

[110] Olmsted, *The Cotton Kingdom*, 37.

[111] Rawick, *The American Slave*, vol. 13, Georgia Narratives, 203.

[112] Rawick, *The American Slave*, vol. 13, Georgia Narratives, 266.

[113] T. B. Thorpe, "Sugar and the Sugar Region of Louisiana," *Harper's New Monthly Magazine* 7 (November 1853), 767. On the antebellum internal economy, see Loren Schweninger, *Black Property Owners in the South, 1790–1915* (Urbana, Ill., 1990), 30–36.

[114] Rawick, *The American Slave*, vol. 4, Texas Narratives, 205; C. W. Larison, *Silvia Dubois: A Biografy of a Slav Who Whipt Her Mistres and Gand Her Freedom*, ed. Jared C. Lobdell (1883; New York, 1988), 91.

[115] Rawick, *The American Slave*, Supplement Series 2, vol. 7, Texas Narratives, 2539.

[116] Rawick, *The American Slave*, vol. 13, Georgia Narratives, 113.

[117] Kemble, *Residence on a Georgian Plantation*, 93–94.

[118] Rawick, *The American Slave*, Supplement Series 2, vol. 7, Texas Narratives, 2493. In the Texas interviews the words "loyal" or "royal" are often used to describe cloth. These words appear to be the interviewers' attempts to render "lowell" on the page. The term "lowell" had come to be a generic one, applying to cloth made on the plantations and not just to that coming from the New England textile manufacturing town.

[119] Rawick, *The American Slave*, vol. 13, Georgia Narratives, 118.

[120] Rawick, *The American Slave*, Supplement Series 2, vol. 6, Texas Narratives, 2096.

[121] Edward Warren, *A Doctor's Experiences in Three Continents* (Baltimore, 1885), 201. The best account of this festival is Elizabeth A. Fenn, "'A Perfect Equality Seemed to Reign': Slave Society and Jonkonnu," *North Carolina Historical Review* 65 (April 1988), 127–53.

[122] Peter H. Wood and Karen C. C. Dalton, *Winslow Homer's Images of Blacks: The Civil War and Reconstruction Years* (Austin, Texas, 1988), 98–106.

[123] Rawick, *The American Slave*, vol. 4, Texas Narratives, 170.

[124] Rawick, *The American Slave*, Supplement Series 1, vol. 10, Mississippi Narratives, 2198.

[125] Rawick, *The American Slave*, vol. 9, Arkansas Narratives, 146.

[126] Quoted in Michael Mullin, *Africa in America: Slave Acculturation and Resistance in the American South and the British Caribbean, 1736–1831* (Urbana, Ill., 1992), 152.

CHAPTER 2

[1] [Joseph H. Ingraham], *The South-West. By a Yankee*, 2 vols. (New York, 1835), vol. 2, 126–27.

[2] Edward C. Carter II, John C. Van Horne, and Charles E. Brownell, eds., *Latrobe's View of America, 1795–1820* (New Haven, Conn., 1985), 102.

[3] Frederick Law Olmsted, *The Cotton Kingdom: A Traveller's Observations on Cotton and Slavery*, ed. Arthur M. Schlesinger (New York, 1953), 162–65.

[4] Roger D. Abrahams, *Singing the Master: The Emergence of African American Culture in the Plantation South* (New York, 1992), 328.

[5] *The Autobiography of Malcolm X*, with the assistance of Alex Haley (New York, 1973), 52–55.

[6] Roger Wilkins, *A Man's Life: An Autobiography* (New York, 1984), 66.

[7] *Baltimore Journal and Baltimore Advertiser*, August 18, 1786 (Windley, *Runaway Slave Advertisements*, vol. 2, 350); *Charleston South-Carolina and American General Gazette*, August 21 to August 28, 1767 (Windley, *Runaway Slave Advertisements*, vol. 3, 422).

[8] *Annapolis Maryland Gazette*, August 6, 1767 (Windley, *Runaway Slave Advertisements*, vol. 2, 70).

[9] Quoted in Charles Joyner, *Down by the Riverside: A South Carolina Slave Community* (Urbana, Illinois, 1984), 52–53.

[10] *Virginia Gazette* (Dixon & Hunter), October 17, 1777 (Windley, *Runaway Slave Ad-

vertisements, vol. 1, 187); *Virginia Gazette* (Rind), May 9, 1771 (Windley, *Runaway Slave Advertisements,* vol. 1, 311).

[11] Esi Sagay, *African Hairstyles: Styles of Yesterday and Today* (Portsmouth, N.H., 1983), Introduction and 1–45; John Thornton, *Africa and Africans in the Making of the Atlantic World, 1400–1680* (New York, 1992), 230.

[12] Willie Morrow, *400 Years without a Comb* (San Diego, 1973), 19.

[13] Runaway slave advertisements have become one of the staples of the historiography of eighteenth-century slavery. See, for example, Gerald W. Mullin, *Flight and Rebellion: Slave Resistance in Eighteenth Century Virginia* (New York, 1972); Peter H. Wood, *Black Majority: Negroes in Colonial South Carolina from 1670 through the Stono Rebellion* (New York, 1974), 239–68; Shane White, "Black Fugitives in Colonial South Carolina," *Australasian Journal of American Studies* 1 (July 1980), 25–40; Michael P. Johnson, "Runaway Slaves and the Slave Communities in South Carolina, 1799 to 1830," *William and Mary Quarterly,* 3d ser., 38 (July 1981), 418–41; Daniel C. Littlefield, *Rice and Slaves: Ethnicity and the Slave Trade to Colonial South Carolina* (Baton Rouge, La., 1981), 115–73; the December 1985 issue of *Slavery and Abolition,* devoted to studies of runaways in various slave societies; Shane White, *Somewhat More Independent: The End of Slavery in New York City, 1770–1810* (Athens, Ga., 1991), 114–49, 187–206; Jonathan Prude, "To Look upon the 'Lower Sort': Runaway Ads and the Appearance of Unfree Laborers in America, 1750–1800," *Journal of American History* 78 (June 1991), 124–59; Michael Mullin, *Africa in America: Slave Acculturation and Resistance in the American South and the British Caribbean, 1776–1831* (Urbana, Ill., 1992). We are using these advertisements for a somewhat different purpose from these authors, with the partial exception of Jonathan Prude.

[14] *Gazette of the State of South Carolina* (Timothy), August 4, 1777 (Windley, *Runaway Slave Advertisements,* vol. 3, 352); *Baltimore Maryland Journal and Baltimore Advertiser,* September 28, 1784 (Windley, *Runaway Slave Advertisements,* vol. 2, 318–19); *Virginia Gazette* (Parks), June 2 to June 9, 1778 (Windley, *Runaway Slave Advertisements,* vol. 1, 6); *South Carolina Gazette* (Timothy), June 16, 1746 (Windley, *Runaway Slave Advertisements,* vol. 3, 84–85); *Virginia Gazette* (Hunter), June 12, 1752 (Windley, *Runaway Slave Advertisements,* vol. 1, 28); *Virginia Gazette* (Purdie & Dixon), March 19, 1767 (Windley, *Runaway Slave Advertisements,* vol. 1, 50); *Virginia Gazette* (Purdie & Dixon), July 9, 1767 (Windley, *Runaway Slave Advertisements,* vol. 1, 54); *Annapolis Maryland Gazette,* October 20, 1763 (Windley, *Runaway Slave Advertisements,* vol. 2, 51); *Virginia Gazette* (Purdie & Dixon), May 7, 1772 (Windley, *Runaway Slave Advertisements,* vol. 1, 114); *Annapolis Maryland Gazette,* December 29, 1785 (Windley, *Runaway Slave Advertisements,* vol. 2, 156–57); *Annapolis Maryland Gazette,* October 20, 1763 (Windley, *Runaway Slave Advertisements,* vol. 2, 51); *Baltimore Maryland Journal and Baltimore Advertiser,* April 12, 1775 (Windley, *Runaway Slave Advertisements,* vol. 2, 191–92); *Annapolis Maryland Gazette,* June 3, 1790 (Windley, *Runaway Slave Advertisements,* vol. 2, 188); *South Carolina Gazette* (Timothy), April 11, 1771 (Windley, *Runaway Slave Advertisements,* vol. 2, 299).

[15] Thornton, *Africa and Africans,* 230.

[16] Kobena Mercer, "Black Hair/Style Politics," in Russell Ferguson, Martha Gever,

Trinh T. Minh-ha, and Cornel West, eds., *Out There: Marginalization and Contemporary Cultures* (Cambridge, Mass., 1990), 252–54, 248–49.

[17] *Virginia Gazette* (Purdie & Dixon), November 14, 1771 (Windley, *Runaway Slave Advertisements*, vol. 1, 103); *Virginia Gazette* (Dixon & Hunter), January 28, 1775 (Windley, *Runaway Slave Advertisements*, vol. 1, 161); *Virginia Gazette* (Purdie), May 2, 1777, Supplement (Windley, *Runaway Slave Advertisements*, vol. 1, 259); *Baltimore Maryland Journal and Baltimore Advertiser*, May 4, 1787 (Windley, *Runaway Slave Advertisements*, vol. 2, 307); *State Gazette of South Carolina* (Timothy), February 18, 1790 (Windley, *Runaway Slave Advertisements*, vol. 3, 410).

[18] *Augusta Georgia State Gazette or Independent Register*, December 23, 1786 (Windley, *Runaway Slave Advertisements*, vol. 4, 183); *South Carolina Gazette* (Timothy), August 27, 1753 (Windley, *Runaway Slave Advertisements*, vol. 3, 122); *South Carolina Gazette*, August 15 to August 27, 1748 (Windley, *Runaway Slave Advertisements*, vol. 3, 84–85); *Annapolis Maryland Gazette*, June 3, 1790 (Windley, *Runaway Slave Advertisements*, vol. 2, 188); *Virginia Gazette or American Advertiser* (Hayes), July 12, 1783 (Windley, *Runaway Slave Advertisements*, vol. 1, 351); *Annapolis Maryland Gazette*, August 20, 1761 (Windley, *Runaway Slave Advertisements*, vol. 2, 41); *Annapolis Maryland Gazette*, August 21, 1771 (Windley, *Runaway Slave Advertisements*, vol. 2, 89–90).

[19] *Virginia Gazette* (Purdie & Dixon), July 9, 1767 (Windley, *Runaway Slave Advertisements*, vol. 1, 54); *Virginia Gazette* (Purdie & Dixon), March 7, 1771 (Windley, *Runaway Slave Advertisements*, vol. 1, 91); *Virginia Gazette* (Purdie & Dixon), November 9, 1769 (Windley, *Runaway Slave Advertisements*, vol. 1, 75); *Virginia Gazette* (Hunter), June 12, 1752 (Windley, *Runaway Slave Advertisements*, vol. 1, 28); *Annapolis Maryland Gazette*, August 28, 1777 (Windley, *Runaway Slave Advertisements*, vol. 2, 118); *Virginia Gazette* (Dixon & Hunter), December 12, 1777 (Windley, *Runaway Slave Advertisements*, vol. 1, 189).

[20] *Virginia Gazette and Weekly Advertiser* (Nicolson), August 20, 1785 (Windley, *Runaway Slave Advertisements*, vol. 1, 233); *South Carolina Gazette* (Timothy), November 15, 1770 (Windley, *Runaway Slave Advertisements*, vol. 3, 294); *Charleston South-Carolina and American General Gazette*, October 24 to November 7, 1776 (Windley, *Runaway Slave Advertisements*, vol. 3, 489); *Baltimore Maryland Journal and Baltimore Advertiser*, June 5, 1787 (Windley, *Runaway Slave Advertisements*, vol. 2, 362); *Annapolis Maryland Gazette*, December 29, 1785 (Windley, *Runaway Slave Advertisements*, vol. 2, 156–57); *Annapolis Maryland Gazette*, August 24, 1786 (Windley, *Runaway Slave Advertisements*, vol. 2, 162).

[21] Mercer, "Black Hair/Style Politics," 256.

[22] Sagay, *African Hairstyles*, 22; Melville J. Herskovits, *The Myth of the Negro Past* (Boston, 1958), 148–49.

[23] The best account of this ideology remains Winthrop D. Jordan, *White Over Black: American Attitudes Toward the Negro, 1550–1812* (Chapel Hill, N.C., 1968).

[24] George P. Rawick, ed., *The American Slave: A Composite Autobiography* (19 vols.; Westport, 1972), vol. 18, 80, 83.

[25] Mercer, "Black Hair/Style Politics," 250–51, 253. Harry, a Maryland slave who ran away in 1771, had "a remarkable long beard'; Dick, who escaped from his Virginia master

the following year, had "short Hair curled close to his Head, [and] a very large black Beard"; and describing his slave Jack, a Virginia owner noted that "his beard grows up his temples, which he generally wears long." The impact of such imposing beards must have been all the greater in a century in which beards were not fashionable among whites. Such "statements" made by bearded African Americans would have lost force by the mid-nineteenth century when beards became common among whites as well as blacks. *Annapolis Maryland Gazette,* May 23, 1771 (Windley, *Runaway Slave Advertisements,* vol. 2, 87); *Virginia Gazette* (Purdie & Dixon), March 5, 1772 (Windley, *Runaway Slave Advertisements,* vol. 1, 109–10); *Virginia Gazette & Weekly Advertiser* (Nicolson), May 28, 1785 (Windley, *Runaway Slave Advertisements,* vol. 1, 230). See Richard Corson, *Fashions in Hair: The First Five Thousand Years* (London, 1965), 402, for Corson's reference to "the beardless eighteenth century."

[26] *Baltimore Maryland Journal and Baltimore Advertiser,* July 30, 1782 (Windley, *Runaway Slave Advertisements,* vol. 2, 266); *Virginia Gazette and Weekly Advertiser* (Nicolson & Prentis), December 11, 1784 (Windley, *Runaway Slave Advertisements,* vol. 1, 229); *Gazette of the State of South Carolina* (Timothy), August 4, 1773 (Windley, *Runaway Slave Advertisements,* vol. 3, 352); *Baltimore Maryland Journal and Baltimore Advertiser,* December 11, 1789 (Windley, *Runaway Slave Advertisements,* vol. 2, 399).

[27] Sagay, *African Hairstyles,* 4, 6, 24, 30; Morrow, *400 Years without a Comb,* 19.

[28] Thornton, *Africa and Africans,* 233; also 230, 232–33.

[29] Marilyn Hammersley Houlberg, "Social Hair: Tradition and Change in Yoruba Hairstyles in Southwestern Nigeria," in Justine M. Cordwell and Ronald A. Schwarz, eds., *The Fabrics of Culture: The Anthropology of Clothing and Adornment* (The Hague, Paris, and New York, 1979), 368–70. See Mullin, *Africa in America,* 41, for a suggestion that Jamaican slaves shaved their heads as a sign of mourning for those who had rebelled and died.

[30] Sylvia Ardyn Boone, *Radiance from the Waters: Ideas of Feminine Beauty in Mende Art* (New Haven, Conn., 1986), 143–44.

[31] Stefan Lorant, ed., *The New World: The First Pictures of America Made by John White and Jacques Le Moyne and Engraved by Theodore De Bry with Contemporary Narratives of the Huguenot Settlement in Florida 1562–1565 and the Virginia Colony 1585–1590* (New York, 1946), on, for example, 51, 57, 59; William Bartram, *Travels through North & South Carolina, Georgia, East & West Florida* (1791; Salt Lake City, Utah, 1980), 318. See also James Merrell, *The Indians' New World: Catawbas and Their Neighbors from European Contact through the Era of Removal* (Chapel Hill, 1989), 126.

[32] James Adair, *The History of the American Indians* (1775; New York, 1968), 123.

[33] Joyce Asser, *Historic Hairdressing* (Bath, England, 1986), 73–74; Corson, *Fashions in Hair,* 181–82, 272, 278–79, 284, 296–97.

[34] Quoted in John F. Kasson, *Rudeness & Civility: Manners in Nineteenth-Century Urban America* (New York, 1990), 26–27. The best analysis of the value system in which Jarratt was embedded is contained in Rhys Isaac, *The Transformation of Virginia, 1740–1790* (Chapel Hill, 1982).

[35] John Donald Duncan, "Servitude and Slavery in Colonial South Carolina" (Ph.D. diss., Emory University, 1973), 241.

[36] *Virginia Gazette* (Purdie & Dixon), May 7, 1767 (Windley, *Runaway Slave Adver-*

tisements, vol. 1, 52); *Annapolis Maryland Gazette,* June 26, 1755 (Windley, *Runaway Slave Advertisements,* vol. 2, 24); *Annapolis Maryland Gazette,* March 24, 1757 (Windley, *Runaway Slave Advertisements,* vol. 2, 27); *Virginia Gazette* (Hunter), January 24, 1752 (Windley, *Runaway Slave Advertisements,* vol. 1, 24–25).

[37] *Baltimore Maryland Journal and Baltimore Advertiser,* August 5, 1785 (Windley, *Runaway Slave Advertisements,* vol. 2, 330–31); *Baltimore Maryland Journal and Baltimore Advertiser,* December 29, 1786 (Windley, *Runaway Slave Advertisements,* vol. 2, 355); *Charleston South-Carolina Gazette and Country Journal,* August 30, 1774 (Windley, *Runaway Slave Advertisements,* vol. 3, 696).

[38] *Annapolis Maryland Gazette,* September 16, 1784 (Windley, *Runaway Slave Advertisements,* vol. 2, 148).

[39] See White, *Somewhat More Independent,* 199.

[40] *Annapolis Maryland Gazette,* October 20, 1763 (Windley, *Runaway Slave Advertisements,* vol. 2, 51); *Virginia Gazette* (Pinkney), June 15, 1775 (Windley, *Runaway Slave Advertisements,* vol. 1, 331–32); *Virginia Gazette* (Purdie & Dixon), March 19, 1767 (Windley, *Runaway Slave Advertisements,* vol. 1, 50); *Baltimore Maryland Journal and Baltimore Advertiser,* February 27, 1787 (Windley, *Runaway Slave Advertisements,* vol. 2, 357); *Virginia Gazette* (Purdie & Dixon), May 7, 1772 (Windley, *Runaway Slave Advertisements,* vol. 1, 114); *Baltimore Maryland Journal and Baltimore Advertiser,* November 16, 1779 (Windley, *Runaway Slave Advertisements,* vol. 2, 234–35).

[41] This paragraph draws, in part, on Shane White, "Digging Up the African-American Past: Historical Archaeology, Photography and Slavery," *Australasian Journal of American Studies* 11 (July 1992), 37–47.

[42] Thomas F. De Voe, *The Market Book: A History of the Public Markets of the City of New York* (1862; New York, 1970), 345.

[43] *Annapolis Maryland Gazette,* August 17, 1769 (Windley, *Runaway Slave Advertisements,* vol. 2, 78); *Virginia Gazette* (Parks), June 2 to June 9, 1738 (Windley, *Runaway Slave Advertisements,* vol. 1, 6).

[44] Sagay, *African Hairstyles,* 22; Boone, *Radiance from the Waters,* 184–86; *Annapolis Maryland Gazette,* December 2, 1762 (Windley, *Runaway Slave Advertisements,* vol. 2, 48); *Virginia Gazette and Weekly Advertiser* (Nicolson & Prentis), October 25, 1783 (Windley, *Runaway Slave Advertisements,* vol. 1, 221).

[45] *Virginia Gazette* (Purdie & Dixon), July 21, 1774 (Windley, *Runaway Slave Advertisements,* vol. 1, 151–52); Gwendolyn Robinson, "Class, Race, and Gender: A Transcultural Theoretical and Sociohistorical Analysis of Cosmetic Institutions and Practices to 1920" (Ph.D. diss., University of Illinois at Chicago, 1984), 84.

[46] Corson, *Fashions in Hair,* 398; Edward C. Carter II, ed., *The Virginia Journals of Benjamin Latrobe 1795–1798* (New Haven, Conn., 1977), 129–30 (entry for May 31, 1796).

[47] *Gazette of the State of South-Carolina* (Timothy), August 4, 1777 (Windley, *Runaway Slave Advertisements,* vol. 3, 352); *Annapolis Maryland Gazette,* March 7, 1771 (Windley, *Runaway Slave Advertisements,* vol. 2, 85–86); *Pennsylvania Gazette,* March 7, 1771 and June 5, 1782, in Billy G. Smith and Richard Wojtowicz, comps., *Blacks Who Stole Themselves: Advertisements for Runaways in the Pennsylvania Gazette, 1728–1790* (Philadelphia, 1989),

143; *Virginia Gazette* (Purdie & Dixon), April 21, 1773 (Windley, *Runaway Slave Advertisements*, vol. 1, 131); *Virginia Gazette* (Purdie & Dixon), March 26, 1767 (Windley, *Runaway Slave Advertisements*, vol. 1, 50–51); *Gazette of the State of South Carolina* (Timothy & Boden), December 16, 1778 (Windley, *Runaway Slave Advertisements*, vol. 3, 361–62).

[48] *Charleston Courier*, May 11, July 3, September 14, and December 22, 1830; *Charleston Times*, July 31, April 5, and June 14, 1810; *Charleston Courier*, July 3, 1830.

[49] See, for example, Edward D. C. Campbell, Jr., ed., *Before Freedom Came: African-American Life in the Antebellum South* (Richmond, Va., 1991), figures 1, 5, 6, 16, 72.

[50] George P. Rawick, ed., *The American Slave: A Composite Autobiography*, Supplement Series 1 (12 vols.; Westport, Conn., 1977), vol. 6, 217–18; George P. Rawick, ed., *The American Slave: A Composite Autobiography*, Supplement Series 2 (10 vols.; Westport, Conn., 1979), vol. 7, 2531.

[51] Sarah Rice, *He Included Me: The Autobiography of Sarah Rice*, transcribed and edited Louise Westling (Athens, Ga., 1989), 1.

[52] Rawick, *The American Slave*, vol. 7, 170; Rawick, *The American Slave*, Supplement Series 1, vol. 9, 1576; Jacob Stroyer, *My Life in the South* (Salem, Mass., 1898), 12–13; Rawick, *The American Slave*, vol. 6, 85.

[53] Quoted in Norrece T. Jones, Jr., *Born a Child of Freedom, Yet a Slave: Mechanisms of Control and Strategies of Resistance in Antebellum South Carolina* (Hanover, N.H., 1990), 110; Rawick, *The American Slave*, Supplement Series 2, vol. 6, 2371; Rawick, *The American Slave*, Supplement Series 2, vol. 4, 90; Rawick, *The American Slave*, vol. 6, 119; Robinson, "Class, Race, and Gender," 83.

[54] Thornton, *Africa and Africans*, 233.

[55] *Pennsylvania Gazette*, September 1, 1763, in Smith and Wojtowicz, *Blacks Who Stole Themselves*, 63.

[56] Boone, *Radiance from the Waters*, 184–86.

[57] *Charleston South-Carolina Gazette and Country Journal*, April 25, 1769 (Windley, *Runaway Slave Advertisements*, vol. 3, 644); *Charleston South-Carolina Gazette and General Advertiser*, April 17 to April 20, 1784 (Windley, *Runaway Slave Advertisements*, vol. 3, 734); *Savannah Gazette of the State of Georgia*, August 23, 1787 (Windley, *Runaway Slave Advertisements*, vol. 4, 150–51).

[58] See, for example, Campbell, *Before Freedom Came*, figures 20, 50, 58, 71, 85, 86, 88, 140, 143.

[59] Olmsted, *The Cotton Kingdom*, 451; quoted in Jones, *Born a Child of Freedom*, 70.

[60] [Anonymous], Travel Journal, 1849–51, of New England School Teacher, South Carolina Historical Society, Charleston (call number 34/606), no pagination; Olmsted, *The Cotton Kingdom*, 206; "An Englishman in South Carolina, December 1860, and July 1862," *Continental Monthly* 2 (1862), 689–94, and 3 (1863), 110–17, in Eugene L. Schwaab, ed., *Travels in the Old South* (2 vols.; Lexington, 1973), vol. 2, 568–69; Elizabeth Ware Pearson, *Letters from Port Royal Written at the Time of the Civil War* (Boston, 1906), 26–27; Whitelaw Reid, *After the War: A Tour of the Southern States, 1865–1866*, ed. C. Vann Woodward (New York, 1965), 81.

[61] Mercer, "Black Hair/Style Politics," 259.

CHAPTER 3

[1] Richard Henry Dana, Jr., *The Journal of Richard Henry Dana, Jr.,* ed. Robert F. Lucid, 2 vols. (Cambridge, Mass., 1968), vol. 2, 625–27.

[2] Ruth Edmonds Hill, ed., *The Black Women Oral History Project,* 10 vols. (Westport, Conn., 1991), vol. 2, 123.

[3] *Charleston South-Carolina and American General Gazette,* February 21, 1781 (Windley, *Runaway Slave Advertisements,* vol. 3, 577); *South-Carolina Gazette* (Timothy), November 7, 1775 (Windley, *Runaway Slave Advertisements,* vol. 3, 345).

[4] Inga Clendinnen, *Aztecs: An Interpretation* (New York, 1991), 285; Frederick Law Olmsted, *The Cotton Kingdom: A Traveller's Observations on Cotton and Slavery in the American Slave States,* ed. Arthur M. Schlesinger (New York, 1953), 28 (emphasis added).

[5] *Baltimore Maryland Journal and Baltimore Advertiser,* September 24, 1790 (Windley, *Runaway Slave Advertisements,* vol. 2, 418); *Annapolis Maryland Gazette,* June 20, 1771 (Windley, *Runaway Slave Advertisements,* vol. 2, 88); *Virginia Gazette or American Advertiser* (Hayes), May 27, 1786 (Windley, *Runaway Slave Advertisements,* vol. 1, 385).

[6] Richard L. Bushman, *The Refinement of America: Persons, Houses, Cities* (New York, 1992), 70–74; Jonathan Prude, "'To Look upon the Lower Sort': Runaway Ads and the Appearance of Unfree Laborers in America, 1750–1800," *Journal of American History* 78 (June 1991), 129–30.

[7] Laura Matilda Towne, *Letters and Diary of Laura M. Towne, Written from the Sea Islands of South Carolina, 1862–1884,* ed. Rupert Sargent Holland (Cambridge, Mass., 1912), 176–77; Charles Ball, *Slavery in the United States: A Narrative of the Life and Adventures of Charles Ball, a Black Man* (1837; New York, 1969), 384.

[8] Quoted in Bertram Wyatt-Brown, "The Mask of Obedience: Male Slave Psychology in the Old South," *American Historical Review* 95 (December 1988), 1248; quoted in Leon F. Litwack, *Been in the Storm So Long: The Aftermath of Slavery* (New York, 1980), 95, 64.

[9] Olmsted, *The Cotton Kingdom,* 459; C. Vann Woodward, ed., *Mary Chesnut's Civil War* (New Haven, Conn., 1981), 233, 113–14, and see also 48, 794; quoted in James C. Cobb, "Does *Mind* No Longer Matter? The South, the Nation, and *The Mind of the South,* 1941–1991," *Journal of Southern History* 57 (November 1991), 698.

[10] Prude, "To Look upon the Lower Sort," 141.

[11] *Savannah Georgia Royal Gazette,* March 1, 1781 (Windley, *Runaway Slave Advertisements,* vol. 4, 86–87); *Virginia Gazette* (Dixon & Hunter), March 23, 1776 (Windley, *Runaway Slave Advertisements,* vol. 1, 175); *Virginia Gazette* (Purdie), April 11, 1777 (Windley, *Runaway Slave Advertisements,* vol. 1, 258); *Baltimore Maryland Journal and Baltimore Advertiser,* June 16, 1789 (Windley, *Runaway Slave Advertisements,* vol. 2, 390–91).

[12] Cited in James Oliver Horton, *Free People of Color: Inside the African American Community* (Washington, D.C., 1993), 82.

[13] *Edenton State Gazette of North-Carolina,* July 9, 1790 (Windley, *Runaway Slave Advertisements,* vol. 1, 459); *Baltimore Maryland Journal and Baltimore Advertiser,* December 11, 1789 (Windley, *Runaway Slave Advertisements,* vol. 2, 399–400); *Baltimore Maryland Journal and Baltimore Advertiser,* August 15, 1783 (Windley, *Runaway Slave Advertisements,* vol. 2, 291).

[14] *Virginia Gazette or American Advertiser* (Hayes), August 14, 1784 (Windley, *Runaway Slave Advertisements*, vol. 1, 362); *Annapolis Maryland Gazette*, July 8, 1784 (Windley, *Runaway Slave Advertisements*, vol. 2, 144); *Annapolis Maryland Gazette*, July 18, 1785 (Windley, *Runaway Slave Advertisements*, vol. 2, 154); *Pennsylvania Gazette*, July 28, 1748, in Billy G. Smith and Richard Wojtowicz, comps., *Blacks Who Stole Themselves: Advertisements for Runaway Slaves in the Pennsylvania Gazette, 1728–1790* (Philadelphia, 1989), 28.

[15] *Gazette of the State of South-Carolina* (Timothy and Boden), July 15, 1779 (Windley, *Runaway Slave Advertisements*, vol. 3, 370); *Baltimore Maryland Journal and Baltimore Advertiser*, November 10, 1788 (Windley, *Runaway Slave Advertisements*, vol. 2, 216); *Baltimore Maryland Journal and Baltimore Advertiser*, July 18, 1783 (Windley, *Runaway Slave Advertisements*, vol. 2, 287–88); *Baltimore Maryland Journal and Baltimore Advertiser*, July 20, 1784 (Windley, *Runaway Slave Advertisements*, vol. 2, 312–13); Ulrich B. Phillips, ed., *Plantation and Frontier, 1649–1863*, 2 vols. (1910; New York, 1962), vol. 2, 88.

[16] Robert Farris Thompson, "Kongo Influences on African-American Artistic Culture," in Joseph E. Holloway, ed., *Africanisms in American Culture* (Bloomington, Ind., 1990), 158–59.

[17] *Virginia Gazette or American Advertiser* (Hayes), May 27, 1786 (Windley, *Slave Runaway Advertisements*, vol. 1, 385); *Virginia Gazette* (Rind), August 8, 1766 (Windley, *Slave Runaway Advertisements*, vol. 1, 282–83); *South-Carolina Gazette* (Timothy), July 21 to July 28, 1766 (Windley, *Slave Runaway Advertisements*, vol. 3, 257–58); *Virginia Independent Chronicle* (Davis), August 29, 1787 (Windley, *Slave Runaway Advertisements*, vol. 1, 391–92); *Virginia Gazette and Weekly Advertiser* (Nicolson), April 17, 1788 (Windley, *Slave Runaway Advertisements*, vol. 1, 240).

[18] *Charleston Royal Gazette*, September 21 to September 28, 1782 (Windley, *Slave Runaway Advertisements*, vol. 3, 598–99); *Virginia Independent Chronicle* (Davis), August 8, 1787 (Windley, *Slave Runaway Advertisements*, vol. 1, 391); *Virginia Gazette* (Purdie), September 6, 1776 (Windley, *Slave Runaway Advertisements*, vol. 1, 253); *Baltimore Maryland Journal and Baltimore Advertiser*, September 24, 1790 (Windley, *Slave Runaway Advertisements*, vol. 2, 418).

[19] On "rolling the eyes," see Kenneth R. Johnson, "Black Kinesics—Some Non-Verbal Communication Patterns in Black Culture," in J. Dillard, ed., *Perspectives on Black English* (The Hague, 1975), 301.

[20] *Baltimore Maryland Journal and Baltimore Advertiser*, August 10, 1779 (Windley, *Slave Runaway Advertisements*, vol. 2, 229); *Savannah Royal Georgia Gazette*, March 15, 1781 (Windley, *Slave Runaway Advertisements*, vol. 4, 89); *Pennsylvania Gazette*, September 2, 1762, in Smith and Wojtowicz, *Blacks Who Stole Themselves*, 58–59; *Baltimore Maryland Journal and Baltimore Advertiser*, August 15, 1783 (Windley, *Slave Runaway Advertisements*, vol. 2, 291); *Annapolis Maryland Gazette* (Timothy), June 20, 1771 (Windley, *Slave Runaway Advertisements*, vol. 2, 88); *South-Carolina Gazette* (Timothy), January 1 to January 5, 1759 (Windley, *Slave Runaway Advertisements*, vol. 3, 169).

[21] Peter H. Wood, "'Gimme de Kneebone Bent': African Body Language and the Evolution of American Dance Forms," in Gerald E. Myers, ed., *The Black Tradition in American Dance* (Durham, N.C., 1988), 7–8.

[22] Towne, *Letters and Diary,* 20; Benjamin A. Botkin, *A Treasury of Southern Folklore* (New York, 1949), 658; Lydia Parrish, *Slave Songs of the Georgia Sea Islands* (1942; Athens, Ga., 1992), 55–56.

[23] Melville J. Herskovits, *The Myth of the Negro Past* (1941; Boston, 1958), 271.

[24] Quoted in Lynne Fawley Emery, *Black Dance: From 1619 to Today* (1972; Princeton, N.J., 1988), 22.

[25] George Pinckard, *Notes on the West Indies* (London, 1806), 266.

[26] Quoted in Emery, *Black Dance,* 25.

[27] The authors wish specifically to acknowledge John Cook, one of our research assistants, for his help in developing these insights.

[28] Quoted in Dena J. Epstein, *Sinful Tunes and Spirituals: Black Folk Music to the Civil War* (Urbana, Ill., 1977), 40.

[29] Quoted in Epstein, *Sinful Tunes,* 42, 45.

[30] Edward C. Carter II, John C. Van Horne, and Lee W. Formwalt, eds., *The Journals of Benjamin Henry Latrobe, 1799–1820: From Philadelphia to New Orleans,* 3 vols. (New Haven, Conn., 1980), vol. 3, 203–4.

[31] Quoted in Emery, *Black Dance,* 163. Emery believes that this dance was probably the Calenda.

[32] Quoted in Emery, *Black Dance,* 165.

[33] Alan Lomax, *The Land Where the Blues Began* (New York, 1993), 365.

[34] George P. Rawick, ed., *The American Slave: A Composite Autobiography,* Series 1 & 2, 19 vols. (Westport, Conn., 1972), vol. 5, 198.

[35] Quoted in Epstein, *Sinful Tunes,* 281.

[36] Towne, *Letters and Diary,* 20; quoted in Epstein, *Sinful Tunes,* 284.

[37] Elizabeth Ware Pearson, ed., *Letters from Port Royal, Written at the Time of the Civil War* (Boston, 1906), 292–93; D. E. Huger Smith, *A Charlestonian's Recollections, 1846–1913* (Charleston, 1950), 31–32 (emphasis added).

[38] Huger Smith, *A Charlestonian's Recollections,* 32.

[39] Charles L. Perdue, Jr., Thomas E. Barden, and Robert K. Phillips, comps. and eds., *Weevils in the Wheat: Interviews with Virginia Ex-Slaves* (Bloomington, Ind., 1980), 14, 49, 316, 265.

[40] C. W. Larison, *Silvia Dubois, A Biografy of the Slav Who Whipt Her Mistres and Gand Her Fredom,* ed. Jared C. Lobdell (1883; New York, 1988), 59–60.

[41] Charles Dickens, *American Notes and Pictures from Italy* (London, 1907), 89–90.

[42] Quoted in Emery, *Black Dance,* 188.

[43] Quoted in Epstein, *Sinful Tunes,* 42, 45; quoted in Emery, *Black Dance,* 96; Lawrence W. Levine, *Black Culture and Black Consciousness: Afro-American Folk Thought from Slavery to Freedom* (Oxford, 1977), 16.

[44] Levine, *Black Culture,* 16; Roger D. Abrahams, *Singing the Master: The Emergence of African-American Culture in the Plantation South* (New York, 1992), 98–100.

[45] John F. Szwed and Morton Marks, "The Afro-American Transformation of European Set Dances and Dance Suites," *Dance Research Journal* 20 (Summer 1988), 29.

[46] Solomon Northup, *Twelve Years a Slave,* ed. Sue Eakin and Joseph Logsdon (1853;

Baton Rouge, La., 1968), 167; Frank Kofsky, "Afro-American Innovation and the Folk Tradition in Jazz: Their Historical Significance," *Journal of Ethnic Studies* 7:1 (1979), 5–6; James Lincoln Collier, *The Making of Jazz: A Comprehensive History* (1978; London, 1991), 6.

[47] Robert Farris Thompson, "An Aesthetic of the Cool: West Indian Dance," *African Forum* 3 (1966), 91; Alan Lomax, "The Homogeneity of African-Afro-American Musical Style," in N. E. P. Whitten and John F. Szwed, eds., *Afro-American Anthropology: Contemporary Perspectives* (New York, 1970), 193.

[48] Quoted in Epstein, *Sinful Tunes,* 134, 204; Lomax, *The Land Where the Blues Began,* 329, 349.

[49] Maude Southwell Wahlman, *Signs and Symbols: African-American Quilts* (New York, 1993), 11, 12.

[50] Wahlman, *Signs and Symbols,* 16.

[51] Quoted in Epstein, *Sinful Tunes,* 277; quoted in Epstein, *Sinful Tunes,* 276; quoted in Eileen Southern, *The Music of Black Americans: A History* (1971; New York, 1983), 210.

[52] Wahlman, *Signs and Symbols,* 12; Olmsted, *The Cotton Kingdom,* 467.

[53] Robert Farris Thompson, *Flash of the Spirit: African and Afro-American Art and Philosophy* (New York, 1984), 207–10; John Miller Chernoff, *African Rhythm and African Sensibility* (Chicago, 1979), 47, 96.

[54] Rawick, *The American Slave,* vol. 5, 191.

[55] *Annapolis Maryland Gazette,* March 24, 1785 (Windley, *Runaway Slave Advertisements,* vol. 2, 151); *Baltimore Maryland Journal and Baltimore Advertiser,* December 11, 1789 (Windley, *Runaway Slave Advertisements,* vol. 2, 399); *Virginia Gazette* (Purdie & Dixon), August 13, 1772 (Windley, *Runaway Slave Advertisements,* vol. 1, 118); *South-Carolina Gazette* (Timothy), October 13 to October 20, 1758 (Windley, *Runaway Slave Advertisements,* vol. 3, 166).

[56] Northup, *Twelve Years a Slave,* 166. On the reconfiguration of the black body in the twentieth century, see bell hooks, "My 'Style' Ain't No Fashion," *Z Magazine,* May–June 1992, 27–29; Robin D. G. Kelley, "'We Are Not What We Seem': Rethinking Black Working-Class Opposition in the Jim Crow South," *Journal of American History* 80 (June 1993), 84–86.

[57] Once again, we are grateful to John Cook for his help with this conclusion.

Chapter 4

[1] Elaine Forman Crane, ed., *The Diary of Elizabeth Drinker,* 3 vols. (Boston, 1991), vol. 2, 1127, 1151–52.

[2] On the ending of slavery in the North, see Graham Russell Hodges, *Slavery and Freedom in the Rural North: African Americans in Monmouth County, New Jersey, 1665–1865* (Madison, Wis., 1997); James Oliver Horton and Lois E. Horton, *In Hope of Liberty: Culture, Community and Protest among Northern Free Blacks, 1700–1860* (New York, 1996); Leon F. Litwack, *North of Slavery: The Negro in the Free States, 1790–1860* (Chicago, 1961); Gary Nash and Jean R. Soderlund, *Freedom by Degrees: Emancipation in Pennsylvania and Its Aftermath* (New York, 1991); Shane White, *Somewhat More Independent: The End of Slav-*

ery in New York City, 1770–1810 (Athens, Ga., 1991); Arthur Zilversmit, *The First Emancipation: The Abolition of Slavery in the North* (Chicago, 1970).

[3] John F. Watson, *Annals of Philadelphia and Pennsylvania, In the Olden Time; Being a Collection of Memoirs, Anecdotes, and Incidents of the City and Its Inhabitants* (Philadelphia, 1845), 261.

[4] Population figures taken from Leonard P. Curry, *The Free Black in Urban America 1800–1850: The Shadow of the Dream* (Chicago, 1981), 1–14 and the tables on 245–57.

[5] On this process, see Betsy Blackmar, "Re-walking the 'Walking City': Housing and Property Relations in New York City, 1780–1840," *Radical History Review* 21 (1979), 131–48; Elizabeth Blackmar, *Manhattan for Rent, 1785–1850* (Ithaca, 1989).

[6] Curry, *The Free Black in Urban America*, 49–80; White, *Somewhat More Independent*, 171–79.

[7] *Montreal Gazette*, reprinted in *New York Evening Post*, July 22, 1829; Joseph Sturge, *A Visit to the United States in 1841* (London, 1842), 40; Francis Pulszky and Theresa Pulszky, *White, Red, Black: Sketches of American Society in the United States*, 2 vols. (New York, 1853), vol. 2, 67; Henry Bradshaw Fearon, *Sketches of America: A Journey of Five Thousand Miles through the Eastern and Western States of America* (London, 1818), 58–60; J. S. Buckingham, *The Slave States of America*, 2 vols. (1842; New York, 1968), vol. 2, 112.

[8] *National Advocate*, May 22, 1817; *New York Evening Post*, August 21, 1829.

[9] Timothy Dwight, *Travels in New York and New England*, ed. Barbara M. Solomon, 4 vols. (Cambridge, Mass., 1969), vol. 3, 431.

[10] Carl Bridenbaugh, ed., "Patrick M'Robert's Tour Through Parts of the North Provinces of America," *Pennsylvania Magazine of History and Biography* 59 (1935), 142; William Strickland, *Journal of a Tour in the United States of America, 1794–1795*, ed. J. E. Strickland (New York, 1971), 63; Fearon, *Sketches of America*, 9; James Stuart, *Three Years in North America*, 2 vols. (Edinburgh, 1833), vol. 1, 29.

[11] Stephen Davis, *Notes of a Tour in America in 1832 & 1833* (Edinburgh, 1833), 75; Lady Emmeline Stuart Wortley, *Travels in the United States etc. During 1849 and 1850*, 3 vols. (London, 1851), vol. 1, 127.

[12] [William Blane], *An Excursion Through the United States and Canada During the Years 1822–23. By an English Gentleman* (London, 1824), 25; S. A. Ferrall, Esq., *A Ramble of Six Thousand Miles Through the United States* (London, 1832), 10.

[13] *National Advocate*, August 3, 1821. Apparently some African Americans hired clothing in order to keep up appearances. In relating the details of a case decided in New York's Police Office in which a black woman was accused of stealing a frock from another black woman, the *National Advocate* of September 28, 1824, noted: "A small piece of intelligence leaked out in the inquiry, which was, that Betsey Freelove hired the gown at two shillings per day, and that a vast portion of our colored fashionables make an appearance in Broadway in 'borrowed robes,' from a similar mode of hiring by day or night."

[14] *National Advocate*, August 3, 1821; *National Advocate*, September 21, 1821. On the African American theater, see Herbert Marshall and Mildred Stock, *Ira Aldridge: The Negro Tragedian* (1958; Washington, D.C., 1993), 28–47; Samuel A. Hay, *African-American Theatre: An Historical and Critical Analysis* (New York, 1994), 5–14.

[15] Carl David Arfwedson, *The United States and Canada in 1832, 1833, and 1834,* 2 vols. (1834; New York, 1969), vol. 1, 27–29. On promenading in New York, see David Scobey, "Anatomy of the Promenade: The Politics of Bourgeois Sociability in Nineteenth-Century New York," *Social History* 17 (May 1992), 203–27.

[16] Geertz quoted in Mary P. Ryan, "The American Parade: Representations of the Nineteenth-Century Social Order," in Lynn Hunt, ed., *The New Cultural History* (Berkeley, 1989), 132. On African American parades, see Shane White, "'It Was a Proud Day': African Americans, Festivals, and Parades in the North, 1741–1834," *Journal of American History* 81 (June 1994), 13–50.

[17] Curry, *The Free Black in Urban America,* 196–215.

[18] White, "It Was a Proud Day"; *Morning Chronicle,* reprinted in *Freedom's Journal,* June 29, 1827; *Daily Adviser,* reprinted in *Long Island Star,* July 12, 1827; James Boardman, *America and the Americans* (London, 1833), 310; *A Memorial Discourse by Reverend Henry Highland Garnet With an Introduction by James McCune Smith, M.D.* (Philadelphia, 1865), 24–26; *Mercantile Advertiser,* reprinted in *New York Evening Post,* July 9, 1829.

[19] *New-York National Advocate,* March 18, 1825.

[20] *Pennsylvania Gazette,* reprinted in *Freedom's Journal,* March 14, 1828; *Democratic Press,* February 29, 1828.

[21] "The African Fancy Ball," *Philadelphia Monthly Magazine* 2 (April 1828), 53–57; on Johnson, see Eileen Southern, *The Music of Black Americans: A History* (1971; New York, 1983, 108–10. The quotation from the white observer is from Robert Waln, *The Hermit in America* (Philadelphia, 1819) and is reprinted in Southern, *Music of Black Americans,* 108.

[22] Boardman, *America and the Americans,* 310; "The African Fancy Ball," 54. On "signifying," see Henry Louis Gates, Jr., *The Signifying Monkey: A Theory of African-American Literary Criticism* (New York, 1988), 44–88.

[23] *New York Evening Post,* March 12, 1830; *Public Ledger,* December 31, 1836. See White, *Somewhat More Independent,* 182–84.

[24] *Freedom's Journal,* July 18, 1828; *The Colored American,* August 26, 1837.

[25] Dorothy Porter, ed., *Early Negro Writing, 1760–1837* (Boston, 1971), 132; *Freedom's Journal,* March 14, 1828.

[26] *Public Ledger,* August 30, 1836; *Public Ledger,* December 3, 1836. See also Graham Hodges, "'Desirable Companions and Lovers': Irish and African Americans in the Sixth Ward, 1830–1870," in Ronald H. Bayor and Timothy J. Meagher, eds., *The New York Irish* (Baltimore, 1996), 107–24.

[27] *New York Evening Post,* June 2, 1827; *National Advocate,* December 18, 1824. On the lurid rumors, see Sean Wilentz, *Chants Democratic: New York City & the Rise of the American Working Class, 1788–1850* (New York, 1984), 264. The reporting of an incident from New York clearly demonstrates the regard in which blacks were held and the way racial hierarchies operated in practice. Lewis Peterson, a black, had stabbed "a good looking Indian" from Oneida Castle, who had seduced Peterson's mulatto wife. The *National Advocate* was less concerned with the crime than with why any Indian would associate with a black woman who was "quite low." The newspaper noted: "They don't seem to relish the unique project of uniting them to the whites, and if they cannot obtain a person of their

own complexion, they take a shade darker. This is a retrograde movement." *National Advocate,* September 10, 1821.

28 *National Advocate,* April 18, 1820. On the convention and black voting rights, see Litwack, *North of Slavery,* 80–84; Horton and Horton, *In Hope of Liberty,* 167–70.

29 *National Advocate,* August 3, 1821; *National Advocate,* September 26, 1821; *National Advocate,* September 25, 1821; *National Advocate,* November 30, 1821.

30 *New-York National Advocate,* March 2, 1825; *National Advocate,* October 7, 1819.

31 *New York American,* July 10, 1827; Arfwedson, *The United States and Canada in 1832, 1833, and 1834,* 27–29.

32 John Palmer, *Journal of Travels in the United States of North America and in Lower Canada, Performed in the Year 1817* (London, 1818), 285–86.

33 *The Annual Report of the Library Company of Philadelphia for the Year 1989* (Philadelphia, 1990), 29–30. On the use of black dialect in the eighteenth-century almanacs, see White, *Somewhat More Independent,* 66–75.

34 "Grand Bobalition, or Great Anniversary Fussible" (1821), Broadside Collection, American Antiquarian Society, Worcester, Mass.

35 *Columbian Centinel,* July 22, 1820.

36 On the sea serpent, see Chandos Michael Brown, "A Natural History of the Gloucester Sea Serpent: Knowledge, Power, and the Culture of Science in Antebellum America," *American Quarterly* 42 (September 1990): 402–36.

37 "Reply to Bobalition" (1821), Broadside Collection, American Antiquarian Society.

38 *New York Evening Post,* July 19, 1822; *National Advocate,* August 27, 1823. See also Phillip Lapsansky, "Graphic Discord: Abolitionist and Antiabolitionist Images," in Jean Fagan Yellin and John C. Van Horne, eds., *The Abolitionist Sisterhood: Women's Political Culture in Antebellum America* (Ithaca, 1994), 201–30.

39 Lapsansky, "Graphic Discord," 216–26; the quotation from Thackera is on 216–17.

40 The standard accounts of the minstrel show are Robert C. Toll, *Blacking Up: The Minstrel Show in Nineteenth-Century America* (New York, 1974); Eric Lott, *Love and Theft: Blackface Minstrelsy and the American Working Class* (New York, 1993). See also Michael Rogin, *Blackface, White Noise: Jewish Immigrants in the Hollywood Melting Pot* (Berkeley, 1996), 19–44; David R. Roediger, *The Wages of Whiteness: Race and the Making of the American Working Class* (London, 1991), 95–131.

41 Hans Nathan, *Dan Emmett and the Rise of Early Negro Minstrelsy* (Norman, Okla., 1962), 67–69.

42 Kenneth Roberts and Anna M. Roberts, trans. and eds., *Moreau de St. Méry's American Journey, [1793–1798]* (Garden City, N.Y., 1947), 303; quoted in Litwack, *North of Slavery,* 99. On racial violence, see Paul A. Gilje, *The Road to Mobocracy: Popular Disorder in New York City, 1763–1834* (Chapel Hill, N.C., 1987), 145–70; Noel Ignatiev, *How the Irish Became White* (New York, 1995); Roediger, *The Wages of Whiteness.*

43 Statement of Jacob Simmons, *People v. John McDonough et al.,* filed January 3, 1827, District Attorney Indictment Papers, Municipal Archives of the City of New York; *Public Ledger,* March 29, 1836.

44 Boardman, *America and the Americans,* 309–11; Julie Winch, *Philadelphia's Black*

Elite: Activism, Accommodation, and the Struggle for Autonomy, 1787–1848 (Philadelphia, 1988), 149–50; Gilje, *The Road to Mobocracy,* 153–69; Roediger, *The Wages of Whiteness,* 109–10.

[45] *Philadelphia Chronicle,* reported in *New York Evening Post,* November 24, 1829.

[46] Boston riot reported in *Carolina Centinel* (Newbern, N.C.), January 15, 1820; *New York Evening Post,* April 19, 1830; *New York Journal of Commerce,* reprinted in *Public Ledger,* December 28, 1836. For other examples, see Gilje, *The Road to Mobocracy,* 147–53.

[47] *Columbian Centinel,* July 18, 1821; *The Liberator,* August 13, 1847.

[48] *Boston Daily Advertiser,* July 15, 1820; Lydia Maria Child quoted in William C. Nell, *The Colored Patriots of the American Revolution, with Sketches of Several Distinguished Colored Persons: To Which is Added a Brief Survey of the Conditions and Prospects of Colored Persons* (Boston, 1855), 26–27. See also White, "It Was a Proud Day," 35–38.

CHAPTER 5

[1] Whitelaw Reid, *After the War: A Tour of the Southern States, 1865–1866* (1866; New York, 1965), 183–84, also 189–93.

[2] The authors wish to acknowledge the valuable assistance of Ivan Coates, a doctoral candidate in the Department of History, University of Sydney, in understanding the deeper meanings behind public displays of blacks' bodies.

[3] Eric Foner, *Reconstruction: America's Unfinished Revolution* (New York, 1988), 79.

[4] Belle Kearney, *A Slaveholder's Daughter* (1900; New York, 1969), 55.

[5] A. G. Bradley, *Other Days: Recollections of Rural England and Old Virginia, 1860–1880* (London, 1913), 396.

[6] Sidney Andrews, *The South Since the War* (1866; New York, 1969), 186–87.

[7] Francis Butler Leigh, *Ten Years on a Georgia Plantation Since the War* (London, 1883), 12.

[8] Andrews, *The South Since the War,* 187.

[9] George P. Rawick, ed., *The American Slave: A Composite Autobiography* (Westport, Conn. 1972), vol. 12, Georgia Narratives, Pt. 1, 325.

[10] Rawick, ed., *The American Slave,* vol. 7, Oklahoma and Mississippi Narratives, 42.

[11] Foner, *Reconstruction,* 200, 120. The Irish woman's complaint is quoted in Wilbert Lee Jenkins, "Chaos, Conflict and Control: The Responses of the Newly-Freed Slaves in Charleston, South Carolina to Emancipation and Reconstruction, 1865–1877" (Ph.D. diss. History, Michigan State University, 1991), vol. 1, 85.

[12] Reid, *After the War,* 419–20.

[13] William D. Piersen, *Black Legacy: America's Hidden Heritage* (Amherst, Mass. 1993), 133.

[14] *Bishop Whipple's Southern Diary, 1843–1844,* ed. Lester B. Shippee (Minneapolis, 1937), 51.

[15] William D. Piersen, "African-American Festive Style," unpublished paper prepared for the conference on Festive Culture and Public Ritual in Early America, Philadelphia, April 1996, 2–7.

[16] *New York Times,* March 30, 1865.

[17] Rawick, ed., *The American Slave,* Supplement, Series 2, vol. 3, Texas Narratives, Pt. 2, 870.

[18] Rawick, ed., *The American Slave,* vol. 14, North Carolina Narratives, Pt. 1, 133.

[19] Rawick, ed., *The American Slave,* vol. 4, Texas Narratives, Pt. 1, 87.

[20] Solomon Northup, *Twelve Years a Slave,* ed. Sue Eakin and Joseph Logsdon (1853; Baton Rouge, La., 1968), 51–52.

[21] Ralph Ellison, "Change the Joke and Slip the Yoke," in Ralph Ellison, *Shadow and Act* (1964; New York, 1972), 49.

[22] Elsa Barkley Brown, "Negotiating and Transforming the Public Sphere: African American Political Life in the Transition from Slavery to Freedom," *Public Culture* 7 (Fall 1994), 120.

[23] Vernon Lane Wharton, *The Negro in Mississippi, 1865–1890* (1947; New York, 1965), 165–66.

[24] Elsa Barkley Brown and Gregg D. Kimball, "Mapping the Terrain of Black Richmond," *Journal of Urban History* 21 (March 1995), 305–8.

[25] *Atlanta Constitution,* August 14, 1878.

[26] Terry John Thornbery, "The Development of Black Atlanta, 1865–1883" (Ph.D. diss., University of Maryland), 1977, 313, 315.

[27] William Barlow, *"Looking Up at Down": The Emergence of Blues Culture* (Philadelphia, 1989), 183.

[28] Foner, *Reconstruction,* 95.

[29] Peter J. Rachleff, *Black Labor in the South: Richmond, Virginia, 1865–1890* (Philadelphia, 1984), 39–40.

[30] Brown and Kimball, "Mapping the Terrain," 305.

[31] "The Streets of Washington," *Harper's New Monthly Magazine* 5, no. 37 (August 1868), 414.

[32] *Atlanta Constitution,* April 21, 1870.

[33] *Washington Star,* April 13, 1870.

[34] George Brown Tindall, *South Carolina Negroes, 1877–1900* (Columbia, S.C., 1952), 188–89).

[35] *Atlanta Constitution,* January 2, 1896.

[36] Quoted in Brown and Kimball, "Mapping the Terrain," p. 305.

[37] *Atlanta Constitution,* July 31, 1868.

[38] *Atlanta Constitution,* August 19, 1868.

[39] George P. Rawick, ed., *The American Slave: A Composite Autobiography,* Supplement, Series 1 (Westport, Conn., 1977), vol. 6, Mississippi Narratives, Pt. 1, 18.

[40] Brown and Kimball, "Mapping the Terrain," 306–7.

[41] Willard B. Gatewood, *Aristocrats of Color: The Black Elite, 1880–1920* (Bloomington, Ind., 1990), 51–52.

[42] Tindall, *South Carolina Negroes,* 288–89.

[43] Brown and Kimball, "Mapping the Terrain," 312.

[44] Barlow, *"Looking Up at Down,"* 183; John W. Blassingame, *Black New Orleans, 1860–1880* (Chicago, 1973), 145; Marjorie Thomas Zander, "The Brass-Band Funeral and Re-

lated Negro Burial Customs" (M.A. thesis, Folklore, University of North Carolina, 1962), 99.

[45] Barlow, "*Looking Up at Down*," 183–84; James Lincoln Collier, *The Making of Jazz: A Comprehensive History* (1978; London, 1981), 26, 64–65; William J. Schafer, *Brass Bands and New Orleans Jazz* (Baton Rouge, La., 1977), 8–10, 17, 39–40, 50.

[46] Ralph Ellison, "That Same Pain, That Same Pleasure: *An Interview*," in Ralph Ellison, *Shadow and Act* (New York, 1972), 10–11.

[47] Sidney Bechet, *Treat It Gentle* (New York, 1975), 61.

[48] Lee Collins, *Oh, Didn't He Ramble: The Life Story of Lee Collins,* as told to Mary Collins, Frank J. Gillis and John W. Miner (Urbana, Ill., 1989), 21.

[49] Danny Barker, *A Life in Jazz,* ed. Alyn Shipton (New York, 1986), 49.

[50] Bechet, *Treat It Gentle,* 61–62.

[51] Barker, *A Life in Jazz,* 51.

[52] Barker, *A Life in Jazz,* 49, 23, 50, 48.

[53] Pleasant "Cousin Joe" Joseph, and Harriet J. Ottenheimer, *Cousin Joe* (Chicago, 1987), 33.

[54] Bechet, *Treat It Gentle,* 66–67.

[55] Louis Armstrong, *Satchmo: My Life in New Orleans* (London, 1955), 29. An interesting indication of the importance placed by some African Americans on the manner in which a person walks appears in Zora Neale Hurston's essay "My People, My People." Discussing the question of whether James Weldon Johnson belongs within this category, Hurston advises: "Watch him! Does he parade when he walks? No, James Weldon Johnson proceeds." See Zora Neale Hurston, "Appendix to *Dust Tracks on a Road,*" in Zora Neale Hurston, *Folklore, Memoirs, and Other Writings,* ed. Cheryl A. Wall (New York, 1995), 775.

[56] Bechet, *Treat It Gentle,* 66–67.

[57] These cultural practices are ubiquitous. Jacqui Malone's account of the famous Florida A&M University's Marching 100 band includes descriptions of the amazing variety of formations and dance steps that invariably make up the band's routine, and the ritual involved in the band's getting onto the field at half time in football matches. "The Marching 100 forms lines along the sides of the field, makes an L-shape, then starts to move at an extraordinarily slow pace (20 steps per minute—1 step every three seconds) known as the 'death cadence.' Then they explode into a spine-tingling pace of 360 steps per minute (6 steps per second)." Jacqui Malone, *Steppin' on the Blues: The Visible Rhythms of African American Dance* (Urbana, Ill., 1996), 159, 162.

[58] Marshall Stearns and Jean Stearns, *Jazz Dance: The Story of American Vernacular Dance* (1968; New York, 1994), 18.

[59] Barker, *A Life in Jazz,* 48, 56.

[60] Reid Mitchell, *All on a Mardi Gras Day: Episodes in the History of New Orleans Carnival* (Cambridge, Mass., 1995), 150–51; Samuel Kinser, *Carnival, American Style: Mardi Gras at New Orleans and Mobile* (Chicago, 1990), 233–35.

[61] F. A. De Caro and Tom Ireland, "Every Man a King: Worldview, Social Tension and Carnival in New Orleans," *International Folklore Review* 6 (1988), 63; Munro S. Edmonson, "Carnival in New Orleans," *Caribbean Quarterly* 14 (March-June, 1956), 244.

[62] Lyle Saxon, *Fabulous New Orleans* (New York, 1928), 26–28.

[63] Mitchell, *All on a Mardi Gras Day*, 119. For a detailed description of elaborate Indian costuming in the 1940 Mardi Gras parade, see Lyle Saxon, Edward Dryer and Robert Tallant, compilers, *Gumbo Ya-Ya* (New York, 1945), 19–20.

[64] George Lipsitz, "Mardi Gras Indians: Carnival and Counter-Narrative in Black New Orleans," in George Lipsitz, *Time Passages: Collective Memory and American Popular Culture* (Minneapolis, 1990), 237, 238.

[65] Barker, *A Life in Jazz*, 48.

[66] Samuel A. Floyd, Jr., *The Power of Black Music: Interpreting Its History from Africa to the United States* (New York, 1995), 21, 35–37. As Floyd points out (on p. 83), the second line in African processions and African American parades is, in effect, the ring straightened out because of the need of participants to move to a distant location.

[67] A more recent example of the fluid and improvisational quality of New Orleans parades is provided by Marshall and Jean Stearns. During a visit to New Orleans in 1959, they followed a black marching band, hoping to hear them play. But the band and club members proceeded pretty much in silence to a distant church, where a conference was being held, and, after waiting several hours, the Stearnses began their weary walk back to their motel. They had stopped to rest on the way home "when suddenly the band came swinging around the corner in full blast. In an instant, our day became glorious. The numbing fatigue vanished, the sun came out, and we half walked, half danced all the way to town." Their account continues: "It was not just the music—we had heard the same or better on recordings—it was the dancing, a fascinating variety of walks, shuffles, grinds, struts, prances, and kicks, improvised by the marchers—official and unofficial—as the residents rushed out of their houses to join the parade. The dancing gave the music a new dimension of joy and vitality." Stearns and Stearns, *Jazz Dance*, 18.

[68] Alan Lomax, *The Land Where the Blues Began* (New York, 1993), xiii, 137, 331–32. Note also Melville Herskovits's observation that dance had "carried over into the New World to a greater degree than almost any other trait of African culture," quoted in Stearns and Stearns, *Jazz Dance*, 14.

[69] Lipsitz, "Mardi Gras Indians," 239; Alan Lomax, *Jazz Parades*, videotape (American Patchwork, 1990).

[70] Saxon, *Fabulous New Orleans*, 33–34.

[71] Kinser, *Carnival, American Style*, 231, 169–70.

[72] Barker, *A Life in Jazz*, 64. The drummer Paul Barbarin, who could recall Buddy Bolden's band, remembered that some pleasure clubs, such as the Jolly Boys, "selected a new uniform every year." Interview with Paul Barbarin, March 27, 1957, reel 2, p. 5, William Ranson Hogan Jazz Archive, Howard Tilton Memorial Library, Tulane University, New Orleans.

[73] Kinser, *Carnival, American Style*, 170–71.

[74] Lipsitz, "Mardi Gras Indians," 235. Robert Farris Thompson has recently pointed to another possible African influence on the festive garb of the "Indians," who, he says, "have long dressed in elaborate versions of Plains Indian apparel, but spread feathers over their entire bodies, as in the Vili tradition, rather than concentrating on the head, as in the Native American one." See Robert Farris Thompson, *Face of the Gods: Art and Altars of Africa and the African Americas* (New York, 1993), 29, 106–7.

[75] Kinser, *Carnival, American Style*, 195.

[76] Michael P. Smith, *Spirit World: Pattern in the Expressive Folk Culture of Afro-American New Orleans* (New Orleans, 1984), 93.

[77] Lomax, *The Land Where the Blues Began*, 137.

CHAPTER 6

[1] Benjamin E. Mays, *Born to Rebel: An Autobiography* (New York, 1971), 45–46.

[2] Trudier Harris, *Exorcising Blackness: Historical and Literary Lynching and Burning Rituals* (Bloomington, Ind., 1984), 18; Neil R. McMillen, *Dark Journey: Black Mississippians in the Age of Jim Crow* (Urbana, Ill., 1990), 24.

[3] Interview with Ted Hunter, Greene County, Georgia, in *The Social World of the Negro Youth: Interviews with Southern Negro Youth on Personal, Social and Racial Adjustment Experiences*, Fisk University: Social Science Institution, Social Science Source Documents No. 5, 1946, p. 47. The words quoted are those of Ted Hunter's father.

[4] "'Millways' Remembered: A Conversation with Kenneth and Margaret Morland," *Southern Cultures* 1 (Winter 1995), 167.

[5] Quoted in Hylan Lewis, *Blackways of Kent* (Chapel Hill, N.C., 1955), 54.

[6] Taylor Gordon, *Born to Be* (New York, 1929), 116–17. As Glenda Elizabeth Gilmore has recently observed, Southern whites "preferred the Uncle Remus of the farm to the 'colored swelldom' of the cities," a class to which Gordon had appeared to the police officer to belong. Glenda Elizabeth Gilmore, *Gender and Jim Crow: Women and the Politics of White Supremacy in North Carolina, 1896–1920* (Chapel Hill, N.C., 1996), 15.

[7] McMillen, *Dark Journey*, 30.

[8] Herbert Shapiro, *White Violence and Black Response: From Reconstruction to Montgomery* (Amherst, Mass., 1988), 147.

[9] Theodore Rosengarten, *All God's Dangers: The Life of Nate Shaw* (New York, 1974), 161.

[10] Allison Davis, Burleigh B. Gardner, and Mary R. Gardner, *Deep South: A Social Anthropological Study of Caste and Class* (Chicago, 1941), 22–24.

[11] Pauli Murray, *The Autobiography of a Black Activist, Feminist, Lawyer, Priest, and Poet* (Knoxville, Tenn., 1989), 32.

[12] Mays, *Born to Rebel*, 25.

[13] Charles S. Johnson, *Growing Up in the Black Belt: Negro Youth in the Rural South* (1941; New York, 1967), 315.

[14] W. Fitzhugh Brundage, *Lynching in the New South: Georgia and Virginia, 1880–1930* (Urbana, Ill., 1993), 5–9.

[15] John Dollard, *Caste and Class in a Southern Town* (1937; New York, 1957), 331.

[16] Richard Wright, *Black Boy: A Record of Childhood and Youth* (1937; New York, 1966), 83.

[17] L. C. Dorsey, "Harder Times than These," address delivered in Atlanta at Campaign for Reflections of Childhood and Youth, 1981, in Dorothy Abbott, ed., *Mississippi Writers*, 2 vols. (Jackson, 1986), vol. 2, 166.

[18] Ray Stannard Baker, *Following the Color Line: American Negro Citizenship in the Progressive Era* (1908; New York, 1964), 8.

[19] Stephen J. Whitfield, *A Death in the Delta: The Story of Emmett Till* (New York, 1988), 7.

[20] Zora Neale Hurston, "Dust Tracks on a Road," in Zora Neale Hurston, *Folklore, Memoirs and Other Writings*, ed. Cheryl A. Wall (New York, 1995), 589.

[21] Maya Angelou, *I Know Why the Caged Bird Sings* (London, 1984), 46.

[22] Tom E. Terrill and Jerrold Hirsch, eds., *Such as Us: Southern Voices of the Thirties* (Chapel Hill, 1978), 255–56.

[23] Charles Evers, *Evers* (New York, 1971), 29.

[24] David H. Cohn, *Where I Was Born and Raised* (Boston, 1947), vii; Wright, *Black Boy*, 175.

[25] Wright, *Black Boy*, 201, 202, 204, 215, 221, 251–52, 256.

[26] Quoted in Franklin M. Garrett, *Atlanta and Environs: A Chronicle of Its People and Events*, 3 vols. (1954; Athens, Ga., 1969), vol. 2, 25–28.

[27] Quoted in Garrett, *Atlanta and Environs*, vol. 2, 607–9.

[28] Perry Bradford, *Born with the Blues: The True Story of the Pioneering Blues Singers and Musicians in the Early Days of Jazz* (New York, 1965), 18.

[29] W. C. Handy, *Father of the Blues: An Autobiography*, ed. Arna Bontemps (1941; New York, 1991), 15, 16.

[30] Quoted in Margaret McKee and Fred Chisenhall, *Beale Black and Blue: Life and Music on Black America's Main Street* (Baton Rouge, La., 1981), 233.

[31] Statement by Rufus Thomas in *All Day and All Night: Memories from Beale Street Musicians*, videocassette, Center for Southern Folklore, Oxford, Miss., 1990.

[32] Shields McIlwaine, *Memphis Down in Dixie* (New York, 1948), 327–28.

[33] Handy, *Father of the Blues*, 118.

[34] George W. Lee, *Beale Street: Where the Blues Began* (New York, 1934), 63–64.

[35] Quoted in Robin D. G. Kelley, *Race Rebels: Culture, Politics, and the Black Working Class* (New York, 1994), 46 (emphasis added).

[36] Alan Lomax, *Mister Jelly Roll* (1950; London, 1991), 18–19; Pops Foster, *Pops Foster: The Autobiography of a New Orleans Jazzman* (Berkeley, 1971), 93–94.

[37] Robert Farris Thompson provides exciting hints as to the relationship between African American modes of walking and physical attributes prized in West and Central African societies. For example, Thompson notes the importance of "moving with flair" in order to display one's beauty and attract the attention of others and of "modes of phrasing the body [that] transform the person into art." Robert Farris Thompson, *African Art in Motion: Icon and Act* (Los Angeles, 1974), 16, XII.

[38] Lomax, *Mister Jelly Roll*, 19.

[39] Clifford H. Kuhn, Harlon E. Joye, and Bernard E. West, *Living Atlanta: An Oral History of the City, 1914–1918* (Athens, Ga., 1990), 39, 55–56.

[40] Kelley, *Race Rebels*, 50.

[41] Quoted in Franklin M. Garrett, *Atlanta and Environs: A Chronicle of Its People and Events*, 3 vols. (1954; Athens, Ga., 1969), vol. 2, 25–28.

[42] Compare Charles W. Joyner, *Down by the Riverside: A South Carolina Slave Community* (Urbana, Ill., 1984), 126. Robin Kelley provides an example of this kind of cultural creativity and affirmation in his recent study of African American working-class culture and

politics. Employed, in the late 1970s, at a McDonald's establishment in Pasadena, he and other African Americans subverted the rigid system of discipline by "stylizing" their work, not only through their "verbal circus and collective dialogues" and subtle modifications to their uniforms, but by "looking cool," "gangster limpin'," and "brandishing a spatula like a walking stick or a microphone." By such means, they "turned work into performance." See Robin D. G. Kelley, *Race Rebels: Culture, Politics and the Black Working Class* (New York, 1994), 1–3.

[43] Quoted in Donald M. Marquis, *In Search of Buddy Bolden: First Man of Jazz* (Baton Rouge, La., 1978), 52.

[44] Danny Barker, *A Life in Jazz* (New York, 1986), 12–16; Albert Murray, *Stomping the Blues* (1976; New York, 1982), 16–17, 45, 258; Jacqui Malone, *Steppin' on the Blues: The Visible Rhythms of African American Dance* (Urbana, Ill., 1996), 27.

[45] Quoted in McKee and Chisenhall, *Beale Black and Blue*, 136–37.

[46] Handy, *Father of the Blues*, 92.

[47] Quoted in McKee and Chisenhall, *Beale Black and Blue*, 34–35.

[48] Quoted in McKee and Chisenhall, *Beale Black and Blue*, 136–37.

[49] Handy, *Father of the Blues*, 97.

[50] Quoted in Kelley, *Race Rebels*, 48.

[51] Danny Barker, *A Life in Jazz* (New York, 1986), 12–16.

[52] Zora Neale Hurston, "Mules and Men," in Hurston, *Folklore, Memoirs, and Other Writings* 140–48.

[53] Hortense Powdermaker, *After Freedom: A Cultural Study in the Deep South* (New York, 1939), 70. The liking for gold teeth provoked generational opposition as well. "Niggers dese days . . . is so uppity," former Alabama slave Mary Rice complained to her WPA interviewer, "callin' derselves 'cullud fokes' an havin' gold teeth. Dey sez de mo' gold teeth dey has, de higher up in church dey sets. Huh!" George P. Rawick, ed., *The American Slave: A Composite Autobiography* (Westport, Conn., 1976), vol. 6, Alabama Narratives, 330.

[54] Thomas L. Johnson and Phillip C. Dunn, eds., *A True Likeness: The Black South of Richard Samuel Roberts, 1920–1936* (Columbia, S.C., and Chapel Hill, N.C., 1986). The reference to the "stylized cathedral window" is on p. 27.

[55] *Louisiana Weekly*, February 13, 1926.

[56] Powdermaker, *After Freedom*, 180.

[57] Gwendolyn Robinson, "Class, Race, and Gender: A Transcultural Theoretical and Sociohistorical Analysis of Cosmetic Institutions and Practices to 1920," (Ph.D. diss., University of Illinois at Chicago, 1984), 453.

[58] Henry Louis Gates, Jr., *Colored People: A Memoir* (New York, 1994), 40–41.

[59] Ruth E. Bass, "Cull'rd Folks," Works Progress Administration, Record Group 60, Mississippi State Archives, Jackson, Mississippi, n.d., 16. See also North Carolina Photographic Archives, Wooten-Moulton Collection, Celia Eudy Group, Wilson Library, University of North Carolina, Chapel Hill, for examples of hair stylings worn by African American women and girls.

[60] Mamie Garvin Fields, with Karen Fields, *Lemon Swamp and Other Places: A Carolina Memoir* (New York, 1983), 218–19.

[61] Rawick, ed., *The American Slave*, vol. 13, Georgia Narratives, Pt. 4, 36.

[62] Rawick, ed., *The American Slave*, vol. 11, Arkansas and Missouri Narratives, Arkansas Narratives, pt. 7, 185.

[63] Angelou, *I Know Why the Caged Bird Sings*, 4.

[64] Fields, *Lemon Swamp*, 187.

[65] Gates Jr., *Colored People*, 40–49.

[66] Arthur Raper, *A Preface to Peasantry* (1936; New York, 1968), 45–46.

[67] Bass, "Cull'rd Folks," 16, 19.

[68] Loyle Hairston, "Growing Up in Mississippi," in Abbott, ed., *Mississippi Writers*, vol. 2, 317.

[69] Evers, *Evers*, 38.

[70] Maurice S. Evans, *Black and White in the Southern States: A Study of the Race Problem in the United States from a South African Point of View* (London, 1915), 89, 119.

[71] Lura Beam, *He Called Them by the Lightning: A Teacher's Odyssey in the Negro South, 1908–1919* (Indianapolis, 1967), 39–40.

[72] Powdermaker, *After Freedom*, 236.

[73] Davis, *Deep South*, 388–89.

[74] Julia Peterkin, *Roll, Jordan, Roll* (New York, 1933), 75–76.

[75] Willa Johnson, "Characteristic Ways of Colored People," n.d., Works Progress Administration, Mississippi State Archives, Record Group 60, Jackson, Mississippi, 1.

[76] Beam, *He Called Them by the Lightning*, 39–40.

[77] Alton Hornsby, Jr., ed., *In the Cage: Eyewitness Accounts of the Freed Negro in Southern Society, 1877–1919* (Chicago, 1971), 75.

[78] Quoted in James C. Cobb, *The Most Southern Place on Earth: The Mississippi Delta and the Roots of Regional Identity* (New York, 1992), 165; Powdermaker, *After Freedom*, 236.

[79] Agnes Brown, "The Negro Churches of Chapel Hill: A Community Study" (M.A. thesis, Sociology, University of North Carolina, Chapel Hill, 1939), 47.

[80] Raper, *Preface to Peasantry*, 45.

[81] R. Emmet Kennedy, *More Mellows* (New York, 1931), 7–8, 10. The Church of God in Christ, also known as the Sanctified Church, was founded in Memphis, Tennessee, in 1895 by a black Baptist, C. H. Mason, and won a large following in the South. The church was charismatic, its members believing in the possibility of sanctification, as evidenced by the possession of such spiritual gifts as the ability to speak in tongues, and services were characterized by enthusiastic participation and expressions of spiritual ecstasy. See Powdermaker, *After Freedom*, 233–34.

[82] Brown, "Negro Churches of Chapel Hill," 56–57.

[83] Powdermaker, *After Freedom*, 244–45.

[84] Kennedy, *More Mellows*, 13.

[85] Zora Neale Hurston, *The Sanctified Church: The Folklore Writings of Zora Neale Hurston* (Berkeley, 1981), 104, 83.

[86] Quoted in Samuel A. Floyd, Jr., *The Power of Black Music: Interpreting Its History from Africa to the United States* (New York, 1995), 21.

[87] Henry H. Mitchell, *Folk Beliefs of Blacks in America and West Africa* (New York, 1975), 146; Albert J. Raboteau, *Slave Religion: The "Invisible Institution" in the Antebellum South* (New York, 1978), 15.

[88] The idea of framing an alternate reality comes from Earl Lewis; see his *In Their Own Interests: Race, Class, and Power in Twentieth-Century Norfolk, Virginia* (Berkeley, 1991), 90.

CHAPTER 7

[1] *Chicago Defender,* August 10, 1912; August 17, 1912, and August 24, 1912.

[2] *Chicago Defender,* August 31, 1912; September 7, 1912.

[3] Lois W. Banner, *American Beauty* (New York, 1983), 255–69; *New York Times,* December 30, 1877; *Philadelphia Evening Item,* November 29, 1900, *Philadelphia Item,* November 30, 1900, December 1, 1900, December 5, 1900, December 6, 1900; *Atlanta Constitution,* July 5, 1892; Sharon Ann Holt, "Making Freedom Pay: Freedpeople Working for Themselves, North Carolina, 1865–1900," *Journal of Southern History* 60 (May 1994), 229–62, quotation on p. 251.

[4] *Age,* February 9, 1911.

[5] *Chicago Defender,* August 5, 1916; see also September 9, 1916 for the company's reply. The editorial "Betrayers of the Race," *Half-Century Magazine,* February 1920, attacks "fake white firms" for making skin preparations and the black press for accepting advertisements from them.

[6] Kathy Peiss, "Making Faces: The Cosmetics Industry and the Cultural Construction of Gender, 1890–1930," *Genders* 7 (Spring 1990), 143–69; Kathy Peiss, "Beauty Culture," in Darlene Clark Hine, ed., *Black Women in America: An Historical Encyclopedia,* 2 vols. (Brooklyn, 1993), vol. 1, 100–104; *Chicago Defender,* September 4, 1915. See also Paula Giddings, *When and Where I Enter: The Impact of Black Women on Race and Sex in America* (New York, 1984), 186–89; Clarence Taylor, *The Black Churches of Brooklyn* (New York, 1994), 79–80.

[7] Ann Douglas, *Terrible Honesty: Mongrel Manhattan in the 1920s* (New York, 1995), 339; Peiss, "Making Faces"; "Race Pride and Cosmetics," *Opportunity* 3 (October 1925), 292–93.

[8] *New York Times,* August 8, 1909.

[9] Lawrence Levine, *Black Culture and Black Consciousness: Afro-American Folk Thought from Slavery to Freedom* (New York, 1977), 284–93; Peiss, "Making Faces."

[10] Paula S. Fass, *The Damned and the Beautiful: American Youth in the 1920's* (New York, 1977), 283–84.

[11] Louis W. George, "Beauty Culture and Colored People," *The Messenger* 2 (July 1918), 25–26.

[12] F. B. Ransom, "Manufacturing Toilet Articles: A Big Negro Business," *The Messenger* 5 (December 1923), 937, 941; *The Chicago Whip,* October 23, 1920 (emphasis added).

[13] See, for example, George Schulyer's almost hagiographic article, "Madame C. J. Walker," *The Messenger* 6 (August 1924), 251–66, reprinted in Gerald Early, ed., *Speech and Power: The African-American Essay and its Cultural Content From Polemics to Pulpit,* 2 vols. (Hopewell, N.J., 1990), vol. 1, 242–54.

[14] Mamie Garvin Fields, *Lemon Swamp and Other Places: A Carolina Memoir* (New York, 1983), 187–89 (emphasis in original).

[15] See Douglas, *Terrible Honesty,* for the mood of the 1920s in New York.

[16] "Balls," *Crisis* 18 (October 1919), 286.

[17] "Types of Racial Beauty," *Half-Century Magazine,* June 1919, 7; "Crowned By the Gods" and "Beauty and Brains," *Half-Century Magazine,* June 1920, 8–9.

[18] *Chicago Whip,* November 5, 1921; *Chicago Whip,* November 19, 1921; *Chicago Whip,* December 17, 1921.

[19] "Exalting Negro Womanhood," *The Messenger* 6 (January 1924), 7.

[20] "Who Is the Prettiest Colored Girl in This Country?" and "Are You One of Those Perfect Types?" *Half-Century Magazine,* September 1921, 9; "Finds the Beauty Contest Helpful," *Half-Century Magazine,* November 1921, 21.

[21] See *The Messenger* 9 (January 1927), 29.

[22] "Baby Contests," *Crisis* 29 (January 1925), 129; "Baby Contests," *Crisis* 30 (March 1926), 233.

[23] Colin Powell, *My American Journey* (New York, 1995).

[24] Chandler Owen, "Good Looks Supremacy," *The Messenger* 6 (March 1924), 80–81; *New York Times,* April 5, 1924; *Crisis* 28 (May 1924), 35. For other scathing comments from the African American press on the cancellation, see "Beauty Contest Called Off," *The Messenger* 6 (May 1924), 137; "When Is a Contest Not a Contest?" *Crisis* 28 (June 1924), 80; *Age,* April 12, 1924.

[25] *Pittsburgh Courier,* May 16, 1925. See Banner, *American Beauty;* Colleen Ballerino Cohen, Richard Wilk and Beverly Stoeltje, eds., *Beauty Queens on the Global Stage: Gender, Contests, and Power* (New York, 1996).

[26] A full account is contained in Kathy Peiss, *Hope in a Jar: The Making of American Beauty Culture* (New York, 1998). We are extremely grateful to Professor Peiss for passing on this information to us prior to the publication of her important book.

[27] Installments of Mamie Hightower's life were printed, in advertisements, in the *Amsterdam News,* April 14, May 26, August 4, and September 15, 1926.

[28] Advertisement in *Pittsburgh Courier,* June 6, 1925. Gerald Early discussed the Miss Golden Brown contest in an essay on Miss Black America, but other than that the contest has been mentioned seldom, if ever, by scholars or writers. See Gerald Early, "The Miss Black America Contest," in Early, *Tuxedo Junction: Essays on American Culture* (New York, 1989), 64–70. In her autobiography, Faith Ringgold, who as a child in the 1930s was taken to Atlantic City, lamented the absence of African Americans in the Miss America contest and pageant. She, along with many others, seems to have been unaware of blacks' attempts during the 1920s to remedy this situation by organizing their own contests, often holding the final ceremony in Atlantic City. See Faith Ringgold, *We Flew Over the Bridge: The Memoirs of Faith Ringgold* (Boston, 1995), 12–13.

[29] *Pittsburgh Courier,* July 11, 1925; *Pittsburgh Courier,* May 16, 1925.

[30] Advertisement in *Amsterdam News,* October 7, 1925. See also news stories in *Amsterdam News,* September 30, 1925 and *Pittsburgh Courier,* October 3, 1925.

[31] See advertisement announcing winners, *Amsterdam News,* June 20, 1928, and news story describing the function on June 22, *Amsterdam News,* June 27, 1928. For other national contests, see *Amsterdam News,* September 19, 1925, where a Miss Beatrice Walker of Chicago was crowned "Miss America" in a contest run by the National Beauty Culturists League, and *Amsterdam News,* December 1, 1926, for a picture of Miss Miriam Walker who

"Won the Verdict as the Colored 'Miss America.'" Compared to Miss Golden Brown, these affairs attracted very little attention.

[32] *Pittsburgh Courier,* November 28, 1925. The link between beauty contests, beauty queens, and the big football games between black colleges appears to date from this time. See, for example, picture and caption in *Pittsburgh Courier,* November 7, 1925, of the young woman "leading the field of beauties entered to represent the state at the Wilberforce-Institute game in Columbus, Thanksgiving."

[33] *Amsterdam News,* August 11, 1926; September 8, 1926; September 15 1926. This was not the only occasion on which the subjective nature of the judging of beauty contests came under fire. See "Judges in Jamaica Beauty Contest Howled Down by Menacing Attitude of Large Gathering," *Amsterdam News,* September 30, 1925.

[34] *Amsterdam News,* February 16, 1926; *Amsterdam News,* July 27, 1927. See also *Amsterdam News,* August 3, 1927, for an account of the winner at one of these nights, who was a "popular beauty and a sure humdinger" wearing a "silk, gorgeously striped one-piece [bathing] suit."

[35] *Heebie Jeebies* 2 (September 4, 1926), cover and 11.

[36] *Louisiana Weekly,* June 30, 1928; *Amsterdam News,* March 16, 1927; May 4, 1927.

[37] William R. Leach, "Transformations in a Culture of Consumption: Women and Department Stores, 1890–1925," *Journal of American History* 71 (September 1984), 319–42, esp. 328; see also William Leach, *Land of Desire: Merchants, Power, and the Rise of a New American Culture* (New York, 1993).

[38] *Chicago Defender,* April 17, 1920; January 8, 1921; April 2, 1921; October 22, 1921.

[39] "Chicago's Fashion Show," *Half-Century Magazine,* March-April 1924; *Pittsburgh Courier,* March 20, 1926; October 31, 1925.

[40] *Pittsburgh Courier* March 27, 1926; April 24, 1926; April 17, 1926; May 1, 1924; May 1, 1926.

[41] *Louisiana Weekly,* March 6, 1926; April 3, 1926; April 10, 1926; April 23, 1927.

[42] Roy Wilkins, *Standing Fast: The Autobiography of Roy Wilkins* (New York, 1982), 77–78.

[43] Gloria T. Hull, ed., *Give Us Each Day: The Diary of Alice Dunbar-Nelson* (New York, 1984), 336; Taylor Gordon, *Born to Be* (New York, 1929), 227–28.

[44] *Amsterdam News,* April 6, 1935; April 13, 1935; June 8, 1935; April 6, 1935; December 14, 1935; May 16, 1936.

[45] St. Clair Drake and Horace R. Cayton, *Black Metropolis: A Study of Negro Life in a Northern City,* 2 vols. (1945; New York, 1962), vol. 2, 694–97; xxiii. For a brief mention of a fashion show associated with a Methodist Church in Brooklyn, see Taylor, *The Black Churches of Brooklyn,* 69.

[46] George Chauncey, *Gay New York: Gender, Urban Culture, and the Making of the Gay Male World 1890–1940* (New York, 1994), 257–64; Langston Hughes, *The Big Sea: An Autobiography* (1940; New York, 1986), 273. For use of the term "Faggots' Ball," see, for example, the interview with Marion Day in Jeff Kisseloff, *You Must Remember This: An Oral History of Manhattan from the 1890s to World War II* (New York, 1989), 323.

[47] Ethel Waters, *His Eye Is on the Sparrow* (Garden City, N.Y., 1951), 149–50; Gordon, *Born to Be,* 228; *Amsterdam News,* March 7 1936.

[48] Gordon, *Born to Be*, 227–28; Hughes, *The Big Sea*, 223; David Levering Lewis, *When Harlem Was in Vogue* (New York, 1981), 208, 210. Also see Lewis A. Erenberg, *Steppin' Out: New York Nightlife and the Transformation of American Culture, 1890–1930* (Chicago, 1984), 206–59. For contemporary comment on the white invasion of Harlem clubs, see Rudolph Fisher, "The Caucasian Storms Harlem," originally published in the *American Mercury* in 1927, reprinted in David Levering Lewis, ed., *The Portable Harlem Renaissance Reader* (New York, 1994), 110–17, and the cooler, more diffident remarks of Langston Hughes in *The Big Sea*, 224–29.

[49] *Pittsburgh Courier*, December 12, 1925.

[50] Gordon, *Born to Be*, 227–28.

CHAPTER 8

[1] Interview with Naomi Washington in Jeff Kisseloff, *You Must Remember This: An Oral History of Manhattan from the 1890s to World War II* (New York, 1989), 272.

[2] Ray Stannard Baker, *Following the Color Line: American Negro Citizenship in the Progressive Era* (1908; New York, 1964), 125–26.

[3] William Pickens, *Bursting Bonds: The Autobiography of a "New Negro"* (1923; Bloomington, Ind., 1991), 14. On etiquette manuals more generally, see John F. Kasson, *Rudeness & Civility: Manners in Nineteenth-Century Urban America* (New York, 1990).

[4] Edward S. Green, *National Capital Code of Etiquette* (Washington, D.C., 1920), 14; E. M. Woods, *The Negro in Etiquette* (St. Louis, 1899), 103, 29.

[5] Quoted in Jervis Anderson, *This Was Harlem: 1900–1950* (New York, 1982), 9; interview with Nora Mair in Kisseloff, *You Must Remember This*, 282; quoted in Anderson, *This Was Harlem*, 74. Dizzy Gillespie explained a related use of the term "stroll," one that also created scope for a virtuoso demonstration of black style: "I made Fletcher Henderson stop playing 'oom-pa, oom-pa, oom-pa,' on the piano during my solos. I stood up to play at the Apollo, and said, 'Stroll!' Stroll is without the piano, just the drums and bass and, if there's one, the guitar. Prez used to stroll a lot; Roy Eldridge used to stroll a lot—piano out. That's where I learned it, because Roy would say 'Strolluh!' in a minute. The piano would be getting in his way. I worked a weekend with Fletcher Henderson in the Apollo and then some one-nighters, but I had to tell him to lay out because the style of piano he played was getting in my way." Dizzy Gillespie with Al Fraser, *Dizzy: The Autobiography of Dizzy Gillespie* (London, 1980), 161.

[6] Ann Douglas, *Terrible Honesty: Mongrel Manhattan in the 1920s* (New York, 1995), 73. On the Great Migration, see James R. Grossman, *Land of Hope: Chicago, Black Southerners, and the Great Migration* (Chicago, 1989).

[7] Quoted in William Howard Kenney, *Chicago Jazz: A Cultural History, 1904–1930* (New York, 1993), 13.

[8] Alan Lomax, *Mister Jelly Roll* (1950; London, 1991), 116.

[9] *Chicago Defender*, May 2, 1914.

[10] Jontyle Theresa Robinson and Wendy Greenhouse, *The Art of Archibald J. Motley, Jr.* (Chicago, 1991), 35.

[11] Quoted in Kenney, *Chicago Jazz*, 15.

[12] *Heebie Jeebies*, November 7, 1925.

[13]*Chicago Whip*, May 22, 1920. This stock joke, based on the stereotype of the Jew as a money-grubbing materialist, can be found in many other locales. See Lawrence W. Levine, *Black Culture and Black Consciousness: Afro-American Folk Thought from Slavery to Freedom* (New York, 1977), 305.

[14]*Chicago Whip*, April 24, 1920.

[15]*Chicago Whip*, April 9, 1921.

[16]*Half-Century Magazine* 6 (June 1919), letters page.

[17]*Chicago Defender*, August 1, 1914.

[18]*Half-Century Magazine* 9 (August-September 1920), editorial page.

[19]*Amsterdam News*, September 23, 1925. Clearly, the street car was one of the important places where race relations were played out. For a series of comments from the time of the 1919 race riot, see Chicago Commission on Race Relations, *The Negro in Chicago: A Study of Race Relations and a Race Riot* (Chicago, 1922), 302–9. For an excellent study of contact between black and white on the buses in the South, see Robin D. G. Kelley, *Race Rebels: Culture, Politics, and the Black Working Class* (New York, 1994), 55–75.

[20]Claude McKay, *Harlem: Negro Metropolis* (New York, 1940), 23.

[21]*Chicago Defender*, August 4, 1917.

[22]Quoted in Anderson, *This Was Harlem*, 322.

[23]*Chicago Defender*, July 9, 1921.

[24]*Pittsburgh Courier*, July 4, 1925; Roy Wilkins, *Standing Fast: The Autobiography of Roy Wilkins* (New York, 1982), 59.

[25]*Amsterdam News*, August 25, 1927.

[26]*New York Times*, August 24, 1927.

[27]*New York Times*, September 6, 1931.

[28]On Palmer Hayden, see Allan M. Gordon, *Echoes of Our Past: The Narrative Artistry of Palmer C. Hayden* (Los Angeles, 1988); Langston Hughes, quoted in Douglas, *Terrible Honesty*, 374; Farah Jasmine Griffin, *"Who Set You Flowin'?": The African American Migration Narrative* (New York, 1995), 64–65.

[29]*Chicago Defender*, July 3, 1920; *Chicago Whip*, June 26, 1920.

[30]*Chicago Defender*, July 3, 1920; James Weldon Johnson, *Black Manhattan* (1930; New York, 1968), 168–69; *Amsterdam News*, November 9, 1927.

[31]Interview with Isabel Washington Powell in Kisseloff, *You Must Remember This*, 282–83.

[32]*Crisis* 27 (January 1924), 129–30.

[33]Interview with Elton Fax in Kisseloff, *You Must Remember This*, 282.

[34]Chester B. Himes, *The Quality of Hurt: The Early Years* (1972; New York, 1990), 36.

[35]Douglas, *Terrible Honesty*, 102; lyric quoted in Anderson, *This Was Harlem*, 141.

[36]*Chicago Defender*, February 4, 1922.

[37]Kenney, *Chicago Jazz*, 38; quoted in Burton W. Peretti, *The Creation of Jazz: Music, Race, and Culture in Urban America* (Urbana, 1992), 135.

[38]Kenney, *Chicago Jazz*, 38; Willie the Lion Smith, *Music on My Mind: The Memoirs of an American Pianist* (London, 1965), 46–47.

[39]Tom Davin, "Conversation with James P. Johnson," in Martin T. Williams, ed., *Jazz Panorama* (1962; New York, 1979), 44–61, 56.

[40] Davin, "Conversation with James P. Johnson," 56; Smith, *Music on My Mind*, 46. On the style of the musicians, see also Jacqui Malone, *Steppin' on the Blues: The Visible Rhythms of African American Dance* (Urbana, In., 1996), especially 23–36.

[41] Smith, *Music on My Mind*, 53.

[42] Davin, "Conversation with James P. Johnson," 59–60.

[43] Smith, *Music on My Mind*, 46–49; Davin, "Conversation with James P. Johnson," 57–58.

[44] Smith, *Music on My Mind*, 99.

[45] Davin, "Conversation with James P. Johnson," 59.

[46] Davin, "Conversation with James P. Johnson," 55.

[47] Bill Crow, *Jazz Anecdotes* (New York, 1990), 124–25.

[48] Quoted in Peretti, *The Creation of Jazz*, 135.

[49] Ralph Ellison, *Going to the Territory* (New York, 1987), 220.

[50] *Chicago Defender*, February 25, 1922.

[51] Miles Davis, *Miles: The Autobiography* (London, 1990), 101.

[52] Robin D. G. Kelley, "'We Are Not What We Seem': Rethinking Black Working-Class Opposition in the Jim Crow South," *Journal of American History* 80 (June 1993), 75–112, quotation on pp. 84–86.

[53] Johnson, *Black Manhattan*, 162–63.

EPILOGUE

[1] Ralph Ellison, *Invisible Man* (1952; London, 1965), 354. Unlike many of the subjects looked at earlier in this work, the zoot suit has an extensive and very good historiography, which has shaped this account. See, in particular, Stuart Cosgrove, "The Zoot-Suit and Style Warfare," *History Workshop Journal* 18 (Autumn 1984), 77–91; Steve Chibnall, "Whistle and Zoot: The Changing Meaning of a Suit of Clothes," *History Workshop Journal* 20 (Autumn 1985), 56–81; Bruce M. Tyler, "Black Jive and White Repression," *Journal of Ethnic Studies* 16 (Winter 1989), 31–66; Robin Kelley, *Race Rebels: Culture, Politics, and the Black Working Class* (New York, 1994), 161–81. See also Eric Lott, "Double V, Double-Time: Bebop's Politics of Style," *Callaloo* 11 (1988), 597–605.

[2] *New York Times*, June 11, 1943.

[3] *Pittsburgh Courier*, June 19, 1943.

[4] *Pittsburgh Courier*, June 26, 1943.

[5] *Amsterdam News*, May 29, 1943.

[6] *Atlanta Daily World*, June 21, 1943.

[7] Ellison, *Invisible Man*, 390.

[8] Malcolm X, with the assistance of Alex Haley, *The Autobiography of Malcolm X* (1965; London, 1968), 135.

[9] *New York Times*, June 11, 1943.

[10] Quoted in Tyler, "Black Jive and White Repression," 34.

[11] Kelley, *Race Rebels*, 162.

[12] Dizzy Gillespie with Al Fraser, *Dizzy: The Autobiography of Dizzy Gillespie* (London, 1980), 279.

[13] *Baltimore Afro-American*, July 17, 1943.

[14] Cosgrove, "The Zoot-Suit and Style Warfare," 77–78.

[15] See Tyler, "Black Jive and White Repression," 35–38; Kelley, *Race Rebels,* 171–73. See also James B. Gilbert, *A Cycle of Outrage: America's Reaction to the Juvenile Delinquent in the 1950s* (New York, 1986), 30–31, for an account of the way the cartoonist Al Capp linked the zoot suit with a criminal culture.

[16] *Atlanta Daily World,* June 21, 1943.

[17] *Amsterdam News,* June 26, 1943.

[18] Hylan Lewis, *Blackways of Kent* (Chapel Hill, N.C., 1955), 254–55.

[19] *Baltimore Afro-American,* November 21, 1942; *Baltimore Afro-American,* May 29, 1943.

[20] See Gilbert, *A Cycle of Outrage,* 30–31.

[21] Faith Ringgold, *We Flew Over the Bridge: The Memoirs of Faith Ringgold* (Boston, 1995), 19.

[22] *Pittsburgh Courier,* June 26, 1943.

[23] Russell Gold, "Guilty of Syncopation, Joy, and Animation: The Closing of Harlem's Savoy Ballroom," *Studies in Dance History* 5 (Spring 1994), 50–64, esp. 52–53.

[24] *Pittsburgh Courier,* June 26, 1943. As many others have done, we can just point to the importance of the cross-racial aspects of the zoot suit, which lies beyond both our expertise and the scope of our study. However, a proper examination of the subject would begin with Carey McWilliams, *North from Mexico: The Spanish-Speaking People of the United States* (New York, 1961), 227–58; Mauricio Mazon, *The Zoot-Suit Riots: The Psychology of Symbolic Annihilation* (Austin, 1984); George J. Sánchez, *Becoming Mexican American: Ethnicity, Culture and Identity in Chicano Los Angeles, 1900–1945* (New York, 1993).

INDEX

CPSIA information can be obtained
at www.ICGtesting.com
Printed in the USA
LVHW080532100722
723125LV00010B/612